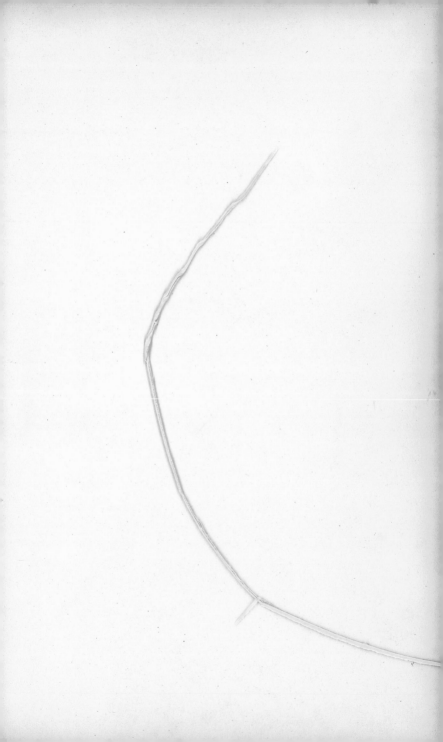

THE STEPS
OF HUMILITY

BY BERNARD, ABBOT OF CLAIRVAUX

TRANSLATED, WITH INTRODUCTION AND NOTES,
AS A STUDY OF HIS EPISTEMOLOGY BY

GEORGE BOSWORTH BURCH

NOTRE DAME, INDIANA
UNIVERSITY OF NOTRE DAME PRESS
1963

248.13
B466gE
1963

First Paperback Edition

152582

INTRODUCTION

AN ANALYSIS OF BERNARD'S EPISTEMOLOGY

TRANSLATOR'S PREFACE

Bernard of Clairvaux, of all the mediaeval Doctors of the Church, best deserves to be called a Lover of Wisdom. By Wisdom I do not mean the wisdom of the world, but that ineffable divine Wisdom, coeternal and consubstantial with God, which is the second person of the Holy Trinity. By Love I do not mean the want of something absent, which is desire, but the enjoyment of something present. Divine Wisdom is to worldly wisdom what reality is to illusion, and love is to desire what understanding is to faith. There are many who love the wisdom of the world, and there are many who desire the Wisdom of God. Bernard was one of the few who truly love the true Wisdom and are therefore truly called Philosophers. Their love of worldly wisdom is transcended, and their desire of divine Wisdom is consummated, in the love of divine Wisdom experienced in the rapture of mystical contemplation. Rapt from the world to the Word, they no longer possess anything but the Word. Possessing it, they no longer seek it, but rest in it and love it as the Bridegroom of the soul.

Bernard's essay on the *Steps of Humility* is an important work of mystical literature because it attempts to describe, not the indescribable mystical experience, but the easily describable steps which lead to the possibility of this experience. Some readers of mystical books feel that the experiences there described, while doubtless of great value to those who have them, are of no significance to themselves, because they do not have them. This feeling is justified only to the extent that mystical books are not of practical value unless they describe the path from the point where the reader finds himself. A description of the last step cannot help one who has not yet taken the first. Bernard wrote this essay to be a practical help for those who are still at the bottom of the path. In fact it is written primarily for those who are not even approaching the possibility of mystical experience, but on the contrary are withdrawing from it, and so it describes the lowest part of the path by means of those landmarks which show by their appearance that we are going in the wrong direction.

The text is substantially the critical text edited by the late Reverend Barton R. V. Mills and published in 1926 by the Cambridge University Press, together with the essay on *Loving God*, under the title *Select Treatises of S. Bernard of Clairvaux*. The reader is referred to the introduction to that edition for a discussion of the manuscripts, and to the footnotes of that edition for the variant readings. All departures from this text have been indicated in the footnotes. Its archaic orthography, which, while of value to the scholar, is only confusing to the general reader interested primarily in the content, has been replaced by the conventional orthography. Mabillon's edition has been followed as a model for punctuation.

The translation has endeavored, first of all, to be accurate. Within the limits set by this primary requirement, however, it has not been felt desirable to observe a word-for-word literalness. It would be impossible to reproduce Bernard's style in English, and it would require a second Bernard even to imitate it successfully, yet the translator has the obligation of imitating it to the best of his ability. Scriptural phrases, since their effectiveness depends primarily on their familiarity to the reader, have been rendered according to the King James version, as being presumably most familiar to the English reader, except where this would alter the sense, but all references are to the chapter and verse of the Vulgate. The translation has been compared with the English version of the late Reverend Barton R. V. Mills, which appeared shortly after it had been completed, and is indebted to this comparison for the correction of certain errors; some differences, however, remain.

The introduction is a systematic analysis of Bernard's epistemological doctrine based on his complete genuine works. Little or no direct use has been made of doubtfully attributed works, translations, or secondary sources. It is an objective presentation of Bernard's actual doctrine without historical or critical commentary. The page references are, in the case of all the sermons except those on Canticles, to the critical text edited by the monks of the Cistercian province of Austria-Hungary and published at Vienna in 1891 under the title *Xenia Bernardina* (cited as "XB"; in all cases "Part I" is to be understood), and in the case of all the other works to the fourth edition of the text edited by Dom John Mabillon, published at Paris in 1839 (cited as "*Opera*"; in all cases "Volume I" is to be understood). Chapter and paragraph are always cited, so that all references can be found in any edition.

The notes are a commentary on certain passages of the essay for the understanding of which it seemed that some explanation might be helpful.

The appendices are notes on certain points of Bernard's epistemological doctrine which, not being based exclusively on his works, have no place in the introduction.

The translator's principal indebtedness is to the late Professor James Haughton Woods for having encouraged him to undertake this work.

G. B. B.

WIDENER MEMORIAL LIBRARY
HARVARD UNIVERSITY
August 20, 1938

The publication of this work has been made possible by a subsidy from the Department of Philosophy of Harvard University. The translator is indebted to Jean Brand for making the drawings and to the Cambridge University Press for permission to use the emendations in its critical text of the *De Gradibus Humilitatis*.

CONTENTS

CONTENTS

CONTENTS

THE STEPS OF HUMILITY

without which it would be a senseless trunk;[13] but the soul is indebted to the body for its very existence, which consists in animating the body.[14]

Section 2. The Human Soul

1. Definition of the soul

The human soul does not *live*, but *is life*, the life of the body.

That which is life and that which has life will not be on the same plane: much less that which is life and those things which lack life. The soul is life, living to be sure, but not by virtue of anything other than itself: and therefore, strictly speaking, not so much *living* as *life*. It follows that, when it is infused in a body, it vivifies the latter, so that the body becomes, from the presence of life, not life but living. Whence it is obvious that, for a body, even if alive, to live is not the same as to be, since it can be without being alive.[1]

The human soul, which is life and has the capacity for blessed life, is intermediate between plant and animal vitality, which is not life but has the capacity for life,[2] and God, who is blessed life.[3] Since it is, rather than has, life, the soul is simple,

---

[13] Sermon 2 for Christmas, 2: Num quid non truncus esset insensibilis caro inanimata? (XB 120.) Cf. Sermon 6 for Advent, 4 (XB 28).

[14] *Ibid.*, 6: Non ex deliberatione propria carni miscetur, sed creando immittitur, immittendo creatur. (XB 123.)

---

[1] Sermon 81 on Canticles, 3: Non stabunt pariter in gradu uno vita et vivens: multo minus vita, et quae sunt sine vita. Vita anima est vivens quidem, sed non aliunde quam se ipsa: ac per hoc non tam vivens, quam vita, ut proprie de ea loquamur. Inde est quod infusa corpori vivificat illud, ut sit corpus de vitae praesentia, non vita, sed vivens. Unde liquet, ne vivo quidem corpori id vivere esse, quod esse: cum esse, et minime vivere possit. (*Opera* 3165.) Cf. Sermon 2 for Easter (to the Abbots), 1 (XB 341).

[2] *Ibid.*, 3: Est pecorum, est et arborum vita, sensu altera vigens, altera carens. At neutri tamen idem esse quod vivere est: cum, ut quidem multorum opinio est, ante in elementis, quam vel illa in membris, vel ista in ramis exstiterint. At secundum hoc cum desinunt vivificare, simul vivere cessant, sed non et esse. (*Opera* 3165.) Cf. Letter 104, 2 (*Opera* 284); Sermon 5 on Canticles, 1 (*Opera* 2683).

[3] *Ibid.*, 2 (*Opera* 3164).

that is, substantially simple; but since it has other attributes not identical with itself, it is not absolutely simple, like God.

Only for God is being identical with being blessed: and this is the first and purest simplicity. But the second is like unto this, namely to have being identical with living: and this pertains to the soul.[4]

For the same reason, it is immortal, that is, ever living; but since it is subject to change in time, it is not eternally immutable, like God.

True and perfect immortality has neither change nor end, because all change is a certain representation of death. For everything which changes, when it passes from one being to another, necessarily dies, in a certain sense, with respect to what it is, in order to begin to be what it is not. But if there are as many deaths as changes, where is immortality? And *the creature was made subject to this vanity, not willingly, but by reason of him who hath subjected the same in hope.* Nevertheless the soul is immortal, for, since it is its own life, it can no more fall from life than it can fall from itself.[5]

2. The "soul" of the soul

However, in another meaning of the word *life*, the soul may acquire its own "life" (knowledge) and its own "sensitivity" (love) by being animated by its own "soul" (God). Thus God bears the same relation to the soul which the soul bears to the body.

[4] *Ibid.*, 2: Soli Deo id est esse, quod beatum esse: atque hoc primum et purissimum simplex. Secundum autem simile est huic, id videlicet habere esse quod vivere: atque hoc animae est. (*Opera* 3164.) Cf. *Conversion* 2, 3 (*Opera* 1135).

[5] *Ibid.*, 5: Vera namque et integra immortalitas tam non recipit mutationem, quam nec finem, quod omnis mutatio quaedam mortis imitatio sit. Omne etenim quod mutatur, dum de uno ad aliud transit esse, quodam modo necesse est moriatur quod est, ut esse incipiat quod non est. Quod si tot mortes quot mutationes, ubi immortalitas? Et huic *vanitati subjecta est ipsa creatura non volens, sed propter eum qui subjecit eam in spe* (Rom. 8. 20). Attamen immortalis anima est: quoniam cum ipsa sibi vita sit; sicut non est quo cadat a se, sic non est quo cadat a vita. (*Opera* 3166.) Cf. Sermon 31 on Canticles, 1 (*Opera* 2862).

A soul which lacks knowledge of truth cannot be said to be alive, but is so far dead in itself; likewise one which does not yet possess love is without sensitivity. The life of the soul, therefore, is truth; its sensitivity, love. You need not wonder that sometimes the souls of wicked men have knowledge of truth and yet are devoid of love, since in some bodies also you find life without sensitivity, as in trees, and such like, which are animated to be sure, but with animation, not with a soul; likewise the souls of wicked men also have knowledge of truth by natural reason, and are sometimes aided by grace, although nowise animated thereby. But in those souls in which their spiritual "soul" infuses both knowledge of truth and love, not in any external way, but as their own "soul," by adhering to which they become one spirit with it; in these souls, I say, the knowledge of truth is undivided, just as was said concerning the life of the body; for you comprehend both great and small things by the same knowledge.

But the love, on the other hand, if you note carefully, you can find varied and perhaps fivefold like the five senses of the body. For there is a pious love, by which we love our parents; there is a pleasant love, by which we love our friends; there is also a just love toward all men, a violent love toward our enemies, a holy or devout love toward God.[1]

[1] Misc. Sermon 10, 1: Neque enim vivere dicenda est anima, quae veritatis non habet cognitionem, sed adhuc mortua est in semet ipsa, quemadmodum et ea sine sensu, quae necdum habet dilectionem. Est ergo animae vita veritas, sensus caritas. Nec mireris, quod interdum animae impiorum notitiam habent veritatis, quae tamen expertes sunt caritatis, quando et in corporibus nonnullis vitam reperis sine sensu, ut sunt arbores ceteraque similia, animata quidem, sed animatione et non anima; quemadmodum et animae iniquorum veritatis habent notitiam naturali ratione, quae tamen interdum adjuvantur a gratia, cum nullatenus sane animentur ab ea. In his autem, quibus et cognitionem veritatis et dilectionem anima spiritualis infundit, non exteriori quolibet modo, sed tamquam anima ipsorum, cui adhaerentes unus spiritus fiunt cum ea, in his — inquam — indivisa est cognitio veritatis, secundum quod dictum est de vita corporis; eadem enim cognitione et minima et maxima comprehendis.

2. Porro dilectionem quidem, si diligenter advertas, variam et fortassis secundum quinque sensus corporis quinquepartitam poteris invenire. Est enim amor pius, quo parentes diligimus; est amor jucundus, quo socios diligimus; est et erga omnes homines amor justus, erga inimicos amor violentus, erga Deum sanctus sive devotus. (XB 777.)

Note how Bernard uses *caritas*, *dilectio*, and *amor* as exact synonyms. Pious, pleasant, just, violent, and holy love are analogous respectively to

With respect to this spiritual "life" the immortal soul is mortal. The body is created dead; becomes alive, acquiring natural life and natural sensitivity, when animated by its soul; dies when separated from this soul; and is resurrected when animated by it again. Likewise the soul is created dead; becomes alive, acquiring spiritual "life" and spiritual "sensitivity," when animated by its "soul" (God); dies when separated from this "soul"; and is resurrected when animated by it again.

There are two deaths and two resurrections. The first death is of the soul, the second of the body; the death of the soul is separation from God, the death of the body is separation of the soul from the body; the former is effected by sin, the latter by the penalty of sin. Moreover, the first resurrection is of the soul, the second of the body; the resurrection of the soul is effected by Christ's humble and secret coming, the resurrection of the body is perfected by Christ's glorious and open coming. But the invisible soul is created in the image of God; wherefore the scripture says: *God made man in his image and likeness*. Upright indeed. Wherefore the outer man also, that is the body, appears upright in its form, having life and sensitivity, so that through this outer and visible man we may understand that inner and invisible one, who is made upright in will, alive in knowledge, sensible in love. And just as the body, that is the outer man, recovers life and sensitivity in its resurrection, so also the soul, that is the inner man, recovers life and sensitivity in its resurrection, that is, knowledge and love. And that knowledge is life, Truth bears witness, saying: *This is life eternal, that they might know thee the true God, and Jesus Christ, whom thou hast sent*.[2]

---

touch, taste, smell, hearing, and sight; but a different theory of the soul's fivefold sensitivity is given in Misc. Sermon 116 (XB 1012). Cf. Sermon 81 on Canticles, 4: Ut nisi creata ab illo non esset, sic nisi ab ipso vivificata non viveret. Non viveret dico, sed spirituali vita, non naturali. Nam naturali quidem, etiam quae non spiritualiter vivit, immortaliter vivat necesse est. (*Opera* 3166.) Cf. *Precept and Dispensation* 20, 60 (*Opera* 1212); Misc. Sermon 47 (XB 915); Misc. Sermon 84, 1 (XB 959).

[2] Misc. Sermon 116: Duae sunt mortes et totidem resurrectiones. Prima mors animae, secunda corporis; mors animae separatio a Deo, mors corporis separatio animae a corpore; hanc operatur peccatum, illam poena peccati. Item, prima resurrectio animae, secunda corporis; resurrectionem animae operatus est humilis et occultus Christi adventus, resurrectionem corporis

This is Bernard's theory of knowledge, that knowledge is the "life" of the mortal soul.

It remains to inquire whether this spiritual "life" is sufficient for the vision of God (that is, without baptism) and whether it is necessary (notwithstanding baptism). It is obviously sufficient because it is union with God.[3] But refusal to obey the command to be baptized would be a sin demonstrating the absence of spiritual "life." Baptism, therefore, is necessary for the spiritually "living" only in the sense that refusal would be a sign that they were not spiritually "living"; it is not itself necessary for the remission of original sin.[4] So far as can be understood by reason, spiritual "life" is necessary. But we believe by faith that in the case of children baptism is sufficient for salvation.[5] The baptism of water is a substitute for

---

gloriosus et manifestus Christi perficiet adventus. Sed anima invisibilis est ad imaginem Dei creata; unde dicit scriptura: *Fecit Deus hominem ad imaginem et similitudinem suam* (Gen. 1. 26). Rectum quidem. Unde et exterior homo, id est corpus, in forma sua rectus apparet, habens vitam et sensum, ut per hunc exteriorem et visibilem illum interiorem et invisibilem intelligeremus, qui rectus factus est in voluntate, vivus in cognitione, sensibilis in amore. Et sicut corpus, id est exterior homo, in resurrectione sua vitam et sensum recipiet, ita et in resurrectione sua vitam et sensum anima, id est interior homo, recipit, id est cognitionem et amorem. Quod autem cognitio vita sit, Veritas attestatur, dicens: *Haec est vita aeterna, ut cognoscant te Deum verum et quem misisti Jesum Christum* (Joan. 17. 3). (XB 1012.) Cf. Sermon 10 on *Qui Habitat*, 3–4 (XB 260).

[3] Faith (not in the epistemological sense of the word, but meaning "the turning of the heart to God") is the condition of salvation. Martyrdom is efficacious because of the faith which makes it possible, not because of the martyrdom itself, which is only a sign proving to men the existence of the faith. The faith is no less efficacious if the circumstances do not require martyrdom. *Baptism* 2, 8–9 (*Opera* 1412).

[4] *Ibid.*

[5] In ancient times the function of baptism was efficaciously fulfilled, among the Jews by circumcision, among the gentiles by their own faith and sacrificial rites. The validity of these rites ceased only when the institution of baptism was sufficiently promulgated. (*Ibid.*, 4 ff.) It would seem to follow (though Bernard does not draw the conclusion) that even today a heathen rite is sufficient for the remission of original sin in non-Christian countries. And from this it would seem to follow, *a fortiori*, that Christian baptism does not require any particular formula; and this is Bernard's opinion (Letter 403, *Opera* 719).

the baptism of desire, miraculously established by God in order that even children may be saved.

Acquiring spiritual "life" by turning to God is a natural process; it is indeed the most natural thing for the human soul. Concerning this process, that is, in his epistemology, Bernard speaks as a philosopher. But salvation by baptism is a miracle which transcends human understanding. Concerning it he speaks as a theologian.

The spiritual creature which we are has need of a body, without which it could nowise attain that knowledge which it obtains as the only approach to those things by knowledge of which it is made blessed. If it be objected to me here concerning regenerate children, that, going from the body without any knowledge of corporeal things, they are nevertheless believed to pass to the blessed life; I reply briefly that grace, not nature, confers this on them. And what have I to do with a miracle of God when I am discussing the processes of nature? [6]

Not that Bernard denies that grace is the sole cause of whatever good we think or do; but he distinguishes between natural grace and miraculous grace.

3. Faculties of the soul

The soul, which is made in the image of God, consists of three faculties: memory, will, and reason.

That blessed and eternal Trinity, Father and Son and Holy Ghost, one God indeed, supreme power, supreme wisdom, supreme goodness, created a certain trinity in its own image and likeness, namely the rational soul, which exhibits a certain trace of that supreme Trinity in this, that it consists of memory, reason, and will.[1]

[6] Sermon 5 on Canticles, 1: Habet ergo necessarium corpus spiritualis creatura quae nos sumus, sine quo nimirum nequaquam illam scientiam assequitur, quam solam accepit gradum ad ea, de quorum fit cognitione beata. Hic si mihi objicitur de parvulis regeneratis, quod absque scientia rerum corporalium exeuntes de corpore, ad beatam vitam nihilominus transire credantur; breviter respondeo hoc illis conferre gratiam, non naturam. Et quid ad me de miraculo Dei, qui de naturalibus dissero? (*Opera* 2683.)

[1] Misc. Sermon 45, 1: Beata illa et sempiterna Trinitas, Pater et Filius et Spiritus sanctus; unus Deus scilicet, summa potentia, summa sapientia, summa

The death of the soul is the death of each faculty.

But this created trinity chose to fall by the force of its own will, rather than to stand by the grace of God through free choice. It fell, therefore, by suggestion, delight, consent [2] from that supreme and beautiful trinity, namely power, wisdom, purity, into a certain contrary and ugly trinity, namely weakness, blindness, impurity; for the memory became impotent and weak, the reason imprudent and obscure, the will impure.[3]

And the resurrection of the soul is the resurrection of each faculty.

Nevertheless that blessed Trinity, mindful of its mercy, unmindful of our guilt, has repaired this fall, so grave, so obscure, so sordid, of our nature. The Son of God, therefore, sent by the Father, came and gave faith; after the Son, was sent the Holy Ghost, who gave and taught love. And so by these two, that is faith and love, was aroused hope of returning to the Father. And this is the trinity, namely faith, hope, love, with which as with a trident that changeless and blessed Trinity has brought back the changeable, fallen, and wretched trinity from the slime of the abyss to its lost beatitude. And faith has illumined the reason, hope has lifted up the memory, love has truly purged the will.[4]

---

benignitas, creavit quamdam trinitatem ad imaginem et similitudinem suam, animam videlicet rationalem, quae in eo praefert vestigium quoddam illius summae Trinitatis, quod ex memoria, ratione et voluntate consistit. (XB 911.) Cf. *Conversion* 6, 11 (*Opera* 1142); Sermon 1 for Easter, 11 (XB 336); Sermon 11 on Canticles, 5 (*Opera* 2717).

[2] These words apply to memory, will, and reason respectively.

[3] *Ibid.*, 1: Sed haec trinitas creata elegit potius per motum propriae voluntatis cadere, quam ex gratia Conditoris per liberum arbitrium stare. Cecidit ergo per suggestionem, delectationem, consensum ab illa summa et pulchra trinitate, scilicet potentia, sapientia, puritate, in quamdam contrariam et foedam trinitatem, scilicet infirmitatem, caecitatem, immunditiam; memoria enim facta est impotens et infirma, ratio imprudens et tenebrosa, voluntas impura. (XB 911.) Cf. *Conversion* 6, 11 (*Opera* 1142).

[4] *Ibid.*, 4: Verumtamen hunc tam gravem, tam tenebrosum, tam sordidum lapsum nostrae naturae reparavit illa beata Trinitas, memor misericordiae suae, immemor culpae nostrae. Venit ergo a Patre missus Dei Filius et dedit fidem; post Filium missus est Spiritus sanctus et dedit docuitque caritatem. Itaque per haec duo, id est fidem et caritatem, facta est spes redeundi ad Patrem. Et haec est trinitas, scilicet fides, spes, caritas, per quam velut per tridentem reduxit de limo profundi ad amissam beatitudinem illa incom-

(1) The *memory* is the thinking faculty. It is the most essential faculty, for without it the soul would not only fail to be a human soul, but would fail to be a soul at all.[5] In the state of spiritual death the memory is devoted to thoughts which are not thoughts of truth; thoughts for the necessities of the body, which cannot be neglected but should be limited; thoughts concerned with our occupations; impure and evil thoughts of various sorts; and frivolous thoughts, which are not in themselves evil but which distract the soul.[6] Sins exist in the memory even when past; and the memory of past sins is what constitutes the torment of hell, which is everlasting because the sins cannot be eradicated from the memory.[7] Even the miraculous forgiveness of sins cannot delete them from the memory, for that would be to destroy the memory, but it brings it about that they no longer hurt the memory in which they exist.[8] Hope of forgiveness, of grace, and of glory restores the dead memory,[9] and in the state of spiritual life it is devoted to thoughts of God.[10]

(2) The *will* is the emotional faculty. Willing is a matter of feeling, not of mere thinking or mere choosing. There is no problem of free will, because the will is free by definition. Freedom is opposed to necessity; to act *freely* is defined as meaning to act *willingly*.[11] Lust of the flesh, lust of the eyes,

mutabilis et beata Trinitas mutabilem, lapsam et miseram trinitatem. Et fides quidem illuminavit rationem, spes erexit memoriam, caritas vero purgavit voluntatem. (XB 913.) Cf. *Grace and Free Choice* 14, 49 (*Opera* 1399); Sermon 1 for Whitsunday, 5 (XB 397); *Les Inédits Bernardins du MS d'Anchin*, "S. Bernard et Son Temps," II (Dijon, 1929), p. 275.

[5] *Consideration* 5, 12, 26 (*Opera* 1090). Irrational souls have the faculty of memory (cf. *Grace and Free Choice* 2, 5, *Opera* 1369); plants, which lack memory, although animated, do not have souls (Misc. Sermon 10, 1, XB 777).

[6] Misc. Sermon 31 (XB 853); Misc. Sermon 45, 1 (XB 912). Cf. *Conversion* 3, 4 (*Opera* 1136).

[7] *Consideration* 5, 12, 25 and 26 (*Opera* 1090).

[8] *Conversion* 15, 28 (*Opera* 1153).

[9] Misc. Sermon 45, 5 (XB 913).

[10] *Ibid.*, 1: Simplicis divinitatis potentiam stans cogitabat. (XB 912.)

[11] *Grace and Free Choice* 2, 4 (*Opera* 1368); *ibid.* 2, 5 (*Opera* 1369); *ibid.* 12, 39 (*Opera* 1391); Sermon 81 on Canticles, 7 (*Opera* 3167). There are

and worldly ambition drive the will into delight for things of the earth; and this is spiritual death.[12] Love restores it to life.[13]

(3) The *reason* is the choosing faculty. It distinguishes good and bad by ethics or moral science, true and false by logic or inspective science, expedient and inexpedient by physics or natural science. It does so infallibly so long as it is illumined by the light which created it. But when it has lost that light it makes errors. Being thus fallible, it cannot restore itself by its own power, but must be aided by faith, which infallibly makes those distinctions which corrupt reason is no longer able to make.[14]

The will and the reason are faculties proper to man and other rational beings, and it is by them that we are distinguished from irrational brutes. They are distinct faculties because their functions are distinct, but they always act together.[15] Willing implies choosing that which is willed; [16] and choosing implies willing that which is chosen.[17] The joint action of will and reason is consent. The consenting faculty, that is, the joint faculty of will and reason, is called *free*

---

several problems of freedom: that of free choice (Do we choose what we will?), that of free counsel (Do we know what we will?), and that of free enjoyment (Do we enjoy what we will?); but the problem of free will (Do we will what we will?) would be meaningless.

[12] Misc. Sermon 45, 3 (XB 912).

[13] *Ibid.*, 4 and 5 (XB 913).

[14] *Ibid.*, 2 and 4 (XB 912). Cf. Sermon 3 for Christmas Eve, 8 (XB 90).

[15] They always act together, but do not always function together. Voluntary action is always rational, but voluntary thinking may be irrational, as in the case of desires which are resisted. Rational action is always voluntary, but rational thinking may be involuntary, as in the case of cognitive humility.

[16] *Grace and Free Choice*, 2, 3: Porro voluntas est motus rationalis, et sensui praesidens, et appetitui. Habet sane, quocumque se volverit, semper rationem comitem, et quodammodo pedissequam: non quod semper ex ratione, sed quod nunquam absque ratione moveatur, ita ut multa faciat per ipsam contra ipsam, hoc est quasi per ejus ministerium, contra ejus consilium sive judicium. (*Opera* 1368.)

[17] *Ibid.* 2, 4: Est vero ratio data voluntati ut instruat illam, non destruat. Destrueret autem, si necessitatem ei ullam imponeret, quominus libere pro arbitrio sese volveret. (*Opera* 1368.)

choice;[18] the word *free* means willing, and the word *choice* means the action of the reason.

Such consent, therefore, on account of the will's inalienable freedom and the reason's inflexible judgment (which it always and everywhere carries with it), is not improperly named, I believe, free choice, free of itself with respect to the will, judge of itself with respect to the reason.[19]

Such voluntary and free consent, from which (as aforesaid) all self-judgment is shown to depend, is not improperly, I think, that which (as defined above) is usually called free choice; so that free refers to the will, choice to the reason.[20]

In the first place, free choice is free because it is voluntary, that is, of the will, and this is precisely what the word "free" means.

It is a disposition of the mind, free of itself. Since it is not forced, it is not extorted. For it is of will, not of necessity; it neither denies nor lends itself to anything, save by will. If on the contrary it can be compelled unwilling, it is violent, not voluntary. But where there is no will, there is no consent either. For there is no consent which is not voluntary. Therefore, where consent is, there will is. But where will is, there freedom is. And this is what I think is named free choice.[21]

[18] *Ibid.* 14, 46: Quid igitur? hoc ergo totum liberi arbitrii opus, hoc solum ejus est meritum quod consentit? Est prorsus. (*Opera* 1396.) *Liberum arbitrium* must not be translated "free will," a rendering which misinterprets the meaning of the phrase, because it is the word *liberum*, not *arbitrium*, which represents the will aspect. The phrase could be rendered with approximate accuracy as "voluntary choice" or "willing choice," but not as "free will."

[19] *Ibid.* 2, 4: Is ergo talis consensus, ob voluntatis inamissibilem libertatem, et rationis quod secum semper et ubique portat, indeclinabile judicium, non incongrue dicetur, ut arbitror, liberum arbitrium, ipse liber sui propter voluntatem, ipse judex sui propter rationem. (*Opera* 1369.)

[20] *Ibid.* 3, 6: Quapropter hujusmodi voluntarium liberumque consensum, ex quo et omne sui (ex his quae dicta sunt) constat pendere judicium; puto non incongrue id esse, ut supra definivimus, quod solet liberum arbitrium appellari: ut liberum ad voluntatem, arbitrium referatur ad rationem. (*Opera* 1370.) Cf. *ibid.* 4, 11 (*Opera* 1373).

[21] *Ibid.* 1, 2: Est enim habitus animi, liber sui. Siquidem non cogitur, non extorquetur. Est quippe voluntatis, non necessitatis; nec negat se, nec praebet cuiquam, nisi ex voluntate. Alioquin si compelli valet invitus, violentus est,

If a person chooses what he does not will, that means only that he wills the consequence of his choice more strongly than he wills the alternative; the stronger will prevails over the weaker will; and so the choice is truly willed and therefore truly free.[22] In the second place, free choice is choice, because it is a distinction between good and bad, that is, it is a rational distinction, and this is precisely what the word "choice" means. The reason judges its choice as being good or bad, and this is how it differs from the non-moral discriminations made by irrational brutes.

And deservedly does judgment accompany liberty; because that which is free of itself certainly judges itself when it sins.[23]

Since it is part of his essential nature, man possesses free choice absolutely. This means in the first place that he possesses it inalienably and under all conditions whatever, whether of innocence, corruption, grace, salvation, damnation, or any other condition; except only the conditions of insanity, infancy, and sleep.[24] It means in the second place that he possesses it to an equal degree with all other rational beings, even God.[25]

The possession of free choice distinguishes man from the brutes. He has life ("an internal and natural movement, flourishing internally only") in common with plants and animals; he has sensitivity ("a vital movement in the body, flourishing also externally") and natural appetite ("a force in the living being, devoted to moving the senses avidly") in common with

---

non voluntarius. Ubi autem voluntas non est, nec consensus. Non enim est consensus, nisi voluntarius. Ubi ergo consensus, ibi voluntas. Porro ubi voluntas, ibi libertas. Et hoc est quod dici puto liberum arbitrium. (*Opera* 1367.) Cf. Thomas Aquinas, *Sum. Theol.* 1, 83, 2, ad secundum.

[22] For example, Peter denied Christ unwillingly, as it seemed, because his will to live was stronger than his will to acknowledge Christ. *Ibid.* 12, 38 (*Opera* 1391).

[23] *Ibid.* 2, 4: Et merito libertatem comitatur judicium: quoniam quidem quod liberum sui est, profecto ubi peccat, ibi se judicat (*Opera* 1369). Cf. *ibid.* 4, 11: Arbitrium quippe judicium est (*Opera* 1373).

[24] *Ibid.* 2, 5 (*Opera* 1369).

[25] *Ibid.* 4, 9: Verum libertas a necessitate aeque et indifferenter Deo universaeque tam malae quam bonae rationali convenit creaturae (*Opera* 1372).

animals. But consent ("a spontaneous nod of the will, or a disposition of the mind, free of itself") is peculiarly human.[26] Life, sensitivity, and appetite pertain to the body. Free choice, which pertains to the soul, rules these faculties of the body.[27] It rules the body in the same way in which divine wisdom rules the world.[28] All other faculties, both of body and of mind, are free insofar as they are dependent on free choice; insofar as they are independent of it, then, as in brutes, they are subject to necessity.[29]

Free choice is the necessary condition of good merit and of bad merit; because we are responsible only for what we do voluntarily. It is therefore the necessary condition of beatitude and of misery, which are awarded to us in accordance with our merits. These concepts have meaning only when attributed to free choice.

If just or unjust things could be done through necessity and without the consent of one's own will, the rational creature neither should for any reason be miserable nor could at all be blessed, since in either case there would be lacking to it that which in it is alone capable of misery or of beatitude, that is, the will.[30]

The consent of the will, being voluntary, not necessary, makes us just or unjust; [31] and free choice, therefore, is the capacity for blessedness or misery.

[26] *Ibid.* 2, 3 and 4 (*Opera* 1367). Cf. Misc. Sermon 16, 3: Quid debet homo homini, quem et ratio docet et trahit affectio? (XB 796.) Cf. Sermon 81 on Canticles, 6 (*Opera* 3167).

[27] *Ibid.* 2, 3: Porro voluntas est motus rationalis, et sensui praesidens et appetitui (*Opera* 1368).

[28] *Ibid.* 10, 33: Forma autem sapientia est; conformatio, ut faciat imago in corpore quod forma facit in orbe (*Opera* 1387).

[29] *Ibid.* 2, 5: Vita, sensus, appetitus, memoria, ingenium, et si qua talia sunt, eo ipso subjacent necessitati, quo non plene subdita sunt voluntati (*Opera* 1369).

[30] *Ibid.* 2, 4: Quod si ex necessitate, et absque consensu propriae voluntatis, justa injustave fieri possent; rationalis creatura aut misera profecto esse nulla ratione deberet; aut beata penitus non posset, cui nimirum in utravis parte id deesset, quod solum in ea miseriae sive beatitudinis capax est, id est voluntas (*Opera* 1368). Cf. *ibid.* 2, 5 (*Opera* 1369); *ibid.* 11, 36 (*Opera* 1389); *ibid.* 14, 46 (*Opera* 1396).

[31] *Ibid.* 2, 4: Cujus voluntatis consensus, utique voluntarius, non neces-

The will alone, therefore, since on account of its innate self-freedom it is compelled by no force, by no necessity, either to dissent with itself or to consent to anything in spite of itself, not unrightly makes a creature just or unjust, worthy and capable of beatitude or misery; that is, according as it has consented to justice or to injustice.[32]

This discussion of free choice and merit, however, does not apply to the case of original sin, for which the individual is not responsible in the same way in which he is responsible for his actual sins.[33]

Free choice is always free, but in another meaning of the word *free* it is "enslaved" and must be "liberated."[34] In the state of nature man is not completely free. The existence of misery shows that he is not free to enjoy what he wills, and the existence of sin shows that he is not even able to will what is good. Misery shows that we lack freedom of enjoyment, and sin shows that we lack freedom of counsel; but we always have freedom of choice, being able to choose what we will.[35]

We believe that free choice takes its name from this freedom by which the will is free to judge itself, either as good if it has consented to good or as evil if to evil (for in neither case does it feel itself to be consenting otherwise than willingly). For that freedom which is from sin might perhaps more appropriately be called free counsel; and again that which is from misery might be called free enjoyment rather than free choice.[36]

---

sarius, dum aut justos probat aut injustos, etiam merito beatos facit vel miseros (*Opera* 1369). Cf. *ibid.* 12, 41 (*Opera* 1393).

[32] *Ibid.* 3, 6: Sola ergo voluntas, quoniam pro sui ingenita libertate, aut dissentire sibi, aut praeter se in aliquo consentire, nulla vi, nulla cogitur necessitate; non immerito justam vel injustam, beatitudine seu miseria dignam ac capacem creaturam constituit; prout scilicet justitiae injustitiaeve consenserit (*Opera* 1370). Cf. Sermon 3 for Easter, 3 (XB 350).

[33] *Ibid.* 2, 5 (*Opera* 1369); *ibid.* 12, 38 (*Opera* 1390); *ibid.* 13, 42 (*Opera* 1394). [34] *Ibid.* 3, 7 (*Opera* 1371); *ibid.* 6, 16 (*Opera* 1376).

[35] Sermon 81 on Canticles, 9: Ita anima miro quodam et malo modo sub hac voluntaria quadam et male libera necessitate, et ancilla tenetur, et libera: ancilla, propter necessitatem; libera, propter voluntatem: et quod magis mirum, magisque miserum est, eo rea quo libera, eoque ancilla quo rea, ac per hoc eo ancilla quo libera (*Opera* 3169).

[36] *Grace and Free Choice* 4, 11: Ex hac ergo tantum libertate, qua liberum

In the state of nature, corrupt reason would be unable to distinguish the good from the evil or the expedient from the inexpedient even if the will were good.[37] Corrupt will would be unable to consent to the good even if it were distinguished by reason.[38] Free choice is the slave of sin, so that the soul is both "dead" by the corruption of the will and "blind" by the corruption of the reason.[39] Nevertheless, the reason, although corrupt, still exists, and distinguishes between licit and illicit, and therefore judges its choice as good or bad.[40] And the will, although corrupt, still exists, and consents freely to its choice.[41]

The liberation of free choice requires a twofold grace, in order that it may be liberated from sin and from misery.

In order that our will, which we have by virtue of free choice, may be had perfect, we have need of a twofold gift of grace, namely, both true wisdom, which is the will's conversion to the good, and also full power, which is its confirmation in the good. Now perfect conversion to the good means that nothing pleases save that which is proper or licit; perfect confirmation in the good, that nothing which pleases is any longer lacking. Then at

---

est voluntati se ipsam judicare: vel bonam, si bono; vel malam, si malo consenserit (quippe quae in neutro, nisi certe volendo, consentire se sentit), liberum arbitrium credimus nominari. Nam ex illa quae dicitur a peccato, congruentius forsitan liberum consilium; et item ex illa quae dicta est a miseria, liberum potius complacitum posset dici, quam liberum arbitrium. (*Opera* 1373.)

[37] Misc. Sermon 45, 2 (XB 912). Cf. Sermon 85 on Canticles, 2 (*Opera* 3186).

[38] *Grace and Free Choice* 2, 3 (*Opera* 1368). Cf. *ibid.* 1, 1: Siquidem non est ejusdem facilitatis scire quid faciendum sit, et facere (*Opera* 1366).

[39] Sermon 85 on Canticles, 2: Nam et malum volendo mortua erat, et bonum ignorando caeca (*Opera* 3186). Cf. *Grace and Free Choice* 1, 1: Porro duo mihi sunt necessaria, doceri ac juvari (*Opera* 1366).

[40] *Grace and Free Choice* 4, 11: Arbitrium quippe judicium est. Sicut vero judicii est discernere quid liceat vel quid non liceat: sic profecto consilii probare quid expediat vel non expediat: sic complaciti quoque experiri quid libeat vel non libeat. Utinam tam libere nobis consuleremus, quam libere de nobis judicamus! ut quemadmodum libere per judicium licita illicitaque decernimus; ita per consilium et licita tanquam commoda nobis eligere, et illicita tanquam noxia respuere liberum haberemus. (*Opera* 1373.)

[41] *Ibid.* 11, 37: At vero quantislibet quis intus forisve tentationibus urgeatur, libera profecto semper, quantum ad arbitrium spectat, voluntas erit: libere quippe de suo nihilo minus consensu judicabit (*Opera* 1390).

last will the will be perfect, when it is fully good and full of good.[42]

The true wisdom which frees us from sin is free counsel; the full power which frees us from misery is free enjoyment.[43] Free counsel, which is consent to the good, involves three elements: the will freely approves the good; [44] the reason truly distinguishes the good; [45] and the free choice resolutely consents to the good.[46] Free counsel makes us good but not necessarily happy. Just as free choice does not imply free counsel, because, although we perceive what ought to be done by our judgment, we do not always choose to do it by our counsel; so likewise free counsel does not imply free enjoyment, because, even though we do what is right willingly, we do not always do it gladly, but rather find it a wearisome duty.[47] Free enjoyment, which is delight in the good, involves two

[42] *Ibid.* 6, 19: Ut ergo velle nostrum, quod ex libero arbitrio habemus, perfectum habeamus; duplici gratiae munere indigemus, et vero videlicet Sapere, quod est voluntatis ad bonum conversio; et pleno etiam Posse, quod est ejusdem in bono confirmatio. Porro perfecta conversio est ad bonum, ut nil libeat nisi quod deceat vel liceat; perfecta in bono confirmatio, ut nil desit jam quod libeat. Tunc demum perfecta erit voluntas, cum plene fuerit bona et bene plena. (*Opera* 1378.)

[43] *Ibid.* 6, 20 (*Opera* 1379). Cf. *ibid.* 3, 7 (*Opera* 1370).

[44] *Ibid.* 6, 16: Itaque liberum arbitrium nos facit volentes, gratia benevolos. . . . Aliud est velle, aliud velle bonum. (*Opera* 1377.) Cf. *ibid.* 6, 17 (*Opera* 1377); Sermon 85 on Canticles, 1 (*Opera* 3185).

[45] *Ibid.* 4, 11 (cited above). Cf. *ibid.* 2, 4: Est vero ratio data voluntati ut instruat illam (*Opera* 1368). Cf. Sermon 85 on Canticles, 2: Nec parum profecit anima tua, cujus immutata voluntas, cujus illuminata ratio est, ut bonum et velit et noverit (*Opera* 3186).

[46] *Ibid.* 1, 1: Ecce enim jam ex ejus munere velle adjacet mihi, perficere autem non invenio; sed nec aliquando me inventurum confido, nisi qui dedit velle det et perficere pro bona voluntate (*Opera* 1366). Cf. Sermon 85 on Canticles, 3–6 (*Opera* 3186).

[47] *Ibid.* 4, 11: Nunc autem cum multa per judicium vel admittenda vel omittenda esse decernamus, quae tamen per consilium nequaquam pro judicii rectitudine aut eligimus aut contemnimus; rursumque non omnia, quae tanquam recta et commoda consulte observamus, etiam ut beneplacita libenter amplectimur, sed insuper quasi dura ac molesta vix aequanimiter ferre perduramus: liquet quia liberum nec consilium habemus, nec complacitum (*Opera* 1373). Cf. Sermon 3 for Ascension, 6 (XB 373); Sermon 85 on Canticles, 7–9 (*Opera* 3189).

elements: it is delight, because it is attended with pleasure; [48] and it is in the good, because pleasure in sins is the truest misery.[49] Free enjoyment is never found in the pleasures of the body, because these consist of the urgency of appetite followed by the boredom of satiety, neither of which is enjoyable in itself; the only enjoyment in ordinary life is the substitution of a lesser misery for a greater one.[50] In ordinary life we are never perfectly free from sin, yet we can, by refusal to consent to it, keep from being conquered by it, and so we can possess wisdom in a large degree; we are never at all free from misery, yet we can, by manly contempt of it, keep from being conquered by it, and so we can possess power in a small degree.[51] Only the just possess the true wisdom which is free counsel, and only those who are experiencing mystical contemplation possess the full power which is free enjoyment.[52] The saints in heaven, even before the resurrection, possess both freedoms fully and perfectly, that is, without any interruption.[53]

Free counsel is a gift of grace.[54] All three kinds of freedom, to be sure, are gifts of grace in the wide sense.[55] But free choice is a gift of creating grace, which creates the soul with all its essential attributes.[56] And free enjoyment is a gift of consummating grace; it is a gift of grace, that is, not an *effect*

[48] *Ibid.* 4, 11: Sed quid si totum solumque quod expediret vel liceret, etiam liberet? Nonne liberi quoque esse complaciti merito diceremur, quippe qui ab omni proinde quod displicere potest, hoc est ab omni nos miseria, liberos sentiremus? (*Opera* 1373.)

[49] *Ibid.* 5, 14 (*Opera* 1375).

[50] *Ibid.* 5, 14 (*Opera* 1375).

[51] *Ibid.* 8, 26 (*Opera* 1383); 9, 29 (*Opera* 1384).

[52] *Ibid.* 5, 15 (*Opera* 1376). Contemplatives possess free enjoyment "ex parte, et parte satis modica, viceque rarissima"; this restriction refers (as the context shows) to the intermittency of contemplation, and does not imply any flaw in the freedom from misery within the experience itself.

[53] *Ibid.* 4, 9 (*Opera* 1372).

[54] *Ibid.* 6, 16: Itaque liberum arbitrium nos facit volentes, gratia benevolos (*Opera* 1377). Cf. *ibid.* 3, 7: Dicatur igitur prima libertas Naturae; secunda, Gratiae; tertia, Vitae vel Gloriae (*Opera* 1370). Cf. *ibid.* 1, 1 (*Opera* 1365); *ibid.* 6, 19 (*Opera* 1378).

[55] *Ibid.* 14, 49 (*Opera* 1398).   [56] *Ibid.* 6, 16 (*Opera* 1376).

of our merit;[57] but it is the kind of grace which can be confidently anticipated because it is owed to us by God in consideration of our merit, that is, it is a *reward* of our merit.[58] Free counsel is a gift of grace in the narrow sense,[59] that is, it is a *merit*.[60] It is natural grace, not miraculous grace (like that of baptism).[61] It is provecting grace,[62] not preventing grace (which inspires good thoughts without affecting the will).[63] God creates the soul by giving it natural life; he then recreates it by giving it spiritual life. This recreating grace liberates or saves the free choice from sin by changing it to free choice of the good, and so is called saving grace.[64]

Saving grace operates salvation, and so, being omnipotent, it is the sufficient condition of salvation.[65] But free choice is the necessary condition of salvation.[66] The inconsistency of these facts presents a dilemma: if grace is sufficient, how can free choice be necessary? Bernard's solution maintains the omnipotence of God. Grace alone saves, and does not need any "cooperation" in the sense of assistance. But while grace is the efficient cause of salvation, free choice is its material cause. Free choice is the very thing which is saved. Salva-

---

[57] *Ibid.* 14, 51: Alioquin si proprie appellentur ea, quae dicimus nostra merita; spei quaedam sunt seminaria, charitatis incentiva, occultae praedestinationis indicia, futurae felicitatis praesagia, via regni, non causa regnandi (*Opera* 1400).

[58] *Ibid.* 13, 43: Deus namque rex noster ante saecula, cum operatus est salutem in medio terrae, dona sua quae dedit hominibus, in merita divisit et praemia: ut et praesentia per liberam possessionem nostra interim fierent merita, et futura per gratuitam sponsionem exspectaremus, imo expeteremus ut debita (*Opera* 1394).

[59] *Ibid.* 6, 18: Deo [nos] subjicit ejus gratia, non nostra voluntas (*Opera* 1378).

[60] *Ibid.* 14, 49: Cum igitur consummatio fieri habeat de nobis, sive etiam in nobis, non autem a nobis; creatio vero facta sit et sine nobis: sola, quae nobiscum quodammodo fit propter consensum voluntarium nostrum, in merita nobis reputabitur reformatio (*Opera* 1398).

[61] Sermon 5 on Canticles, 1 (*Opera* 2683).

[62] *Grace and Free Choice* 1, 1 (*Opera* 1365).

[63] *Ibid.* 14, 46 (*Opera* 1396).

[64] *Ibid.* 6, 16 (*Opera* 1377).

[65] *Ibid.* 13, 42: Sola salvat misericordia (*Opera* 1394).

[66] *Ibid.* 11, 36: Nemo quippe salvatur invitus (*Opera* 1389).

tion is the liberation of free choice from sin. To be saved means to consent to grace; and consenting is the function of free choice. God cannot save without free choice, for without it there would be nothing to save. The necessity of free choice for salvation, therefore, does not violate the divine omnipotence, because it is a logical, not a psychological, necessity.

What, then, you ask, does free choice do? I reply briefly: It is saved. Take away free choice, and there will be nothing to be saved; take away grace, there will be nothing by which it is saved. This work cannot be accomplished without two things: one by which it is done; the other to which or in which it is done. God is the author of salvation; free choice is merely receptive of it; nothing can give it except God; nothing can receive it except free choice. Because, therefore, it is given only by God and only to free choice, it cannot be accomplished either without the consent of the receiver or without the grace of the giver. And so free choice is said to cooperate with grace which is operating salvation, when it consents, that is, when it is saved. For to consent is to be saved.[67]

Since grace gives freedom, the problem of grace and freedom becomes reoriented in the course of the essay on *Grace and Free Choice*; the original problem, how can we be free when subject to grace, gives way to the problem, how can we be free even when not subject to grace; but both solutions are necessary, the former to justify salvation, the latter to justify damnation.

[67] *Ibid.* 1, 2: Quid igitur agit, ais, liberum arbitrium? Breviter respondeo: Salvatur. Tolle liberum arbitrium, et non erit quod salvetur: tolle gratiam, non erit unde salvetur. Opus hoc sine duobus effici non potest: uno a quo fit; altero cui, vel in quo fit. Deus auctor est salutis, liberum arbitrium tantum capax: nec dare illam, nisi Deus; nec capere valet, nisi liberum arbitrium. Quod ergo a solo Deo, et soli datur libero arbitrio; tam absque consensu esse [*alias*, effici] non potest accipientis, quam absque gratia dantis. Et ita gratiae operanti salutem cooperari dicitur liberum arbitrium, dum consentit, hoc est dum salvatur. Consentire enim salvari est. (*Opera* 1367.) Cf. *ibid.* 6, 16: Velle etenim bonum, profectus est; velle malum defectus. Velle vero simpliciter, ipsum est quod vel proficit vel deficit (*Opera* 1377). Cf. *ibid.* 13, 42 (*Opera* 1393).

Freedom in the sense of indeterminism, which is defined as equal power or facility to choose either good or evil, is not possessed by man, either in the state of nature or in the state of grace. It is not possessed by any being whatsoever — God, angels, men, or devils.[68] Indeterminism existed only in our first parents in the state of innocence; it was lost irrecoverably at the fall. Salvation elevates man from the state of nature (*non posse non peccare*) to the state of grace (*non posse peccare*), which is superior to the state of innocence in which man was originally (*posse non peccare*) [69] but inferior to the state in which he would have been if he had not fallen (*non peccare cum peccare posset*).[70]

4. Functions of the soul

There are three functions of the soul: thought, emotion, and intention; residing respectively in the memory, the will, and the reason.[1]

(1) *Thoughts* arise from three sources: they originate in our own souls, or they are inspired in us by evil spirits, or they are inspired in us by God. We "speak," as it were, the thoughts which originate in us; that is, we are the cause of them. But we "hear" the thoughts which are inspired in us, for something external is the cause of them, and we are merely receptive. Our original thoughts are always evil, because of the corruption of our nature; inspired thoughts are good or evil, depending on their source.[2] Therefore, it is hard (in fact impossible for Bernard himself) to distinguish between the first kind and the second kind of thoughts, both being evil; [3]

[68] *Ibid.* 10, 35 (*Opera* 1388).
[69] *Ibid.* 7, 21 (*Opera* 1380).
[70] *Ibid.* 7, 22 (*Opera* 1381).

[1] Misc. Sermon 32, 2: Sunt autem tria ista, id est cogitatio, affectio, et intentio, in anima, sed in ea quoque propriis singula locis distincta videntur; nam cogitatio in memoria est, affectio in voluntate, intentio in ratione consistit (XB 856).
[2] Sermon 32 on Canticles, 5 (*Opera* 2872).
[3] *Ibid.* 6 (*Opera* 2873).

but it is easy to distinguish between the first or second kind and the third kind, the former being evil and the latter good.[4] Chastity and peaceableness are criteria by which divinely inspired thoughts can be recognized.[5]

All good thoughts are brought about in us by God's preventing grace; that is, God alone causes them, without our cooperation or predisposition.[6] Therefore, they are not to our merit; but they are a necessary preliminary [7] to the operation of provecting grace which causes in us good will and good choice, that is, consent to the good, in which alone our merit consists.[8]

(2) There are four *emotions*: love, joy, fear, and sadness.[9] These exist in every human soul, but in different ways: if purified and rightly ordered, they become virtues; if not, they become vices.[10] Love and fear are purified when objects are loved and feared in proportion to their intrinsic loveableness and fearfulness; joy and sadness are purified when we rejoice or grieve in proportion to the goodness of the situation which

[4] *Ibid*. 7: Ergo quantum distat bonum a malo, tantum ista duo a se (*Opera* 2873). Cf. *ibid*. 5: Itaque pacem, pietatem, justitiam Deus in nobis loquitur: nec talia nos cogitamus ex nobis, sed in nobis audimus. Caeterum homicidia, adulteria, furta, blasphemiae, et his similia, de corde exeunt, nec audimus ea sed dicimus. (*Opera* 2872.)

[5] Misc. Sermon 24, 1 (XB 828).

[6] *Grace and Free Choice* 14, 46: Si ergo Deus tria haec, hoc est bonum cogitare, velle, perficere, operatur in nobis: primum profecto sine nobis; secundum, nobiscum; tertium, per nos facit. Siquidem immittendo bonam cogitationem, nos praevenit; immutando etiam malam voluntatem, sibi per consensum jungit; ministrando et consensui facultatem, foris per apertum opus nostrum internus opifex innotescit. (*Opera* 1396.) Cf. Sermon 82 on Canticles, 1 (*Opera* 3171).

[7] *Ibid*. 14, 46: Qui autem bonum neminem invenit, neminem salvat quem non praevenit (*Opera* 1396).

[8] *Ibid*. 14, 46: Valet itaque intentio ad meritum; actio, ad exemplum; utramque praeveniens cogitatio, tantummodo ad excitandum (*Opera* 1397).

[9] Misc. Sermon 50, 2: Sunt autem affectiones istae quatuor notissimae: amor et laetitia, timor et tristitia (XB 919).

[10] *Ibid*. 2: Absque his non subsistit humana anima, sed quibusdam sunt in coronam, quibusdam in confusionem; purgatae enim et ordinatae gloriosam in virtutum corona reddunt animam, inordinatae per confusionem dejectam et ignominiosam (XB 919).

Without love, we deliberately choose as expedient that which we correctly know to be wrong.[25] Without wisdom, we ignorantly choose as expedient that which we incorrectly believe to be right.[26]

(b) Intention on the good is called *religion*.[27] Fundamentally, this is the same as intention on the expedient, because the good is in fact the expedient; to know this is to possess free counsel.[28] But all men do not know this; therefore, although all men seek the expedient, all men do not seek the good. Only men of upright will prefer what appears to be the good. Only men of upright and strong will perform what appears to be the good, instead of the evil preferred by the flesh.[29] Only men of upright and strong will and enlightened understanding perform what is in fact the good. True religion being the same as true counsel, the fundamental requirements of true religion are the same as those of true counsel, namely, love and wisdom, that is, good will and enlightened understanding.[30] The understanding is enlightened by the Word of God, and the will is purified by the Spirit of God.[31] But without love we do not will to perform the

[25] *Grace and Free Choice* 4, 11 (*Opera* 1373). Cf. Sermon 3 for Easter, 3 (XB 350).

[26] Sermon 3 for Easter, 4: Lepra vero proprii consilii eo perniciosior est quo magis occulta, et quanto plus abundat, tanto sibi quisque sanior esse videtur. Haec illorum est, qui zelum Dei habent, sed non secundum scientiam; sequentes errorem suum et obstinati in eo ita, ut nullis velint consiliis acquiescere. (XB 351.)

[27] Sermon 3 for Ascension, 4: Sic ergo eorum intelligentia per Christum illuminata est et voluntas emundata per Spiritum, ut, sicut bonum noverint, sic et velint; quod solum perfecta religio vel religiosa perfectio est (XB 372).

[28] *Grace and Free Choice* 4, 11 (*Opera* 1373).

[29] Misc. Sermon 124, 2: In primo gradu anima mente legi Dei consentit, sed carne repugnante bonum, quod diligit, perficere non invenit (Rom. 7. 18), sed saepe malum, quod odit, per infirmitatem facit (XB 1019). The will, while always retaining perfect freedom of choice, may lack strength to control the body.

[30] *Precept and Dispensation* 14, 36: Ut interior oculus vere simplex sit, duo illi esse arbitror necessaria, charitatem in intentione, et in electione veritatem (*Opera* 1199).

[31] *Steps of Humility* 7, 21. Cf. Sermon 3 for Ascension, 2 (XB 371).

good which we know.[32] And without understanding, the stronger our good will the more we err.[33]

(c) Intention on the true is called *consideration*.

Consideration is thought intent on research, or the intention of the mind when it is searching for the true.[34]

There are three kinds of consideration: dispensative, estimative, and speculative; characteristic respectively of the active life, the academic life, and the contemplative life.

Great is he whose business is to distribute the use of the senses, like public funds, dispensing it for the salvation of himself and of many. And no less great is he who has made the use of the senses a step toward those things which are invisible, by philosophising; save that the latter is more pleasant, the former more useful; the latter is always the happier way, the former the sturdier. But greatest of all is he who spurns all use of things and of the senses, so far as is permitted to human weakness, and is accustomed to fly to those heights by contemplating, not by ascending steps but by unexpected raptures. To this last class I think Paul's raptures belong. Raptures, not ascents; for he himself asserts that he was caught up, rather than ascended. This is why he said, *Whether we be transported in mind, it is to God.* Now these three things happen thus when consideration, becoming dominant even in the place of its pilgrimage by zeal for virtue and help of grace, either represses sensibility lest it exult or restrains it lest it wander or flees it lest it corrupt. In the first case it is stronger, in the second freer, in the third purer. For that flight is made on the two wings of purity and ecstasy.

Do you wish these species of consideration to be distinguished

[32] Sermon 3 for Ascension, 7: Affectus id est voluntas eorum nondum purgata est nec bonum sic volunt sicut noverunt (XB 374).

[33] Sermon 4 for first Sunday of November, 2: *Scienti bonum et non facienti peccatum est illi* (Jac. 4. 17). Sic et zelus absque scientia, quo vehementius irruit, eo gravius corruit, impingens nimirum atque resiliens; ubi vero intelligentiam caritas, agnitionem devotio comitatur, volet secure, quisquis ejusmodi est, volet sine fine, quia volat in aeternitatem (XB 435).

[34] *Consideration* 2, 2, 5: Consideratio autem, intensa ad investigandum cogitatio, vel intentio animi vestigantis verum (*Opera* 1024). *Intensa cogitatio*, "thought intent," is a paraphrase for *intentio*, thought being the ever present substratum of all conscious activity; it does not mean "intense thought." Cf. Sermon 2 on Canticles, 3: Intendite [i.e., consider] (*Opera* 2672).

by different names? The first, if you please, let us call dispensative, the second estimative, the third speculative.[35]

Dispensative consideration is that which uses the senses and sensible things methodically and unselfishly in order to merit God.[36] This is the active life; it is the most necessary and important kind of consideration.

Rachel is more fair, but Leah is more fertile. So do not insist too much on the kisses of contemplation, for the breasts of preaching are better.[37]

But it has no epistemological value; it produces welfare, not knowledge, which it merits indeed, but does not itself attain.[38]

Estimative consideration is that which examines and ponders everything wisely and diligently in order to investigate God.[39] This includes science, philosophy, and theology. It proceeds

[35] *Consideration* 5, 2, 3: Magnus ille, qui usum sensuum, quasdam veluti civium opes, expendere satagit, dispensando in suam et multorum salutem. Nec ille minor, qui hunc sibi gradum ad illa invisibilia philosophando constituit: nisi quod hoc dulcius, illud utilius; hoc felicius, illud fortius esse constat. At omnium maximus, qui spreto ipso usu rerum et sensuum, quantum quidem humanae fragilitati fas est, non ascensoriis gradibus, sed inopinatis excessibus, avolare interdum contemplando ad illa sublimia consuevit. Ad hoc ultimum genus illos pertinere reor excessus Pauli. Excessus, non ascensus: nam raptum potius fuisse, quam ascendisse ipse se perhibet (2 Cor. 12. 1-4). Inde est quod dicebat: *Sive mente excedimus, Deo* (2 Cor. 5. 13). Porro haec tria ita contingunt, cum consideratio, etsi in loco peregrinationis suae, virtutis studio, et adjutorio gratiae facta superior, sensualitatem aut premit ne insolescat, aut cogit ne evagetur, aut fugit ne inquinet. In primo potentior, in secundo liberior, in tertio purior. Puritatis siquidem et alacritatis pariter alis fit ille volatus. 4. Vis tibi has considerationis species propriis distingui nominibus? Dicamus, si placet, primam dispensativam, secundam aestimativam, tertiam speculativam. (*Opera* 1073.)
[36] *Ibid.* 5, 2, 4: Dispensativa est consideratio sensibus sensibilibusque rebus ordinate et socialiter utens ad promerendum Deum (*Opera* 1074).
[37] Sermon 9 on Canticles, 8: Nam etsi Rachel formosior, sed Lia fecundior est. Noli ergo nimis insistere osculis contemplationis; quia meliora sunt ubera praedicationis. (*Opera* 2707.) Preaching is a typical expression of the active life, especially in the case of the monks to whom Bernard's writings were addressed.
[38] *Consideration* 5, 2, 4: Et prior quidem absque intuitu hujus multa serit et nihil metit (*Opera* 1074).
[39] *Ibid.* 5, 2, 4: Aestimativa est consideratio prudenter ac diligenter quaeque scrutans et ponderans ad vestigandum Deum (*Opera* 1074).

from the investigation of visible things to the investigation of invisible ones.[40]

Visible things are investigated by means of sense-perception, which reveals corporeal objects not as they are in themselves but as they appear to our sensitivity.[41] Sense-perception is made possible by a similarity between the sense organ and the object. Vision, the loftiest of the five senses,[42] is made possible by the similarity between the light in the eye and the light in the object.[43] Because this similarity is imperfect, sense-perception is imperfect.[44] Empirical knowledge, therefore, is fallible.[45] But it is a necessary preliminary to intellectual knowledge, which is derived from it.

We live indeed after the body; but we have no means of access to the conditions of blessed living save through the body. This fact was realized by him who said, *The invisible things of God are clearly seen, being understood by the things that are made.* But these things that are made, that is, visible corporeal things, do not come to our knowledge unless sensed by means of the body. Therefore the spiritual creature which we are has need of a body, without which it nowise attains that knowledge which it has acquired as the only approach to those things by knowledge of which it is made blessed.[46]

[40] *Ibid.* 5, 2, 3 (Opera 1073).

[41] Sermon 31 on Canticles, 2: Nam neque hoc luminare magnum (solem loquor istum, quem quotidie vides) vidisti tamen aliquando sicuti est, sed tantum sicut illuminat, verbi causa aerem, montem, parietem (*Opera* 2863).

[42] Misc. Sermon 10, 4 (XB 779).

[43] Sermon 31 on Canticles, 2: Quod nec ipsum quidem aliquatenus posses, si non aliqua ex parte ipsum lumen corporis tui, pro sui ingenita serenitate et perspicuitate, coelesti lumini simile esset (*Opera* 2863).

[44] *Ibid.* 2: Profecto si pari prorsus puritate vigeret, videret omnino inoffensa acie eum, sicuti est, propter omnimodam similitudinem (*Opera* 2864).   [45] Sermon 28 on Canticles, 8 and 9 (*Opera* 2842).

[46] Sermon 5 on Canticles, 1: Verum nos vivimus quidem post corpus: sed ad ea quibus beate vivitur, nullus nobis accessus patet, nisi per corpus. Senserat hoc qui dicebat: *Invisibilia Dei, per ea quae facta sunt, intellecta conspiciuntur* (Rom. 1. 20). Ipsa siquidem quae facta sunt, id est corporalia et visibilia ista, nonnisi per corporis instrumentum sensa, in nostram notitiam veniunt. Habet ergo necessarium corpus spiritualis creatura quae nos sumus, sine quo nimirum nequaquam illam scientiam assequitur, quam solam accepit gradum ad ea, de quorum fit cognitione beata. (*Opera* 2683.)

The possibility of a priori knowledge is not denied; but it is asserted that such knowledge (the subject-matter of pure mathematics) is useless; all useful intellectual knowledge is derived from empirical knowledge.

Invisible things are investigated by means of opinion, faith, and understanding.[47] It is important not to confuse these.[48] *Opinion* is to hold as true something you do not know to be false.[49] It is based on *plausibility*.[50] It differs from faith and understanding in being fallible; it seeks, rather than grasps, truth.[51] Each person is justified in holding his own opinion in matters which are not subject to faith or understanding.[52] But such opinions should be held and asserted tentatively, not dogmatically; we must avoid the common error of confusing opinion with understanding, believing that we apprehend by reason a judgment we merely hold because plausible, and so believing something concerning which we should remain in doubt.[53] Bernard, in his writings, always expressly labels his opinions as such, so that they may not be confused with his doctrine.[54] Whoever declares what his opinion is, speaks the

[47] *Consideration* 5, 3, 5 (*Opera* 1074).

[48] *Ibid.* 5, 3, 6: Omnino in his cavenda confusio, ne aut incertum opinionis fides figat, aut quod firmum fixumque est fidei, opinio revocet in quaestionem. Et hoc sciendum, quia opinio, si habet assertionem, temeraria est: fides, si habet haesitationem, infirma est: item intellectus, si signata fidei tentet irrumpere, reputatur effractor, scrutator majestatis. (*Opera* 1075.)

[49] *Ibid.* 5, 3, 6: Opinio est quasi pro vero habere aliquid, quod falsum esse nescias (*Opera* 1075).

[50] *Ibid.* 5, 3, 5: Opinio sola veri similitudine se tuetur (*Opera* 1075).

[51] *Ibid.* 5, 3, 5: Opinio certi nihil habens, verum per verisimilia quaerit potius quam apprehendit (*Opera* 1075).

[52] *Baptism* 5, 18: Sane ibi unusquisque in suo sensu securus abundat, ubi aut certae rationi aut non contemnendae auctoritati quod sentitur non obviat (*Opera* 1421).

[53] *Consideration* 5, 3, 6: Multi suam opinionem intellectum putaverunt, et erraverunt (*Opera* 1075).

[54] Notably, in his denial of the immaculate conception of the Virgin Mary, the contrary not being known either by faith or by reason. Letter 174, 1: Celebritatem, quam ritus Ecclesiae nescit, non probat ratio, non commendat antiqua traditio (*Opera* 389). Cf. *Consideration* 5, 4, 7 (*Opera* 1075); *Steps of Humility*, Retractation; *Baptism* 5, 18 (*Opera* 1420); Sermon 17 on Canticles, 5 (*Opera* 2757); Sermon 41 on Canticles, 3 (*Opera* 2922).

truth, even though his opinion be false; but whoever asserts dogmatically a judgment of opinion, lies, even though the opinion be true.[55] *Faith* is a sort of foretaste, voluntary and certain, of a truth not yet become obvious.[56] It is based on *authority*.[57] It differs from opinion in being infallible, and from understanding in being unintelligible.[58] Its tenets are certain, although obscure.[59] It involves three aspects: faith in precepts, by which we believe in God, loving him and putting our trust in him; faith in signs, by which we believe God, who can perform such miracles; and faith in promises, by which we have belief in God, who will fulfill his promises.[60] Faith is necessary for us.[61] On the one hand, it reveals truths undiscoverable empirically because of the fallibility of empirical knowledge or because the objects are not sensible things.[62] On the other hand, it reveals truths undiscoverable rationally because of the limits of human understanding.[63] *Understanding* is the certain and evident knowledge of some

[55] Sermon 17 on Canticles, 3 (*Opera* 2757).

[56] *Consideration* 5, 3, 6: Fides est voluntaria quaedam et certa praelibatio necdum propalatae veritatis (*Opera* 1075).

[57] *Ibid.* 5, 3, 5: Fides auctoritati (*Opera* 1075).

[58] *Ibid.* 5, 3, 5: Habent illa duo certam veritatem: sed fides clausam et involutam, intelligentia nudam et manifestam (*Opera* 1075).

[59] *Ibid.* 5, 3, 6: Etsi non habet incertum non magis quam intellectus, habet tamen involucrum, quod non intellectus (*Opera* 1075). Cf. *Abelard's Errors* 4, 9: Denique in primo limine Theologiae, vel potius Stultologiae suae, fidem definit aestimationem. Quasi cuique in ea sentire et loqui quae libeat liceat; aut pendeant sub incerto in vagis ac variis opinionibus nostrae fidei sacramenta, et non magis certa veritate subsistant. (*Opera* 1449.)

[60] Misc. Sermon 45, 5 (XB 913).

[61] Sermon 18 on Canticles, 1: Fides, spes, charitas nobis propter nos dantur: absque his quippe salvi esse non possumus (*Opera* 2760). Cf. Misc. Sermon 28, 3: Longe minus salvare poterunt opera sine fide (XB 846).

[62] Sermon 28 on Canticles, 8: At experimentum fallax.

9. Mittitur ergo ad certiorem fidei cognitionem; quae utique apprehendit quod sensus nescit, experimentum non invenit. (*Opera* 2843.)

[63] Sermon 76 on Canticles, 6: Quid non inveniat fides? Attingit inaccessa, deprehendit ignota, comprehendit immensa, apprehendit novissima; ipsam denique aeternitatem suo illo vastissimo sinu quodam modo circumcludit. Fidenter dixerim, aeternam beatamque Trinitatem, quam non intelligo, credo; et fide teneo, quam non capio mente. (*Opera* 3140.)

invisible thing.[64] It is based on *reason*.[65] It cannot be mistaken either objectively or subjectively; when we understand, we possess the truth and we know that we possess it.[66]

Speculative consideration is that which collects itself in itself and, so far as divinely assisted, withdraws itself from human affairs in order to contemplate God.[67] It is not mystical contemplation [68] but mystical recollection, the first step of mysticism. This is the monk's vocation: [69] he should, like Lazarus, be devoted to humble self-examination; although the more proficient monk may, like Mary, be devoted to contemplation, and the abbot must, like Martha, be devoted to dispensative consideration.[70] Speculative consideration is the only true consideration.[71] The others do not attain their goal.[72] Dispensative consideration prepares the feast of wisdom, estimative consideration smells it, but speculative consideration tastes it.[73] The active and the academic life may lead to the vision of God in the next world, but only the contemplative life achieves it in this world.[74]

There are, then, including the subdivisions, six kinds of consideration. These are identical with the six "ways of know-

[64] *Consideration* 5, 3, 6: Intellectus est rei cujuscumque invisibilis certa et manifesta notitia (*Opera* 1075).

[65] *Ibid*. 5, 3, 5: Intellectus rationi innititur (*Opera* 1075).

[66] *Ibid*. 5, 3, 6: Verus nempe intellectus certam habet non modo veritatem sed notitiam veritatis (*Opera* 1075).

[67] *Ibid*. 5, 2, 4: Speculativa est consideratio se in se colligens, et, quantum divinitus adjuvatur, rebus humanis eximens ad contemplandum Deum (*Opera* 1074).

[68] *Ibid*. 2, 2, 5 (*Opera* 1024).

[69] Sermon 40 on Canticles, 4 (*Opera* 2918).

[70] Sermon 3 for Assumption, 4 (XB 567).

[71] *Consideration* 5, 2, 4: Caeteras, si non referantur ad istam, quod dicuntur videri posse, sed non esse (*Opera* 1074).

[72] *Ibid*. 5, 2, 4: Et prior quidem absque intuitu hujus multa serit, et nihil metit: sequens vero nisi ad istam se dirigat, vadit, sed non evadit (*Opera* 1074).

[73] *Ibid*. 5, 2, 4: Quod prima aptat, secunda odorat, tertia gustat (*Opera* 1074).

[74] *Ibid*. 5, 2, 4: Ad quem tamen gustum perducunt et caeterae, etsi tardius (*Opera* 1074).

ing" of modern philosophy: dispensative consideration is "pragmatism"; estimative consideration of visible things is "empiricism"; estimative consideration of invisible things by opinion is "scepticism"; that by faith is "authoritarianism"; that by understanding is "rationalism"; speculative consideration is "mysticism." [75] Each kind of consideration is supreme in its own domain. Error results from the attempt to consider an object in a way which is not appropriate to that object.

Thought is, as it were, the "skin" of the soul, emotion the "flesh" of the soul, and intention the "bone" of the soul.[76] In the case of the body, if some blemish discolors the skin, it makes the body ugly; if a tumor infects the flesh, it destroys the body's health; and if the disease penetrates to the bones, then life itself must be despaired of. Likewise in the case of the soul, if a sin is suggested to the memory by thought, that is a blemish in the soul, although not a disease. But if the will is moved to the sin by an emotional desire for it, then the soul is diseased, although not fatally. But if the reason also is inclined to the sin by intention, so that the sin is consented to, then the soul dies.[77] On the other hand, right intention produces the soul's life, pure emotion its health, and holy thought its beauty.[78] The soul's life is good reason, which is knowledge of truth.[79] The soul's health is good will; just as normal sense-perception is the result of bodily health, so perfect love, which is the sensitivity of the soul,[80] is the result of spiritual health. The soul's beauty is good memory or conscience; this consists of humility joined to innocence.[81]

[75] W. P. Montague: *The Ways of Knowing, or The Methods of Philosophy* (London, 1925).   [76] Misc. Sermon 6, 1 (XB 763).

[77] Misc. Sermon 32, 3 (XB 856). Cf. Misc. Sermon 6, 1: Sicut enim peccati cogitatio decolorat, affectio vulnerat, sic consensus omnino animam necat (XB 763). Cf. *Steps of Humility* 10, 30; *ibid.* 10, 38.

[78] *Ibid.* 2: Cogitatio debet esse sancta, . . . affectio pura et intentio recta (XB 856). Misc. Sermon 6, 1: Erit in ossis integritate animae vita, in carnis incorruptione sanitas, in cutis specie pulchritudo (XB 763).

[79] Misc. Sermon 10, 1 (XB 777); Misc. Sermon 116 (XB 1012).

[80] *Ibid.; ibid.*

[81] Sermon 45 on Canticles, 2 (*Opera* 2940). Cf. *Office of Bishops* 4, 13

The resurrection of the soul is the resurrection of each faculty, and that is accomplished by the renewal of each function.

The intention, bowed under worldly cares, slowly rises from the depths to the heights; and the emotion, sick with the lusts of the flesh, gradually convalesces into the love of the spirit; and the memory, defiled by the infamy of old deeds, daily grows joyous as it is cleansed by new good acts. For it is in these three things that inner renewal consists: namely, in rightness of intention, purity of emotion, and remembrance of good work by which the memory becomes clear in good conscience.[82]

(*Opera* 1110); Misc. Sermon 45, 5 (XB 914). The soul's beauty together with its outer manifestation is called honor and defined as nobility of soul careful to preserve integrity of reputation along with good conscience. Sermon 85 on Canticles, 11 (*Opera* 3192).

[82] *Grace and Free Choice* 14, 49: Intentio terrenis incurvata curis, de imis paulatim ad superna resurgit; et affectio circa carnis desideria languens, sensim in amorem spiritus convalescit; et memoria veterum operum turpitudine sordens, novis bonisque actibus candidata in dies hilarescit. In his namque tribus interior renovatio consistit: rectitudine scilicet intentionis, puritate affectionis, recordatione bonae operationis, per quam sibi bene conscia memoria enitescit. (*Opera* 1399.) Cf. *Conversion* 16, 29 (*Opera* 1154).

PART II

THE OBJECT OF KNOWLEDGE

Section 1. Truths

1. Why we should know

The object of knowledge is truth. Knowledge of any truth is good, and an end in itself. But we cannot know all particular truths, for life is short and they are infinite in number. Although science for its own sake is theoretically justifiable, it is practically impossible, for that principle would justify wasting our lives on any sort of frivolous knowledge. Knowledge requires, therefore, some sanction beyond itself. In order to be worth knowing, a particular truth must be not only an end in itself, as all truths are, but also a means to something further. Some truths are means required by the practical necessities of life, and therefore knowledge of them is necessary. But some truths are means to the knowledge of Truth in itself. All truths are good, but Truth in itself is the highest good, and knowledge of it is salvation. Therefore the monk, that is, the man who is devoting his life to seeking the highest good, must, on account of the brevity of human life, devote himself primarily to that knowledge which is a means to this end. The wise man avoids secular science not because it is bad (for it is good) but because there is something better.

All knowledge, in itself, is good, provided it be true. But you who with fear and trembling are hastening, on account of the shortness of time, to work out your own salvation should take care to know first and most fully those things which you feel are concerned with salvation.[1]

---

[1] Sermon 36 on Canticles, 2: Est autem, quod in se est, omnis scientia bona, quae tamen veritate subnixa sit: sed tu qui cum timore et tremore tuam ipsius operari salutem pro temporis brevitate festinas, ea scire prius ampliusque curato, quae senseris viciniora saluti (*Opera* 2898). Cf. Sermon 2 for the dedication of a church, 4: Cognitio quidem perfecta in hac vita

Knowledge of particular truths, therefore, should be sought for the sake of salvation, inspiration, and edification, and not as an end in itself.

If any man think that he knoweth any thing, he knoweth nothing yet as he ought to know. You see how he disapproves one who knows much, if he knows not the manner of knowing. You see, I say, how he put the profit and utility of knowledge in the manner of knowing. What, then, does he call the manner of knowing? What, save to know in what order, with what zeal, and for what end you ought to have knowledge of anything? In what order: that first which leads more quickly to salvation. With what zeal: that more ardently which inspires more strongly to love. For what end: not for vainglory, or curiosity, or anything of the sort, but only for the edification of yourself or your neighbor. For there are some who desire to know only for the sake of knowing; and this is disgraceful curiosity. And there are some who desire to know, that they may become known themselves; and this is disgraceful vanity. These do not escape the mocking satirist who sings to whoever is of this sort:

> Knowledge is nothing to you, unless others know of
> your knowledge.

And there are also some who desire to know in order to sell their knowledge, as for money, or for degrees; and this is disgraceful commercialism. But there are also some who desire to know in order to edify; and this is charity. And also some who desire to know in order to be edified; and this is prudence.[2]

---

haberi non potest, forsitan nec oportet. In coelesti siquidem domo cognitio dilectionis est nutrimentum, hic vero esse poterat detrimentum. (XB 699.)

   [2] *Ibid.* 3: *Qui se*, inquit, *putat aliquid scire, nondum scit quomodo oporteat eum scire* (1 Cor. 8. 2). Vides quoniam non probat multa scientem, si sciendi modum nescierit. Vides, inquam, quomodo fructum et utilitatem scientiae in modo sciendi constituit? Quid ergo dicit modum sciendi? Quid, nisi ut scias, quo ordine, quo studio, quo fine quaeque nosse oporteat? Quo ordine; ut id prius, quod maturius ad salutem: quo studio; ut id ardentius, quod vehementius ad amorem: quo fine; ut non ad inanem gloriam, aut curiositatem, aut aliquid simile, sed tantum ad aedificationem tuam vel proximi. Sunt namque qui scire volunt eo fine tantum, ut sciant; et turpis curiositas est. Et sunt qui scire volunt, ut sciantur ipsi; et turpis vanitas est. Qui profecto non evadent subsannantem satyricum, et ei qui ejusmodi est decantantem:

A knowledge of literature is an ornament of the soul, which it both instructs and makes capable of instructing others.[3] The liberal arts are honorable and useful subjects to study or to practice.[4] But both are unnecessary for salvation, that is, for the knowledge of Truth in itself; and so both must be considered optional subjects in the monk's curriculum. The same applies to portions of theology, such as that concerning the nature of angels.[5] Particularly useless and frivolous is philosophy. Its subject-matter is foolish;[6] its doctrines are false;[7] and its teachers are interested less in the truth than in their own reputation as philosophers.[8] Particularly useful and indispensable, on the other hand, is the study of the sacred scriptures, which are full of divine mysteries and overflowing with celestial sweetness, provided the reader knows how to suck honey out of the rock and oil out of the flinty rock.[9] In them and in the writings of the Fathers [10] will be found such wisdom as can be learned from books.

Scire tuum nihil est, nisi te scire hoc sciat alter (Persius, satyra 1, vers. 27). Et sunt item qui scire volunt, ut scientiam suam vendant; verbi causa, pro pecunia, pro honoribus: et turpis quaestus est. Sed sunt quoque qui scire volunt, ut aedificent; et charitas est. Et item qui scire volunt, ut aedificentur; et prudentia est. (*Opera* 2898.)

[3] Sermon 37 on Canticles, 2 (*Opera* 2902).

[4] Sermon 36 on Canticles, 1 (*Opera* 2897).

[5] Sermon 5 on Canticles, 7 (*Opera* 2686).

[6] Sermon 3 for Whitsunday, 5: Platonis argutias, Aristotelis versutias (XB 407).

[7] Sermon 41 on Canticles, 1 (*Opera* 2920).

[8] Misc. Sermon 7, 1 (XB 765); Misc. Sermon 40, 1 (XB 886).

[9] Sermon 1 in praise of the Virgin Mary, 1: Plena quippe sunt omnia supernis mysteriis ac coelesti singula dulcedine redundantia, si tamen diligentem habeant inspectorem, qui noverit *sugere mel de petra oleumque de saxo durissimo* (Deut. 32. 13) (XB 33). Cf. Sermon 3 for Palm Sunday, 1 (XB 311); Sermon 23 on Canticles, 3 (*Opera* 2794); Sermon 51 on Canticles, 4 (*Opera* 2974); Sermon 72 on Canticles, 6 (*Opera* 3113). The version authorized by the Church, even if differing from the original, is authoritative. Sermon 3 for Christmas Eve, 1 (XB 85).

[10] *Baptism*, Preface: Patrum tantum opponimus sententias, ac verba proferimus, et non nostra: nec enim sapientiores sumus quam patres nostri (*Opera* 1405). Cf. Sermon 4 in praise of the Virgin Mary, 11: Sed si quid dictum est post patres, quod non sit contra patres, nec patribus arbitror nec cuiquam displicere debere (XB 74).

2. What we should know

The particular objects knowledge concerning which is useful include, first of all, yourself. To know yourself is the beginning of wisdom; to know God is its consummation.[1] Self-knowledge comes first in the rational order of knowledge, because our first concern is naturally to know what we ourselves are; and it comes first in the order of utility, because it destroys pride and produces humility, which is the necessary condition of spiritual progress.[2]

In the second place, it is useful to know other men. Although in one sermon Bernard commends the Augustinian doctrine that your own self is the only desirable particular object for consideration,[3] this must be regarded as an exaggerated reference to the priority of self-knowledge, for his consistent doctrine is much broader. We can know our neighbors only by love, and this purifies the mind's eye so as to make it able to contemplate Truth in itself. Knowledge of other men is, therefore, the path which leads from knowledge of yourself to knowledge of God.[4]

In the third place, it is useful to know any creatures whatever, provided they be studied not for their own sakes, but for the light which their teleological aspects throw on the nature of their creator. Carnal men, filled with sensuality, investigate things themselves, in order to use them. Philosophers, filled with vanity, investigate the arrangement and order of things, in order to gratify their scientific curiosity. Spiritual men, filled with truth, investigate the functions of things, in order to seek God. The being of things reveals God's power, the arrangement of things reveals God's wis-

[1] Sermon 37 on Canticles, 1 (Opera 2902).
[2] Sermon 36 on Canticles, 5 (Opera 2900).
[3] Misc. Sermon 2, 1: Huic duplici considerationi tota haec vestra vocatio tribuatur, sicut sanctus orabat: "Deus, noverim me, noverim te" (XB 744).
[4] Steps of Humility 6, 19. In this essay three things are commended to the monk's attention: himself, his neighbors, and God. In the essay on Consideration six things are commended to the pope's consideration: himself, the Church, the Romans, the papal household, angels, and God. All spiritual beings — men, angels, and God — are proper objects for consideration.

dom, and the utility of things reveals God's goodness.[5] The
only study which Bernard disapproves is positivism, the study
of the phenomenal world without reference to the source or
function of things. This is curiosity, the first step of the path
which leads away from truth.

[5] Sermon 3 for Whitsunday, 3: Tria in magno hujus mundi opere cogitare debemus, videlicet: quid sit, quomodo sit, ad quid constitutus. Et in
esse quidem rerum inaestimabilis potentia commendatur, quod tam multa, tam
magna, tam multipliciter, tam magnifice sunt creata. Sane in modo ipso
sapientia singularis elucet, quod haec quidem sursum, haec vero deorsum,
haec in medio ordinatissime sint locata. Si vero, ad quid factus sit, mediteris,
occurrit tam utilis benignitas, tam benigna utilitas, quae etiam ingratissimos
quosque multitudine et magnitudine beneficiorum possit obruere; potentis-
sime siquidem ex nihilo omnia, sapientissime pulchra, benignissime utilia
sunt creata. Verumtamen et fuisse novimus ab initio et adhuc multos esse
videmus in filiis hominum, qui in bonis inferioribus sensibilis mundi hujus
tota sensualitate depressi totos se dederunt his, quae facta sunt, quonam
modo vel ad quid facta sint negligentes. Quid istos nisi carnales dicamus?
Paucissimos esse jam arbitror; legimus tamen, nonnullos quandoque fuisse,
quibus summum studium fuit atque unica sollicitudo, modum et ordinem
investigare factorum, adeo ut plerique non modo utilitatem rerum perquirere
dissimulaverint, sed et ipsas magnanimiter spreverint, cibo parvissimo vilis-
simoque contenti. Ipsi quidem sese philosophos vocant, sed a nobis curiosi
et vani rectius appellantur.

4. Utrisque igitur successerunt viri prudentiores utrisque, qui nimirum,
et quae facta sunt et quomodo facta sunt transsilientes, intenderunt aciem
mentis, ut, ad quid facta sunt, viderent. Nec latuit eos, quoniam omnia
propter semet ipsum fecit Deus, omnia propter suos; aliter tamen propter se,
aliter propter suos. In eo quippe, quod dicitur: *Omnia propter se*, praeveniens commendatur origo; in eo autem, quod dicitur: *Omnia propter suos*
(cf. Prov. 16. 4; Gen. 1. 29), magis exprimitur fructus sequens. Omnia fecit
propter semet ipsum, gratuita videlicet bonitate; omnia propter electos suos,
pro eorum scilicet utilitate, ut illa quidem efficiens causa sit, haec finis. Hi
sunt spirituales viri, sic *utentes hoc mundo tamquam non utentes* (1 Cor. 7. 31),
sed *in simplicitate cordis sui quaerentes Deum* (Sap. 1. 1), ne illud quidem
magnopere vestigantes, quonam modo mundialis haec machina volveretur;
primi voluptate, secundi vanitate, tertii veritate impleti. (XB 406.) Cf. Sermon 3 for Christmas Eve, 8 (XB 90). For the vanity of the philosophers,
cf. Sermon 9 on Canticles, 7 (*Opera* 2707). For the false asceticism of the
philosophers, cf. Sermon 66 on Canticles, 6–7 (*Opera* 3069). For the utility
of the study of biology, cf. Sermon 5 on Canticles, 6 (*Opera* 2685).

Section 2. Truth

1. Our knowledge of God's existence

The existence of God is demonstrated by the cosmological argument. Just as the existence of brilliant objects proves the existence of the sun which is the source of their light, so the existence of all creatures proves the existence of the God who created them, without, however, proving anything about his essence.

What are this great variety of forms and multitude of species in creation but definite rays of Deity, demonstrating the existence of their source, although not defining its essence? And so you see his effects but not himself. But since you see other things, effects of that which you do not see; you know indubitably the existence of that which is to be sought, so that grace will not disappoint you if you seek, nor ignorance excuse you if you neglect to. Now this kind of vision is universal. For it is easy for every rational creature, according to the Apostle, to see clearly the invisible things of God, being understood by the things that are made.[1]

2. Our knowledge of God's essence

The essence of God is determined by the ontological argument. What God is in himself is unknowable.[1] But the human intellect, endeavoring to comprehend God as he appears to it, defines him as that than which nothing greater or better can be thought.[2] This definition of God implies that he has no attributes. For example, God cannot be called

---

[1] Sermon 31 on Canticles, 3: Tanta haec formarum varietas, atque numerositas specierum in rebus conditis, quid nisi quidam sunt radii Deitatis, monstrantes quidem quia vere sit a quo sunt, non tamen quid sit prorsus definientes? Itaque de ipso vides, sed non ipsum. Cum autem de eo, quem non vides, caetera vides; scis indubitanter existere quem oportet inquirere, ut inquirentem non fraudet gratia, negligentem ignorantia non excuset. Verum hoc genus videndi commune. In promptu enim est, juxta Apostolum, omni utenti ratione, invisibilia Dei, per ea quae facta sunt, intellecta conspicere (Rom. 1. 20). (*Opera* 2864.) Cf. *Loving God* 2, 6 (*Opera* 1333).

---

[1] *Consideration* 5, 11, 24: Quid ergo est Deus? Quod ad universum spectat, finis: quod ad electionem, salus: quod ad se, ipse novit. (*Opera* 1089.)

[2] *Ibid.* 5, 7, 15: Quo nihil melius cogitari potest (*Opera* 1082). *Abelard's*

good, in the same sense in which other things are good, because he is that very goodness by participation in which good things are good; otherwise goodness would be something greater than God. To predicate any attribute of God, is to commit the fallacy of confusion of types. God cannot be called great, good, just, or wise; because he is greatness, goodness, justice, and wisdom.[3] Since, therefore, God is every form in which he participates, there is no diversity in him. This substantial unity of God is more profound than the collective unity of a pile of stones or the organic unity of a body or the conjugal unity of husband and wife or the natural unity of soul and body or the moral unity of a virtuous man or the spiritual unity of mutual lovers or the mystic unity of the soul and God or the miraculous unity of two natures in Christ.[4] Except in God, no form is identical with that of which it is a form;[5] every creature, although it may be one in the sense that it is an individual, has an intrinsic diversity of substance and accidents and, if it is material, of matter and form. But the substantial unity of God is absolute unity.

God is not formed; he is form. God is not affected; he is affection. God has no composition; he is pure simplicity. And

---

Errors 2, 4: Quidquid namque illud est quod Deus sit, id sine dubio est, quo non possit majus aliquid cogitari (*Opera* 1445). So far as I know, Bernard never drew any inference concerning God's existence from this definition.

[3] Sermon 80 on Canticles, 7: Sed dicit haereticus: Quid? Deum divinitate esse negas? Non, sed eamdem divinitatem, qua est, Deum nihilominus assero, ne Deo excellentius aliquid esse assentiar. Nam et magnitudine dico magnum, sed quae ipse est, ne majus aliquid Deo ponam: et bonitate fateor bonum, sed non alia, quam ipse est, ne melius ipso aliquid mihi videar invenisse: et de caeteris in hunc modum. Securus et libens pergo inoffenso, ut aiunt, pede in ejus sententiam qui dicebat: "Deus nonnisi ea magnitudine magnus est, quae est quod ipse. Alioquin illa erit major magnitudo, quam Deus." Augustinus hic est, validissimus malleus haereticorum (*De Trinitate* 5, 10, 11). Si quid itaque de Deo proprie dici possit, rectius congruentiusque dicetur, Deus est magnitudo, bonitas, justitia, sapientia, quam, Deus est magnus, bonus, justus aut sapiens. (*Opera* 3162.) Cf. *Consideration* 5, 5, 12 (*Opera* 1080).

[4] *Consideration* 5, 8, 18 (*Opera* 1085); Misc. Sermon 80, 1 (XB 955).

[5] Sermon 80 on Canticles, 5: Nulla forma est id, cujus est forma (*Opera* 3161).

that you may understand clearly what I mean by simplicity: it is the same as unity. God is as simple as he is one. But he is one in a way in which naught else is. He is, so to speak, the most one. The sun is one, because there is no other; the moon is one, likewise because there is no other. So is God, but more besides. What more? He is also intrinsically one. Do you wish this also to be explained to you? He is always the same, and in one way. Not so is the sun one, not so is the moon one. Each cries aloud that it is not intrinsically one; the former by its motions, the latter by its phases also. But God is not only intrinsically one; he is also one in himself. He has nothing in himself besides himself. He has no alteration in time, no alterity in substance. Hence Boethius says of him: "That is truly one in which there is no plurality, and there is nothing else in it besides that which it is. For it cannot become a subject, because it is a form." Compare with this one everything else which can be called one, and it will not be one.[6]

In particular, this definition implies that the being by which God is is not something other than God, for if it were it would be better than God.[7] God, therefore, is being. All things

[6] *Consideration* 5, 7, 17: Non est formatus Deus: forma est. Non est affectus Deus: affectio est. Non est compositus Deus: merum simplex est. Et ut liquido noveris, quid simplex dicam: idem quod unum. Tam simplex Deus, quam unus est. Est autem unus, et quo modo aliud nihil. Si dici possit, unissimus est. Unus est sol, quod non sit alter: una luna, quod aeque altera non sit. Atque id quidem Deus, sed plus. Quid plus? Unus est etiam sibi. Et hoc vis tibi declarari? Idem est semper, et uno modo. Non sic unus sol, non sic una luna. Clamat uterque non esse unum sibi; ille motibus, illa et defectibus suis. Deus autem non modo unus sibi: et in se unus est. Nihil in se nisi se habet. Non ex tempore alterationem habet, non in substantia alteritatem. Hinc de eo Boetius: "Hoc vere unum, in quo nullus est numerus, nullum in eo aliud praeter id quod est: Neque enim subjectum fieri potest: forma enim est." (Boethius, *De Unitate Trinitatis*, 2, *Pat. Lat.* 64, 1250.) Compara huic uni omne quod unum dici potest; et unum non erit. (*Opera* 1084.) Cf. Misc. Sermon 8, 1 (XB 768); Sermon 80 on Canticles, 5 (*Opera* 3160); Sermon 81 on Canticles, 2 (*Opera* 3164). That God is, nevertheless, three, transcends reason and must be believed by faith. *Consideration* 5, 8, 18 (*Opera* 1085). Cf. Sermon 71 on Canticles, 8: Sunt in sese Pater et Filius, non solum ineffabili, sed etiam incomprehensibili modo sui ipsorum capabiles pariter et capaces (*Opera* 3104).

[7] *Consideration* 5, 7, 15: Quid est Deus? Quo nihil melius cogitari potest. Si approbas, non oportet assentiaris esse aliquid, quo Deus sit, et quod Deus non sit. Hoc enim sine dubio melius. Quomodo non melius Deo, si Deus non est, quod dat Deo ut sit? (*Opera* 1082.)

which are are by participation in being. God is; but he is in a different and higher sense than that in which creatures are, because he, being being, is, not by participation in something other than himself, but by participation in himself.

Who is he? I can think of no better answer than, *He who is.* He himself wished this answer to be given, he himself taught this, when Moses spoke to the people at his command, *He who is, hath sent me to you.* And rightly. Nothing is more appropriate to the eternity which God is. If you call God good, or great, or blessed, or wise, or anything of the sort; it is included in these words, namely, *He is.* For to him it is the same to be as to be all these. Even if you add a hundred such things, you have not transcended being. By saying them you have added nothing; by not saying them you have detracted nothing. Now if you regard this being so peculiar, so supreme; do you not consider that, by comparison with this, whatever is not this is not rather than is? What then is God? That without which nothing is. A thing can no more be without him than he can be without himself. He is, for himself and for all things. And therefore, in a certain sense, only he is, who is the being of himself and of all things.[8]

This does not mean that God is the substance of all things — which would be pantheism; he is the necessary and sufficient cause of all things — which is monotheism.

What is God? Of whom all things, by whom all things, in whom all things. Of whom all things, by creation, not generation. By whom all things, lest you suppose there be any other author

[8] *Ibid.* 5, 6, 13: Quis est? Non sane occurrit melius, quam *Qui est.* Hoc ipse de se voluit responderi, hoc docuit, dicente Moyse ad populum, ipso quidem injungente: *Qui est, misit me ad vos* (Ex. 3. 14). Merito quidem. Nil competentius aeternitati, quae Deus est. Si bonum, si magnum, si beatum, si sapientem, vel quidquid tale de Deo dixeris; in hoc verbo instauratur, quod est, *Est.* Nempe hoc est ei esse, quod haec omnia esse. Si et centum talia addas, non recessisti ab esse. Si ea dixeris, nihil addidisti: si non dixeris, nihil minuisti. Jam si vidisti hoc tam singulare, tam summum esse; nonne in comparatione hujus quidquid hoc non est, judicas potius non esse, quam esse? Quid item Deus? Sine quo nihil est. Tam nihil esse sine ipso, quam nec ipse sine se potest. Ipse sibi, ipse omnibus est. Ac per hoc quodammodo ipse solus est, qui suum ipsius est, et omnium esse. (*Opera* 1081.) Cf. Sermon 86 on Canticles, 3: Sine causa ergo aliud a Verbo petitur, cum ipsum sit omnia (*Opera* 3196). Cf. Misc. Sermon 4, 2 (XB 757).

and maker. In whom all things, not spatially, but virtually. Of
whom all things, as the sole principle and author of all things. By
whom all things, lest a demiurge be introduced as a second principle. In whom all things, lest space be introduced as a third. Of
whom all things, not out of whom, because God is not matter: he
is the efficient, not the material cause.[9]

As being, God was not, nor will be, but is — uncreated, un-
ending, invariable.[10] As efficient cause, he creates all things,
not by emanation or from coeternal matter, but from nothing.[11]

The definition likewise implies that God is Truth.[12] Unlike
particular truths, Truth should be sought only as an end in
itself. If the soul is intent on Truth but for some ulterior
purpose, such as desire for fame or some temporal good, that
is hypocrisy or pusillanimity; if it is intent on some object

[9] *Ibid.* 5, 6, 14: Quid est Deus? Ex quo omnia, per quem omnia, in quo
omnia (Rom. 11. 36). Ex quo omnia, creabiliter, non seminabiliter. Per quem
omnia, ne alium auctorem atque alium opificem arbitreris. In quo omnia,
non quasi in loco, sed quasi in virtute. Ex quo omnia, tanquam uno principio, auctore omnium. Per quem omnia, ne alterum inducatur principium
artifex. In quo omnia, ne tertium inducatur, locus. Ex quo omnia, non de
quo, quia non est materia Deus: efficiens causa est, non materialis. (*Opera*
1081.) Cf. *ibid.* 5, 5, 12 (*Opera* 1080); *ibid.* 5, 6, 13 (*Opera* 1081). Cf. Sermon 4 on Canticles, 4: Sane esse omnium dixerim Deum, non quia illa sunt
quod est ille; sed quia ex ipso, et per ipsum, et in ipso sunt omnia. Esse est
ergo omnium quae facta sunt ipse factor eorum, sed causale, non materiale.
Tali proinde modo dignatur illa majestas suis esse creaturis, omnibus quidem
quod sunt; animantibus autem quod et vivunt; porro ratione utentibus lux,
recte vero utentibus virtus, vincentibus gloria. (*Opera* 2682.)

[10] Sermon 31 on Canticles, 1 (*Opera* 2862).

[11] *Consideration* 5, 6, 14 (*Opera* 1082).

[12] Sermon 80 on Canticles, 8: "Pater est veritas, id est verus: Filius est
veritas, id est verus: Spiritus sanctus est veritas, id est verus. Et hi tres simul
non tres veritates, sed una veritas, id est unus verus." (Gilbertus Porreta,
In Boetii de Trinitate librum, Pat. Lat. 64, 1307.) O obscuram perversamque
explanationem! Quam verius saniusque per contrarium ita dixisset: Pater est
verus, id est veritas: Filius est verus, id est veritas: Spiritus sanctus est verus,
id est veritas. Et hi tres unus verus, id est una veritas. Quod quidem
fecisset, si sanctum dignaretur Fulgentium imitari, qui ait: "Una quippe
veritas unius Dei, imo una veritas unus Deus non patitur servitium atque
culturam creatoris creaturaeque conjungi." (Fulgentius, Letter 8, 5, 12,
Pat. Lat. 65, 365.) (*Opera* 3162.) Cf. Sermon 4 for Christmas Eve, 5: Ecce
infans sine sorde, solus inter homines verax, immo et veritas ipsa (XB 96).
Cf. *Steps of Humility* 7, 20.

other than Truth, yet for the sake of God, that is the active
life; if it is intent on some object other than Truth, and for
its own sake, that is the carnal life; if it is intent on Truth,
and for the sake of Truth, that is the contemplative life.[13]
Truth is the object of knowledge, and the knowledge of Truth
is the highest good for the human soul, being the fulfillment of
the capacity for knowledge which is its peculiar endowment.[14] Particular truths can delight the soul, but only the
universal Truth can satisfy it.[15]

3. Our knowledge of God

The knowledge that Truth exists, the knowledge of its
essence which we discover by reason, the further knowledge
of its essence which we receive by revelation and believe by
faith — these do not satisfy the soul. The soul seeks direct
acquaintance. And that Truth which it seeks direct acquaintance with, is being. But how can being be known? The very
question presents a paradox. Nothing is so incomprehensible
as the being of all things. Yet nothing is so immediately
knowable as your own being. But these are identical, for
there is only one being, which is the being of yourself and
of all things which are.[1] The problem of knowledge having
been stated in these terms, it is clear that its solution will be
by mysticism; for mysticism is that introspection whereby a
man, by understanding his own being, comes also to comprehend the being of all things, which he finds to be the
same as his own.[2] Although God is the being of all things,
he is not comprehended by all things, because they lack the
capacity for knowledge. Only by rational creatures is he

[13] Sermon 40 on Canticles, 2–3 (*Opera* 2916).
[14] Sermon 77 on Canticles, 5 (*Opera* 3146).
[15] *Loving God* 7, 19 (*Opera* 1344).

[1] Sermon 4 on Canticles, 4: Non quod longe ab unoquoque sit qui esse
omnium est, sine quo omnia nihil: sed (ut tu plus mireris) et nil eo praesentius, et nil incomprehensibilius. Quid nempe cuique rei praesentius, quam
esse suum? Quid cuique tamen incomprehensibilius, quam esse omnium?
(*Opera* 2682.)
[2] Pantheistic mysticism maintains that you are the same being as all things;
monotheistic mysticism maintains that you have the same being as all things.

comprehended at all; they have a partial comprehension of
him insofar as they know him by reason. But only by mystics
is he comprehended by acquaintance; they comprehend him
by both reason and will, that is, by both understanding and
love, the two arms of the soul.[3]

For God, who, in his simple substance, is all everywhere equally,
nevertheless, in efficacy, is in rational creatures in a different way
than he is in others; and in the good ones in a different way than
he is in the bad. He is in irrational creatures in such a way as not
to be comprehended by them, by all rational ones, however, he
can be comprehended through knowledge, but only by the good is
he comprehended also through love. Only in the good, therefore,
he is, in such a way as to be also with them by harmony of will;
for as they subdue their own wills to justice so that it is not un-
worthy of God to will what they will, they are particularly joined
to God by not dissenting from his will.[4]

Intuitive acquaintance, either perceptual or mystical, is
based on a similarity between subject and object. The more
brilliant the light in the bodily eye, the more clearly do we
see the sun. The more brilliant the light in the mind's eye,
the more clearly do we see God.[5] Dropping the metaphor,
this means: the more ardent the love in the will, the more
clearly do we contemplate God. God is love; and love is the
sensitivity of the soul. Both bodily and spiritual vision give
intuitive acquaintance with, not discursive knowledge about,
their objects. The object of contemplative knowledge, therefore, is Truth in itself, not a particular truth.[6] This does not

[3] Letter 18, 3 (*Opera* 161).
[4] Sermon 3 in praise of the Virgin Mary, 4: Deus enim, qui ubique
aequaliter totus est per suam simplicem substantiam, aliter tamen in rationalibus creaturis quam in ceteris, et ipsarum creaturis aliter in bonis quam in malis est
per efficaciam. Ita sane est in irrationalibus creaturis, ut tamen non capiatur
ab ipsis; a rationalibus autem omnibus quidem capi potest per cognitionem,
sed a bonis tantum capitur etiam per amorem. In solis ergo bonis ita est, ut
etiam sit cum ipsis propter concordiam voluntatis; nam dum suas voluntates
ita justitiae subdunt, ut Deum non dedeceat velle, quod ipsi volunt, per hoc,
quod ab ejus voluntate non dissentiunt, Deum sibi specialiter jungunt.
(XB 55.)
[5] Sermon 31 on Canticles, 2 (*Opera* 2863). [6] *Steps of Humility* 3, 6.

mean that contemplation reveals God as he is in himself. Just as perception reveals, not the thing in itself, but the thing as it appears to the perceiver; so contemplation reveals, not God as he is, but God as he manifests himself to the contemplator. But in both cases the appearance is not utterly unlike the reality.[7] And in both cases, the greater the similarity between subject and object, the closer is the resemblance between appearance and reality.[8] We can come to know God, therefore, by making ourselves more like him.

We must draw near to him, therefore, not rush upon him, lest the irreverent searcher of majesty be overwhelmed by glory. We must draw near not by a change of place but by an increase of brilliance, and that not physical but spiritual.[9]

The subject is not the object of knowledge, but it is like it.

[7] Sermon 31 on Canticles, 7: Non tamen adhuc illum dixerim apparere sicuti est, quamvis non omnino aliud hoc modo exhibeat, quam quod est (*Opera* 2866).

[8] *Ibid.* 2: Profecto si pari prorsus puritate vigeret, videret omnino inoffensa acie eum, sicuti est, propter omnimodam similitudinem (*Opera* 2864). *Ibid.* 3: Qui itaque clarior, ille propinquior: esse autem clarissimum, pervenisse est. Porro jam praesentibus non aliud est videre sicuti est, quam esse sicuti est, et aliqua dissimilitudine non confundi. Sed id tunc, ut dixi. (*Opera* 2864.)

[9] *Ibid.* 3: Ergo accedendum ad eum, non irruendum, ne irreverens scrutator majestatis opprimatur a gloria (Prov. 25. 27). Nec locis sane accedendum, sed claritatibus; ipsisque non corporeis, sed spiritualibus. (*Opera* 2864.)

PART III

THE METHOD OF KNOWLEDGE

Section 1. Humility

1. Definition of humility

No one is wise who is not wise to himself.[1]

Knowledge of God is the end of the anagogic path; but the practical problem is: what is its beginning? Bernard answers, "Know thyself." [2] And this is why humility is the preeminent monastic virtue, because it is through humility that we know ourselves by seeing how miserable we are.

There are two kinds of humility: cognitive and conative.[3] Cognitive humility, which is the beginning of knowledge, is that thorough self-examination which makes a man contemptible in his own sight.[4] This is not inconsistent with Plotinus's doctrine that honoring yourself is the beginning of knowledge.[5] Both mystics teach that we must know ourselves as we really are before we can proceed to seek Truth. Plotinus, living in a materialistic age, feared that his readers would underestimate themselves, believing themselves to be

---

[1] *Consideration* 2, 3, 6: Non ergo sapiens, qui sibi non est (*Opera* 1024). Cf. Prov. 9. 12: Si sapiens fueris, tibimetipsi eris.

[2] Misc. Sermon 40, 3: De coelo cecidit ista sententia: Nosce te ipsum, homo (XB 887).

[3] Where not otherwise specified, the word *humility* is to be understood as meaning cognitive humility.

[4] *Steps of Humility* 1, 2; 4, 14. Cf. *Office of Bishops* 5, 19: Humilitas est contemptus propriae excellentiae (*Opera* 1114). Misc. Sermon 12, 1: Cogita unde veneris et erubesce; ubi sis et ingemisce; quo vadas et contremisce (XB 782). Misc. Sermon 25, 4: Quanto quisque plus proficit, eo minus se reputet profecisse (XB 832).

[5] Plotinus, *Ennead* 5, 1, 2: τὴν δὴ θεοῖς αἰτίαν τοῦ θεοῖς εἶναι ἀνάγκη πρεσβυτέραν αὐτῶν εἶναι· ὁμοειδὴς δὲ καὶ ἡ ἡμετέρα, καὶ ὅταν ἄνευ τῶν προσελθόντων σκοπῆς λαβὼν κεκαθαρμένην, εὑρήσεις τὸ αὐτὸ τίμιον, ὃ ἦν ψυχή, καὶ τιμιώτερον παντὸς τοῦ ὃ ἂν σωματικὸν ᾖ . . . . εἰ δ' ὅτι ἔμψυχον διωκτὸν ἔσται, τί παρεὶς τις ἑαυτὸν ἄλλον διώκει; τὴν δὲ ἐν ἄλλῳ ψυχὴν ἀγάμενος σεαυτὸν ἄγασαι.

soulless animals, and so urged them to consider that they were souls. Bernard feared the other extreme; his monks knew they were men, not animals, but were apt to forget that they were sinful, ignorant, and wretched. Bernard agrees that knowledge is impossible for a man who does not know that he is made in the image of God, nor should a man believe himself to be worse than he really is. The virtue is to know yourself as you really are: that you are a soul made in the image of God but separated from him by sin, ignorance, and wretchedness.[6] This virtue is a mean between two extremes. One extreme is pride, love of your own excellence, which is ignorance of yourself by overestimating your own merit.[7] The other extreme, equally false although not equally dangerous,[8] is false humility, which is ignorance of yourself by underestimating your own merit.[9]

It is therefore necessary to know both what you are and that you are not of yourself, lest you either glory not at all or glory vainly. It is said accordingly: *If thou know not thyself, go forth after the flocks of thy companions.* It does happen like that. Man made in honor, when he understands not this honor, deserves by such ignorance to be likened to the sheep, as sharers in his present corruption and mortality. So it comes to pass that by not knowing himself the creature marked off by the gift of reason begins to be herded with the flocks of irrational beings, when, ignorant of his own glory which is within, he is led away by his own curiosity to be conformed outwardly to sensible things; and he becomes one of the rest, because he understands not that he

[6] Sermon 37 on Canticles, 6: Si enim in quonam statu unumquemque nostrum habeat Deus, liquido cognosceremus; nec supra sane, nec infra secedere deberemus, veritati in omnibus acquiescentes (*Opera* 2905).

[7] *Steps of Humility* 4, 14. Cf. *Office of Bishops* 5, 19: Superbia est appetitus propriae excellentiae (*Opera* 1114). Sermon 37 on Canticles, 6: Sic autem superbiam parit tibi ignorantia tui, cum meliorem quam sis, decepta et deceptrix tua cogitatio te esse mentitur. Hoc quippe est superbia, hoc initium omnis peccati, cum major es in tuis oculis quam apud Deum, quam in veritate. (*Opera* 2905.)

[8] Sermon 37 on Canticles, 7 (*Opera* 2905).

[9] Letter 201, 2: Nam nec sterilis verecundia grata est, nec humilitas praeter veritatem laudabilis (*Opera* 430). Cf. Sermon 2 for Christmas, 1: Agnosce, o homo, dignitatem tuam; agnosce gloriam conditionis humanae (XB 120).

has received something beyond the rest. And so we must greatly beware of this ignorance, by which we may think of ourselves less than ourselves; but not less, nay even more, of that by which we attribute more to ourselves; which happens if we fallaciously think any good which is in us is also of us.[10]

Conative humility is desiring others to have similar contempt for you. Unlike cognitive humility, which is involuntary because produced only by reason, this is voluntary because produced by love.

There is a humility which truth engenders in us, and it has no warmth; there is also a humility which love produces and warms. The latter has its place in affection, the former in knowledge. For if you examine yourself inwardly by the light of truth and without dissimulation, and judge yourself without flattery; no doubt you will be humbled in your own eyes, becoming contemptible in your own sight as a result of this true knowledge of yourself, although perhaps you cannot yet endure that it should be so in the eyes of others. You will be humble, therefore, but only by the working of truth, and not yet by the infusion of love. For if you were affected by love as well as illumined by the light of truth itself, which has shown you yourself truly and profit-

---

[10] *Loving God* 2, 4: Utrumque ergo scias necesse est, et quid sis, et quod a te ipso non sis: ne aut omnino videlicet * non glorieris, aut inaniter glorieris. Denique *si non cognoveris*, inquit, *te ipsam, egredere post greges sodalium tuorum* (Cant. 1. 6, 7). Revera ita fit. Homo factus in honore, cum honorem ipsum non intelligit, talis suae ignorantiae merito comparatur pecoribus, velut quibusdam praesentis suae corruptionis et mortalitatis consortibus. Fit igitur ut sese non agnoscendo egregia rationis munere creatura, irrationabilium gregibus aggregari incipiat, dum ignara propriae gloriae, quae ab intus est, conformanda foris rebus sensibilibus, sua ipsius curiositate abducitur: efficiturque una de caeteris, quod se prae caeteris nihil accepisse intelligat. Itaque valde cavenda haec ignorantia, qua de nobis minus nobis forte sentimus: sed non minus, imo et plus illa, qua plus nobis tribuimus: quod fit, si bonum quodcumque in nobis esse, et a nobis, decepti putemus. (*Opera* 1332.) Cf. *Consideration* 2, 7, 14: Volo glorieris testimonio conscientiae tuae, sed non minus ut eodem ipso humilieris (*Opera* 1031). Cf. Misc. Sermon 7, 3 (XB 767).

* The superfluous word *videlicet* is explained by the hypothesis that *videlicet non* ("He obviously means not") is a gloss, and this is confirmed by its absence in the Clairvaux MSS followed in the Cambridge edition of this essay. But he obviously does mean not; the original must have been *ne aut omnino non glorieris* or possibly *ne aut omni non glorieris*.

ably; you would, no doubt, so far as possible, desire all to hold the very same opinion of you which you know that truth has with you.[11]

2. Cause of humility

Cognitive humility is the first step of the anagogic path.[1] Therefore it has no psychological cause or antecedent. Its only cause is God's preventing grace.[2] The giving of this grace does not require or presuppose any antecedent predisposition on the part of the recipient; it is given to those who are completely immersed in sin and ignorance.

First, when the Son of God, who is the Word and wisdom of the Father, finds that faculty of our soul called reason weighed down by the flesh, captive to sin, blinded by ignorance, and given over to external things; he gently lifts it up, powerfully strengthens it, prudently instructs it, and turns it to internal things. Miraculously making the reason his vicar, as it were, he appoints it judge of itself, so that, out of reverence for the Word to which it is joined, prosecutor and witness and judge of itself,

[11] Sermon 42 on Canticles, 6: Est humilitas quam nobis veritas parit, et non habet calorem: et est humilitas quam charitas format et inflammat. Atque haec quidem in affectu, illa in cognitione consistit. Etenim tu si temetipsum intus ad lumen veritatis et sine dissimulatione inspicias, et sine palpatione dijudices; non dubito quin humilieris et tu in oculis tuis, factus vilior tibi ex hac vera cognitione tui, quamvis necdum fortasse id esse patiaris in oculis aliorum. Eris igitur humilis, sed de opere interim veritatis, et minime adhuc de amoris infusione. Nam si veritatis ipsius, quae te tibi veraciter atque salubriter demonstravit, sicut splendore illuminatus, ita affectus amore fuisses; voluisses procul dubio, quod in te est, eamdem de te omnes tenere sententiam, quam ipsam apud te Veritatem habere cognoscis. (*Opera* 2927.) Cf. *Office of Bishops* 5, 19: Duabus quoque superbiae speciebus, duae nihilominus humilitatis opponuntur: contra caecam, ut quis de se noverit sentire humiliter; contra vanam, nec consentire aliter sentientibus (*Opera* 1114). Cf. Sermon 4 for Advent, 4: Humilitas duplex est: altera cognitionis, altera affectionis (XB 22). Cf. Sermon 11 on *Qui Habitat*, 9 (XB 269).

[1] The fear of the Lord, which is the beginning of wisdom, is reckoned not as antecedent to, but rather as the first step of, humility.

[2] Sermon 20 on Canticles, 1: Sed, Deus, tu scis insipientiam meam; nisi quod hoc ipsum fortasse sapere est, quod et ego agnosco eam, et quidem ex munere tuo (*Opera* 2771).

it performs the office of Truth against itself. From this first conjunction of the Word and the reason is born humility.[3]

Humility is a kind of consideration; that is, it is a function of the reason, not of the will.[4] Therefore it is not voluntary but necessary; free choice does not cooperate in it, and so it is not a merit.[5]

3. Steps of humility

For a monk, there are twelve steps of humility, as distinguished in the Benedictine Rule: fear of the Lord, ignoring desire, submission to a superior, perfect obedience, complete confession, admission of your inferiority, belief in your inferiority, conventionality, silence, gravity, restrained speech, and downcast eyes.[1] The first step is that fear of the Lord which makes a man attentive to his own peril; the last is that perfect introversion which prevents his even looking at external things.[2] The usual opposite of humility is pride, and the opposite of each step of humility is a step of pride.[3] The first step of pride is that curiosity which is manifested by looking around;[4] it is the beginning of sin and ignorance;[5] its classical examples are Satan,[6] Eve,[7] and Dinah.[8] The last step of pride is that habitual sinning which has no consciousness of sin.[9]

[3] Steps of Humility 7, 21.
[4] Cf. Letter 393, 3: Humilitas enim duos habet pedes: considerationem divinae potentiae, et propriae infirmitatis (Opera 706).
[5] Sermon 42 on Canticles, 6–7 (Opera 2927). Cf. Grace and Free Choice 14, 46 (Opera 1396); Sermon 85 on Canticles, 14 (Opera 3194).

[1] Benedictus, Regula, cap. 7.
[2] Steps of Humility 10, 28.
[3] Ibid. 9, 27. Cf. ibid. 22, 57.
[4] Ibid. 10, 28. Cf. Sermon 2 for Ash Wednesday, 2: Miser homo, qui totus pergens in ea quae foris sunt, et ignarus interiorum suorum, putans aliquid se esse, cum nihil sit, ipse se seducit! (XB 190.)
[5] Ibid. 10, 38. Cf. Sermon 4 for Ascension, 4 (XB 378).
[6] Ibid. 10, 31.
[7] Ibid. 10, 30.
[8] Ibid. 10, 29.
[9] Ibid. 21, 51.

4. Fruits of humility

God gives grace to the humble; [1] pride is always a reason
for the withdrawal of grace; [2] humility, therefore, is a necessary condition of grace.[3] But both *humility* and *grace* are
homonyms, and this doctrine has two distinct meanings. In
the first place, *cognitive* humility is necessary, not voluntary,
and therefore not a merit. The grace which is given to it is
not a deserved reward, because there is no merit to reward,
but is itself a merit. This humility is merely good thought,
that is, not a function of the will.[4] It is a necessary condition
of grace because it makes the soul receptive of grace; that
is, good thought is a necessary condition of good will.[5] In
this sense, conative humility is itself one of the graces which
are given to the humble. In the second place, *conative* humility is voluntary, and therefore a merit. The grace which is
given to it is a deserved reward. This humility is a sort of
love. It is a necessary condition of grace because it purifies
the soul; that is, good will is a necessary condition of blessedness, which is the plenitude of grace.[6] These two meanings
of the doctrine that God gives grace to the humble are clearly
shown in the 34th sermon on Canticles, where three stages
of grace are distinguished: (1) To a man in the state of nature
God may, by preventing grace, give "humiliation," realization
of his misery, that is, cognitive humility.[7] (2) To a man in

[1] Jac. 4. 6. Letter 372: Humilitas enim est, cui gratia datur; fides, in qua
suscipitur; timor, a quo custoditur (*Opera* 675). Cf. Sermon 4 in praise of
the Virgin Mary, 9 (XB 71); Misc. Sermon 46 (XB 915).

[2] Sermon 54 on Canticles, 10: Superbia tamen semper causa erit subtractae
gratiae (*Opera* 2996).

[3] Sermon 1 in praise of the Virgin Mary, 5 (XB 35).

[4] Sermon 54 on Canticles, 9: Haec cogitatio tollit extollentiam oculorum,
conciliat gratiam, sponsi saltibus praeparat (*Opera* 2994).

[5] *Grace and Free Choice* 14, 46 (*Opera* 1396).

[6] Sermon 3 for Annunciation, 9: Merito proinde humilibus dat gratiam,
merito respexit Deus humilitatem ancillae suae. Quonam merito, quaeris?
Eo utique, quo animum humilem meritum non occuparet humanum,
quominus libere influeret divinae gratiae plenitudo. (XB 530.)

[7] Sermon 34 on Canticles, 2: At parum est cum per se ipsum humiliat nos
Deus, si tunc libenter accipimus, nisi quando et per alium hoc facit, sapiamus

this state God may, by provecting grace, give "true humility,"
delight in humiliation, that is, conative humility.[8] (3) To a
man in this meritorious state God will, by rewarding grace,
give "exaltation." [9]

Any desirable state of mind has a twofold cause: first, God's
grace, which is its efficient cause; second, the antecedent state
which makes the mind receptive of this grace. The effect is
called, with reference to grace, a *gift*; and with reference to
receptivity, a *fruit*. Humility itself is a gift of preventing
grace and a fruit of nothing. The gifts of provecting grace
which are given to the humble are the fruits of humility.

Five fruits of humility mark the soul's progress toward
knowledge. (1) Knowledge of yourself is the immediate
fruit of humility.[10] This is the first step of truth,[11] and like
all knowledge an end in itself.[12]

He, therefore, who wants to know truth in himself fully must
first get rid of the beam of pride, which prevents him from seeing
the light, and then erect a way of ascent in his heart by which to
seek himself in himself; and thus after the twelfth step of humility
he will come to the first step of truth.[13]

But knowledge of yourself is more than mere *rational* cog-
nition. It involves also acceptance of the fact that you are a
man and therefore *willingness* to undergo that for which man
is born — toil and sorrow.[14] (2) Sorrow is the fruit of that

similiter (*Opera* 2888). Cf. Misc. Sermon 20, 4: Humiliat eos veritas, exaltat
vanitas (XB 814).

[8] *Ibid.* 1: Et quia nisi humilitatis merito maxima minime obtinentur,
propterea qui provehendus est, correptione humiliatur, humilitate meretur.
Tu ergo cum te humiliari videris, habeto id signum in bonum omnino
argumentum gratiae propinquantis. (*Opera* 2887.) Cf. *ibid.* 3: Est autem
humilis, qui humiliationem convertit in humilitatem, et ipse est qui dicit Deo:
Bonum mihi quod humiliasti me (Ps. 118. 71). (*Opera* 2888.) Cf. *Conversion*
7, 12 (*Opera* 1142).

[9] *Ibid.* 4: Ita ergo non qui humiliatur, sed qui sponte se humiliat, exaltabi-
tur; utique ob meritum voluntatis (*Opera* 2889).

[10] *Steps of Humility* 1, 1.   [11] *Ibid.* 3, 6.

[12] Sermon 36 on Canticles, 2 (*Opera* 2898).

[13] *Steps of Humility* 4, 15.

[14] Misc. Sermon 2, 1: Quomodo enim notus sibi videtur homo, laboris
fugitans et doloris? (XB 744.)

self-examination which makes a man contemptible in his own sight.[15]

Humility too has its banquet in the same palanquin, the bread of sorrow, namely, and the wine of remorse.[16]

(3) Conative humility is the fruit of cognitive humility. This is justice.[17]

This virtue consists peculiarly in humility, it purifies the intention, it also obtains every merit the more truly and effectively the less it arrogates to itself.[18]

The warning against hypocritical humility does not apply to conative humility: strict justice (rendering to each his due) is not to prefer yourself to your equal nor compare yourself to your superior; higher justice is not to compare yourself to your equal nor prefer yourself to your inferior; the highest justice is to show yourself inferior even to your inferior.[19] (4) Charity [20] is the fruit of the self-examination which makes a man recognize in himself the weaknesses which he sees so clearly in his neighbors, and so leads him to show mercy to them.

Observe what you are, that you are wretched indeed, and so learn to be merciful, a thing you cannot know in any other way. For if you regard your neighbor's faults but do not observe your own, you are likely to be moved not to ruth but to wrath, not to condole but to condemn, not to restore in the spirit of meekness but to destroy in the spirit of anger.[21]

---

[15] Sermon 36 on Canticles, 5: Convertetur, inquam, ad lacrymas, convertetur ad planctus et gemitus (*Opera* 2900). Cf. Sermon 11 on *Qui Habitat*, 9 (XB 269).

[16] *Steps of Humility* 2, 4.

[17] Sermon 34 on Canticles, 3: Alii cum rancore humiliantur, alii patienter, alii et libenter. Primi rei sunt, sequentes innoxii, ultimi justi. (*Opera* 2888.)

[18] Sermon 14 on *Qui Habitat*, 10: Haec enim virtus specialiter in humilitate consistit, haec intentionem purgat, haec quoque meritum omne eo veracius et efficacius obtinet, quo minus arrogat sibi (XB 289). Fear (the first step of humility) is the cause of justice. Misc. Sermon 50, 2 (XB 919).

[19] Sermon for the octave of Epiphany, 4 (XB 167).

[20] Active, not emotional, charity.

[21] *Steps of Humility* 4, 13. Cf. Sermon 44 on Canticles, 4: Ex considera-

(5) Desire for God is the fruit of the knowledge that apart from God we are nothing.

At first, therefore, a man loves himself for his own sake, for he is flesh and can delight in nothing but himself. And when he sees that he cannot subsist through himself, he begins to seek by faith and to love God as necessary to himself. And so on the second step he loves God — but for his own sake, not God's sake.[22]

Sorrow, conative humility, and charity purify the reason from the three impediments which alienate it from truth — willfulness, weakness, and ignorance respectively.

Those who persevere, therefore, in these three things, the re-morse of repentance,[23] desire of justice,[24] and works of mercy,[25] may then pass through contemplation to the third step, having purged the spiritual vision of the three obstacles arising from ignorance and weakness and willfulness. . . . Those who feel themselves alienated from truth by delight and gladness in sinning and overcome by weakness and ignorance, must change their delight to despite, their gladness to sadness, conquer the weakness of the flesh with the zeal of justice, and resist ignorance with philanthropy. . . . From every blemish, therefore, arising from weakness or ignorance or willfulness the eye of the heart is puri-fied by weeping, hungering for justice, and devotion to works of mercy.[26]

---

tione sui ipsius cuique veniat mansuetum esse ad omnes (*Opera* 2936). Cf. Sermon 50 on Canticles, 5: Moveamur ad bene operandum magis quodam vividae veritatis impulsu, quam sapidae illius charitatis affectu (*Opera* 2969). Cf. Sermon 2 for Easter (to the Abbots), 4 (XB 343).

[22] *Loving God* 15, 39: In primis ergo diligit se ipsum homo propter se; caro quippe est, et nil sapere valet praeter se. Cumque se videt per se non posse subsistere; Deum quasi sibi necessarium incipit per fidem inquirere, et diligere. Diligit itaque in secundo gradu Deum, sed propter se, non propter ipsum. (*Opera* 1360.) Cf. *Conversion* 11, 23 (Opera 1149).

[23] That is, sorrow.

[24] That is, conative humility.

[25] That is, charity.

[26] *Steps of Humility* 6, 19. Cf. Misc. Sermon 18, 1: Erit, quando omni-modis erit gaudium spirituale, ut nullis jam corporeis occasionibus excitetur, non operibus misericordiae, non lacrimis poenitentiae, non exercitatione justitiae, non probatione patientiae (XB 805).

Section 2. Love

1. Definition of love

Love (*dilectio*) is spiritual passion (*amor spiritualis*) or emotional charity (*charitas affectualis*). It is distinguished from passion which is not spiritual but carnal, and from charity which is not emotional but active.[1]

On the one hand, to cultivate the spiritual rather than the carnal is the fundamental rule of monastic life.[2] The two are incompatible with each other.[3] The body is to the soul as a wife, to be loved but disciplined.[4] In the domain of works, the care of the body is medicine, the care of the soul is charity. To seek his own well-being by physical methods is utterly opposed to the monk's vocation.

But to buy drugs, summon doctors, take medicines, is unbecoming to religion and opposed to purity, and is especially inconsistent with the character and purity of our order.[5]

[1] The scheme may be represented as follows:

	actualis (Ratio) OPERA	affectualis (Voluntas) AMOR
carnalis SENSUALITAS	opera carnalia sensualitas actualis MEDICINA	amor carnalis sensualitas affectualis CONCUPISCENTIA
spiritualis CHARITAS	opera spiritualia charitas actualis BENEFICIUM	amor spiritualis charitas affectualis BENEVOLENTIA DILECTIO

[2] Letter 385, 4 (*Opera* 691); *Apology* 6, 12 (*Opera* 1231). Cf. *Grace and Free Choice* 12, 41 (*Opera* 1393); Sermon 3 for Christmas, 1 (XB 125).

[3] Letter 2, 10: Quomodo ignis et aqua simul esse non possunt, sic spirituales et carnales deliciae in eodem se non patiuntur (*Opera* 119). Cf. Sermon 29 on Canticles, 7 (*Opera* 2852); Sermon 35 on Canticles, 2 (*Opera* 2891).

[4] Sermon 1 for All Saints', 11 (XB 615). Cf. Sermon 10 on *Qui Habitat*, 3 (XB 260); Misc. Sermon 23, 1 (XB 823).

[5] Letter 345, 2: At vero species emere, quaerere medicos, accipere potiones, religioni indecens est, et contrarium puritati, maximeque Ordinis nostri nec honestati congruit, nec puritati (*Opera* 641). Cf. Sermon 30 on Canticles, 12: Puta te, quaeso, monachum esse, non medicum; nec de complexione judicandum, sed de professione (*Opera* 2861). Cf. Letter 1, 11 (*Opera* 109); Misc. Sermon 16, 5 (XB 797).

Giving medical care to others is not the monk's business,[6] but may even imperil his salvation.[7] In the domain of emotion, carnal passion is concupiscence, spiritual passion is love.

It is a beautiful sentiment when the bride says, not "Whom I love," but *Whom my soul loveth*; because that love by which it loves anything spiritually, for example God, an angel, or a soul, truly and properly pertains to the soul alone. And to love justice, truth, piety, wisdom, and other virtues is also of this sort. For when the soul loves, or rather craves, something according to the flesh, for example food, clothing, power, and such material and mundane things, the love should be attributed to the flesh rather than to the soul.[8]

By concupiscence, which infects mind and body,[9] we voluntarily enslave ourselves.[10] It is natural to our sinful state, but it can evolve into spiritual passion.

Since we are flesh and born of the lust of the flesh, it must needs be that our desire or love begins from the flesh; and if it is rightly directed and advances by its several degrees under guidance of grace, it will finally be consummated in the spirit; because *that was not first which is spiritual, but that which is natural, and afterward that which is spiritual.*[11]

[6] Letter 67, 2 (*Opera* 215).

[7] Letter 68, 3 (*Opera* 217). Cf. Sermon 46 on Canticles, 8 (*Opera* 2950).

[8] Sermon 75 on Canticles, 9: Pulchre vero sponsa, non Quem diligo ego, sed *quem diligit anima mea* (Cant. 3. 1), inquit: quod vere et proprie ad solam pertineat animam illa dilectio, qua aliquid spiritualiter diligit, verbi gratia, Deum, angelum, animam. Sed et diligere justitiam, veritatem, pietatem, sapientiam, virtutesque alias, ejusmodi est. Nam cum secundum carnem quidpiam diligit, vel potius appetit anima, verbi gratia cibum, vestimentum, dominium, et quae istiusmodi sunt corporalia sive terrena, carnis potius quam animae amor dicendus est. (*Opera* 3134.) Cf. Misc. Sermon 10, 4 (XB 779); Sermon 20 on Canticles, 8 (*Opera* 2776).

[9] Misc. Sermon 28, 4: Mentem desideriis afficit, membra illecebris inficit (XB 846).

[10] Sermon 81 on Canticles, 7 (*Opera* 3167). Cf. *Grace and Free Choice* 11, 36 (*Opera* 1390).

[11] *Loving God* 15, 39: Verumtamen quia carnales sumus, et de carnis concupiscentia nascimur, necesse est ut cupiditas vel amor noster a carne incipiat; quae si recto ordine dirigitur, quibusdam suis gradibus duce gratia proficiens, spiritu tandem consummabitur: quia *non prius quod spirituale, sed quod animale; deinde quod spirituale* (1 Cor. 15. 46). (*Opera* 1360.)

The principal reason why God became flesh was in order to win the love of those who know how to love only carnally.[12] Spiritual passion replaces concupiscence,[13] and this is charity.[14]

On the other hand, action may be purely rational, emotion is essentially voluntary. Unemotional action, although requiring the will's consent, is subject to reason. Emotion, although requiring the reason's service in acting, is itself a function of the will. Passion, one of the four natural emotions,[15] is not subject to reason.[16] On the carnal level, works are medicine, passion is concupiscence. We owe our bodies health, and nothing else.[17] Both medicine, which seeks to increase bodily vigor beyond what health requires,[18] and concupiscence, which seeks those pleasures which destroy health,[19] are to be avoided. On the spiritual level, active charity is beneficence, emotional charity is benevolence, that is, love.[20] Rightly

[12] Sermon 20 on Canticles, 6: Ut carnalium videlicet, qui nisi carnaliter amare non poterant, cunctas primo ad suae carnis salutarem amorem affectiones retraheret, atque ita gradatim ad amorem perduceret spiritualem (*Opera* 2774). Cf. Sermon 3 for Ascension, 3 (XB 371).

[13] Sermon 7 on Canticles, 3: Amat sancte, quia non in concupiscentia carnis, sed in puritate spiritus (*Opera* 2694). Cf. Sermon 3 for Ascension, 7 (XB 374); Misc. Sermon 29, 4 (XB 851).

[14] Letter 90, 1: Porro amare in Deo, charitatem habere est (*Opera* 264). Cf. Sermon 9 on Canticles, 10 (*Opera* 2708).

[15] *Loving God* 8, 23: Amor est affectio naturalis una de quatuor (*Opera* 1347).

[16] Sermon 9 on Canticles, 2: Praeceps amor nec judicium praestolatur, nec consilio temperatur, nec pudore frenatur, nec rationi subjicitur (*Opera* 2704). Cf. Letter 70: Potest quidem ratio vel voluntas affectui effectum subtrahere: sed numquid ipsum affectum evellere? (*Opera* 222.)

[17] Misc. Sermon 16, 2: Sunt autem omnia bona corporis et quae ei solummodo debeamus, sanitas. Nihil autem ultra ei dandum est vel quaerendum, sed hoc termino ligandum et frenandum est, cum fructus ejus nullus sit et mors sit finis illius. (XB 795.)

[18] Sermon 30 on Canticles, 11: Videsne hac sententia Magistri mei carnis sapientiam condemnari, per quam utique aut in luxum voluptatis diffluitur, aut ipsa quoque bona valetudo corporis ultra quam oporteat appetitur? (*Opera* 2861.)

[19] Misc. Sermon 16, 2: Insidiatur enim voluptas sanitati (XB 795).

[20] Sermon 50 on Canticles, 2: Est charitas in actu, est et in affectu (*Opera* 2967). Cf. Sermon 4 for Assumption, 8: Sic [in B. V. Maria] potentissima et piissima caritas et affectu compatiendi et subveniendi abundat effectu, aeque locuples in utroque (XB 575). Cf. Sermon 1 for Whitsunday, 5 (XB 397).

ordered beneficence is proportional to the inferiority of its objects, because the inferior is the needier; whereas rightly ordered love is proportional to the superiority of its objects, because the superior is the more loveable.[21] It is possible to perform works of mercy without any emotion of love.[22] Emotional charity is a sufficient, but not necessary, condition of active charity.[23] But good works are seasoned by love, if it accompanies them.[24]

Where there is love there is not labor but savor.[25]

Love, being good will, makes us free.[26] Fear and cupidity compel the soul to act against its will. But love "converts the soul," [27] that is, converts the free will itself; and so whatever is done by love is done voluntarily.

There are, then, three kinds of love — that which is emotional but not spiritual, that which is spiritual but not emotional, and that which is both emotional and spiritual; only the last is love in the strict sense.[28]

There is one sort of emotion which is born of the flesh, and there is one which is ruled by reason, and there is one which is seasoned with wisdom. The first is that which the Apostle says is not subject to the law of God, neither indeed can be; the second, that which he describes, on the other hand, as consenting unto the law of God, that it is good; and surely contending and consenting are different from each other. But very different from either is

[21] *Ibid.* 5 (*Opera* 2969).

[22] Cf. Misc. Sermon 3, 6 (XB 373).

[23] Sermon 50 on Canticles, 3: Supervacue autem de opere monuisset, si in affectione jam fuisset dilectio (*Opera* 2968).

[24] Sermon 1 for Christmas, 6: Bona opera fervore devotionis et dulcedine spiritualis gratiae condiantur (XB 117).

[25] Sermon 85 on Canticles, 8: Ubi autem amor est, labor non est, sed sapor (*Opera* 3190).

[26] Letter 143, 3: Charitas libertatem donat (*Opera* 354). Cf. Sermon 59 on Canticles, 1: Amor loquitur, qui dominum nescit (*Opera* 3020).

[27] *Loving God* 12, 34: Charitas vero convertit animas, quas facit et voluntarias (*Opera* 1356). Ps. 18. 8: Lex Domini immaculata convertens animas.

[28] The specific word for love in the strict sense is *dilectio*. But frequently, where there is no ambiguity, Bernard uses the generic words *amor* and *charitas* for the species. In practice, therefore, *dilectio*, *amor*, and *charitas* are used interchangeably. Cf., e.g., Misc. Sermon 10, 1-2 (XB 777).

the third, which tastes and savors the sweetness of the Lord, banishing the first, rewarding the second. For the first is delightful, but vile; the second is dry, but powerful; the last is unctuous, and sweet. It is by the second, therefore, that works are performed; and it is in it that charity consists — not emotional charity, which, unctuous and seasoned with the salt of wisdom, brings to the mind the great abundance of divine delight; but rather an active sort which, while not yet refreshing sweetly with that delightful love, nevertheless inflames with love of love itself.[29]

The commandment, "Thou shalt love the Lord thy God with all thy heart, and with all thy soul, and with all thy mind; and thou shalt love thy neighbor as thyself," refers only to active charity. Carnal passion is not commanded; it is natural.[30] Love in the strict sense is not commanded, because it would not be in our power to fulfill the command;[31] love is essentially spontaneous.[32] Active charity is commanded. Toward God it is keeping his commandments; toward your neighbor it is doing unto others as you would that they should do unto you.[33]

Love in the strict sense is benevolence, which is goodness of will. Insofar as it is an objective emotion, with an object outside the lover himself, it is also consensus or sympathy,

[29] Sermon 50 on Canticles, 4: Sed est affectio quam caro gignit; et est quam ratio regit, et est quam condit sapientia. Prima est, quam Apostolus legi Dei dicit non esse subjectam, nec esse posse (Rom. 8. 7); secunda, quam perhibet e regione consentientem legi Dei, quoniam bona est (Rom. 7. 16): nec dubium distare inter se contentiosam et consentaneam. Longe vero tertia ab utraque distat, quae et gustat et sapit quoniam suavis est Dominus (Ps. 33. 9), primam eliminans, secundam remunerans. Nam prima quidem dulcis, sed turpis: secunda sicca, sed fortis: ultima pinguis, et suavis est. Igitur per secundam opera fiunt, et in ipsa charitas sedet, non illa affectualis, quae sale sapientiae condita pinguescens magnam menti importat multitudinem dulcedinis Domini: sed quaedam potius actualis, quae etsi nondum dulci illo amore suaviter reficit, amore tamen amoris ipsius vehementer accendit. (Opera 2968.)

[30] Loving God 8, 23: Nec praecepto indicitur, sed naturae inscritur (Opera 1347).

[31] Sermon 50 on Canticles, 2 (Opera 2967). Cf. Loving God 10, 29 (Opera 1352).

[32] Loving God 12, 34 (Opera 1356).

[33] Sermon 50 on Canticles, 3 (Opera 2968).

which is community of will between lover and beloved.[34] This requires a psychological union of wills.[35] Just as marriage makes two bodies to be one flesh, so love makes two souls to be one spirit.[36] Neither the separation nor even the death of the bodies can part the lover from his beloved.[37]

2. Objects of love

The proper objects of a man's love are himself, his neighbors, and God.

(1) All men naturally love their own bodies by physical love, that is, desire those things which are good for the body.[1] Some men also love their own souls by spiritual love.[2] But such self-love involves only half the connotation of spiritual emotional love; that is, it is benevolence but not sympathy. It is benevolence, because it is desire for those things which are good for the soul.[3] But it is not sympathy, because sympathy requires two wills; lover and beloved must be distinct substances.[4] This consideration applies even to God's self-love. There is no love, strictly speaking, between Father and Son, because there is no union of wills.

[34] Sermon 2 for Easter (to the Abbots), 8: Communis voluntas caritas est (XB 345). Cf. Misc. Sermon 87, 5: Duo sunt ubera sponsae, unum congratulationis, alterum compassionis (XB 964).

[35] Sermon 83 on Canticles, 3: Complexus plane, ubi idem velle, et nolle idem, unum facit spiritum de duobus (*Opera* 3178).

[36] Letter 53 (*Opera* 200); Sermon 8 on Canticles, 9 (*Opera* 2702). Cf. Letter 387 (*Opera* 694).

[37] Letter 65, 2: Nec locorum distantia, nec corporum vel mors vel absentia disjungere poterit, quos unus spiritus vegetat, una charitas ligat (*Opera* 211). Cf. Letter 91, 1 (*Opera* 265); Letter 107, 2 (*Opera* 290); Letter 324 (*Opera* 613).

---

[1] *Loving God* 8, 23 (*Opera* 1347).

[2] Misc. Sermon 103, 1: Quatuor gradibus distinguitur omnium electorum profectus; primo enim fit quisque amicus suae animae (XB 995).

[3] *Ibid*. 1: In primo profectu vitat omnia, quae animam possunt offendere, et diligit ea, quae eam possunt mulcere; horret ergo infernum et coelum concupiscit (XB 995).

[4] Sermon 71 on Canticles, 7: Unus spiritus dicitur et est cum Deo, anima adhaerens Deo; nec praejudicat rerum pluralitas unitati huic, quam facit non confusio naturarum sed voluntatum consensio. Propter hanc quoque multa corda unum, et multae animae una dicuntur. (*Opera* 3104.)

Consent [5] requires at least two wills; conjunction or union by consent requires two essences. There is nothing of the sort in Father and Son, who have neither two essences nor two wills.[6]

When the Holy Ghost is called the love which unites Father and Son,[7] that is meant only in the limited sense of self-love, that is, self-benevolence.[8] The incompatibility of love with consubstantiality is the epistemological basis of Bernard's rejection of pantheism.[9]

Self-benevolence is not only good in itself but is the only source of any benevolence.[10] Just as God's love for creatures is only an overflowing of the superabundance of his self-love, so our love for our neighbors can only be an overflowing of our self-love, springing from it without exhausting it.

The Fountain of Life itself, full in itself and full from itself — did it not first, bubbling over and leaping forth into the hidden places of the heavens, which are nearest to it, fill them all with goodness; and only then, when the loftier and hidden places had been filled, burst forth onto the lands to bring salvation [11] to men and beasts from its superfluity, multiplying its mercy? First it filled the inner places; and thereby overflowing in the multitude of its mercies *visited the earth, and watered it, and greatly enriched it.* Therefore do thou likewise. First be filled, and then seek to pour forth. Kind and prudent love is accustomed to flow over, not to flow away.[12]

[5] Consent (*consensus*), i.e. consensus (*consensio*; cf. *ibid.* 7–8, *Opera* 3104) — not the "consent" of free choice.

[6] Sermon 71 on Canticles, 9: Duas esse oportet ad minus voluntates, ut sit consensus; duas aeque essentias, ut sit conjunctio sive unitio per consensum. Horum nihil in Patre et Filio, quippe nec essentias duas, nec duas habentibus voluntates. (*Opera* 3105.)

[7] Sermon 8 on Canticles, 2 (*Opera* 2698).

[8] Sermon 71 on Canticles, 9: Si quis tamen inter Patrem et Filium dicat esse consensum; non contendo, dummodo non voluntatum unionem, sed unitatem intelligat voluntatis (*Opera* 3105).

[9] *Ibid.* 8 (*Opera* 3104).

[10] *Office of Bishops* 4, 13: Sed et ordinis exigit ratio, ut qui ad sui mensuram proximum jubetur diligere, prius se ipsum diligere norit (*Opera* 1110). Cf. Sermon 11 on *Qui Habitat*, 8: Qui sibi nequam, cui bonus? (XB 269.) Ecclus. 14. 5. Cf. *Consideration* 1, 5, 6 (*Opera* 1012); Letter 8, 1 (*Opera* 143). [11] That is, creation.

[12] Sermon 18 on Canticles, 4: Denique ipse Fons vitae plenus in se ipso,

(2) The overflowing of our superabundant love seeks its object in those persons with whom we come in contact, that is, in our neighbors.[13] Uniting us with them, it becomes love in the full sense of the word. It is benevolence, desiring their good for their sake, not ours,[14] or rather for the sake of the good itself.[15] It is sympathy, rejoicing and grieving as they rejoice or grieve.

The merciful quickly grasp truth in their neighbors, extending their own feelings to them and conforming themselves to them through love, so that they feel *their* joys or troubles as their own. They are weak with the weak; they burn with the offended. They *rejoice with them that do rejoice, and weep with them that weep.*[16]

Love of neighbor, like all love, is pure only when proportioned to the loveableness of its object. You should "love your neighbor as yourself," [17] but not more than yourself.[18] The soul should be loved more than the body.[19] That is, you

---

et plenus se ipso, nonne primum quidem ebulliens et saliens in proxima secreta coelorum, omnia implevit bonitate; et tunc demum impletis superioribus secretioribusque partibus erupit ad terras, ac de superfluo homines et jumenta salvavit, quemadmodum multiplicavit misericordiam suam? Prius interna replevit: et sic exundans in multis miserationibus suis *visitavit terram, et inebriavit eam, multiplicavit locupletare eam* (Ps. 64. 10). Ergo et tu fac similiter. Implere prius, et sic curato effundere. Benigna prudensque charitas affluere consuevit, non effluere. (*Opera* 2763.)

[13] *Ibid.* 3: Vult abundare sibi, ut possit et omnibus; servat sibi quantum sufficiat, ut nulli deficiat (*Opera* 2762).

[14] Sermon 42 on Canticles, 5: Dicas forsan mihi, quod bonum meum ad me revertatur, et quia liberavi animam meam, et mundus sum a sanguine hominis, cui annuntiavi et locutus sum, ut averteretur a via sua mala, et viveret. Sed etsi innumera talia addas, me tamen minime ista consolabuntur, mortem filii intuentem. Quasi vero meam illa reprehensione liberationem quaesierim, et non magis illius! (*Opera* 2926.)

[15] *Loving God* 12, 34: Nam qui magis, aut certe solum diligit suum, convincitur non caste diligere bonum, quod utique propter se diligit, non propter ipsum (*Opera* 1356).

[16] *Steps of Humility* 3, 6.

[17] As a commandment, this applies only to active charity; but as a counsel of perfection, it applies to emotional love also.

[18] Sermon 18 on Canticles, 4 (*Opera* 2762).

[19] *Apology* 8, 16: Quae etenim charitas est, carnem diligere, et spiritum negligere? (*Opera* 1235.) Cf. *Loving God* 14, 38 (*Opera* 1360).

should love your neighbor not in the flesh but in God.[20] His loveableness, like your own, is measured by the extent to which he loves God.[21] Sinners, who do not love God, are not to be loved. Having withdrawn from God, who is their being, they are nothing;[22] and that which is nothing is not a proper object of love.[23] Curable sinners are actually nothing but potentially something; they should be loved only in order that they may love.[24] That is, you should have benevolence but not sympathy for them, for sympathy would be malevolence in the case of those who will their own evil. Only in this way can you love your enemies, whose hatred for you shows their hatred for God.[25] Incurable sinners are absolutely nothing; they should not be loved at all, but rather hated.[26] Sympathy for them would be to join yourself to their sin; benevolence for them would be to oppose God's justice and so be out of sympathy with God. Therefore you should have no compassion for the damned, and no pity for them disturbs the blessedness of the saints.[27] This applies equally to incurable sinners still living, but in practice this fact is unknowable; even excommunicated persons, although not to be prayed for, are to be presumed to be curable and so loved.[28]

(3) Only the love of that which is most loveable can finally satisfy us, for we naturally seek ever something more desirable until we attain that which is most desirable.[29] Love,

[20] *Loving God* 8, 25: Alioquin proximum pure diligere quomodo potest, qui in Deo non diligit? (*Opera* 1348.)

[21] Sermon 50 on Canticles, 8 (*Opera* 2971).

[22] Cf. 1 Cor. 13. 2.   [23] Letter 18, 1 (*Opera* 160).

[24] Sermon 50 on Canticles, 7: Porro inimicum hominem, quoniam nihil est, pro eo quod non diligit Deum; non potes quidem diligere tanquam te ipsum, qui Deum diligis: diliges tamen ut diligat (*Opera* 2970).

[25] The commandment to love your enemies refers to active charity. *Ibid.* 3 (*Opera* 2968).

[26] Sermon 50 on Canticles, 7 (*Opera* 2970).

[27] *Loving God* 15, 40 (*Opera* 1362).

[28] *Steps of Humility* 22, 56.

[29] *Loving God* 7, 18: Inest omni utenti ratione naturaliter pro sua semper aestimatione atque intentione appetere potiora, et nulla re esse contentum, cui quod deest, judicet praeferendum (*Opera* 1343). Cf. Sermon 9 on *Qui Habitat*, 8: Perfecta caritas solum sitit quod summum est (XB 257).

by which we love and are loved, is itself the most loveable object.[30] Only those who love God, that is, Love,[31] are satisfied; those who do not are constantly seeking.[32]

The *reason* for loving God is twofold: his merit and our advantage.[33] To the infidel, reason teaches that God is to be loved as the creator of mankind and the giver of all good gifts.[34] To the Christian, faith teaches that God is to be loved as the redeemer who laid down his life for those who were not even his friends.[35] And we find that loving God is sweet, even when it is imperfect and partial.

Thou art good, O Lord, to the soul that seeketh thee; if to it, how much more to that which findeth thee! If the anticipation is so sweet, what must the reality be! If honey and milk are sweet under the tongue, what must they be on the tongue! [36]

The *manner* of loving God is threefold. He should be loved emotionally, lest the lover be seduced by the emotions of physical love. He should be loved wisely, lest the lover be deceived by the errors of heresy. He should be loved strongly, lest the lover be overcome by adversities.[37]

[30] *Consideration* 5, 14, 30: Quid item tam amabile, quam amor ipse, quo amas, et quo amaris? (*Opera* 1094.) Cf. Sermon 77 on Canticles, 5 (*Opera* 3146).

[31] Sermon 83 on Canticles, 4 (*Opera* 3179).

[32] *Loving God* 7, 19 (Opera 1344).

[33] *Ibid.* 1, 1 (*Opera* 1330). Cf. Sermon 11 on Canticles, 3 (*Opera* 2717).

[34] *Ibid.* 2, 6 (*Opera* 1333); *ibid.* 5, 15 (*Opera* 1341).

[35] *Ibid.* 3, 7 (*Opera* 1334); Sermon 1 for Annunciation, 13 (XB 520); Misc. Sermon 29, 2 (XB 849). Cf. Sermon 20 on Canticles, 1: Pro his ergo ita sum amans te, quantum possum. 2. Sed est quod me plus movet, plus urget, plus accendit. Super omnia, inquam, reddit amabilem te mihi, Jesu bone, calix quem bibisti, opus nostrae redemptionis (*Opera* 2771). Cf. Letter 107, 8 (*Opera* 294).

[36] Misc. Sermon 4, 1: *Bonus es, Domine! animae quaerenti te* (Lam. 3. 25); si quaerenti, quanto magis invenienti? Si tam dulcis est memoria, qualis erit praesentia? Si mel et lac dulce est sub lingua (Cant. 4. 11), quid erit super linguam? (XB 756.) Cf. *Loving God* 7, 22: Sed enim in hoc est mirum, quod nemo te quaerere valet, nisi qui prius invenerit (*Opera* 1347).

[37] Sermon 20 on Canticles, 4: Dulciter, ne illecti; prudenter, ne decepti; fortiter, ne oppressi ab amore Domini avertamur (*Opera* 2772). Cf. Misc. Sermon 29, 1: Diliges dulciter sive affectuose, diliges prudenter, diliges fortiter (XB 849).

The *extent* of our love for God, if proportioned to the loveableness of its object, must be infinite.

You wish to hear from me why and in what way God is to be loved? I reply: The cause [38] of loving God is God; the way, to love always.[39]

3. Cause of love

The cause [1] of love, even of self-love,[2] is God's grace.[3] For God, love is his substance; each person of the Trinity loves [4] and is love.[5] But for man, love is an accident, present in some men and lacking in others.[6]

And so love gives love, the substantial giving the accidental. Where it signifies the giver, it refers to the substance; where it signifies the gift, to a quality.[7]

It is a gift of the Holy Ghost, by whom it is diffused in our hearts.[8]

Another faculty, called the will, infected to be sure with the poison of the flesh but now under the control of the reason, is graciously visited, gently purged, ardently energized, and made merciful by the Holy Ghost; so that, like a skin which is anointed

---

[38] That is, the final cause.

[39] *Loving God* 1, 1: Vultis ergo a me audire, quare, et quomodo diligendus sit Deus? Et ego: Causa diligendi Deum, Deus est; modus, sine modo diligere. (*Opera* 1330.)

[1] That is, the efficient cause. *Loving God* 7, 22 (*Opera* 1346).

[2] Misc. Sermon 103, 1: Hoc modo fit amator animae suae per Spiritum sanctum, quem ex fide accepit (XB 996).

[3] Distinguish between the source of love and the cause of love. The source of love is that physical self-love naturally implanted in all men. The cause of love (God's grace) is the efficient cause which makes that physical love become spiritual and makes that love of self become love of others.

[4] *Loving God* 4, 13 (*Opera* 1339).

[5] Letter 18, 3 (*Opera* 162).

[6] Cf. Misc. Sermon 10, 1 (XB 777).

[7] *Loving God* 12, 35: Itaque charitas dat charitatem, substantiva accidentalem. Ubi dantem significat, nomen substantiae est: ubi donum, qualitatis. (*Opera* 1357.)

[8] Letter 107, 8–9 (*Opera* 294); Letter 362, 1 (*Opera* 659); Letter 368, 1 (*Opera* 670); *Steps of Humility* 7, 20; Sermon 1 for Michaelmas, 6 (XB 604).

and stretched, it, divinely anointed, is extended in affection even to its enemies. And thus, by this second conjunction of the Spirit of God and the human will, love is created.[9]

The condition of receptivity of this grace is humility.[10] This applies to love of self, love of neighbor, and love of God.

(1) Those who, instead of humility, have false humility, believing themselves to be soulless animals, love only their bodies by physical love, not their souls by spiritual love — just as the animals do.[11] Those who, instead of humility, have the other extreme, pride, believing themselves to be good by their own natural unassisted merit, love themselves excessively — proceeding from belief in their own excellence (blind pride or contumacy, the opposite of cognitive humility) to delight in their own praises (vain pride or vanity, the opposite of conative humility).[12] Only the truly humble, therefore, love themselves with a love which is *purified*, that is, in proportion to the loveableness of its object, and *rightly ordered*, that is, accompanied by fear and sadness rather than joy.[13]

(2) Sorrow, conative humility, and active charity lead us to love our neighbors; these are the fruits of humility, which is therefore the necessary condition of love of neighbor.[14]

(a) Christ, although God, became man, in order that, knowing by his own experience what it is to be a man, he might be able to sympathize with and love other men, as he could not do otherwise, for only through passion [15] can compassion be learned.[16] We too should learn what it is to be a man, by humbly lowering ourselves from what we proudly think we are down to what we really are. Recognizing our own weaknesses, we can then sympathize with the similar faults of others, and this is the essence of love.

[9] *Steps of Humility* 7, 21.
[10] *Ibid.* 2, 3. Cf. *Office of Bishops* 5, 17 (*Opera* 1113).
[11] *Loving God* 2, 4 (*Opera* 1332).
[12] *Office of Bishops* 5, 19 (*Opera* 1114).
[13] Cf. Sermon 3 for Assumption, 4 (XB 567).
[14] *Steps of Humility* 5, 18. Cf. Sermon 37 on Canticles, 2 (*Opera* 2903).
[15] Passion (*passio*), that is, suffering or sorrow — not the "passion" used above to translate *amor*.   [16] *Ibid. cap.* 3.

Just as pure truth is seen only with a pure heart, so a brother's misery is truly felt with a miserable heart. But in order to have a miserable heart because of another's misery, you must first know your own; so that you may find your neighbor's mind in your own and know from yourself how to help him, by the example of our Savior, who willed his passion in order to learn compassion; his misery, to learn commiseration.[17]

(b) Just as the zeal for justice which rises from conative humility is the perfection of humility,[18] so charity is the perfection of justice. Active justice is expressed in active charity or beneficence — keeping God's commandments and doing unto others as you would that they should do unto you.[19] Emotional or perfect justice is expressed in emotional fear and love.[20] Love, therefore, is the fruit of justice.[21]

(c) Emotional charity is the reward, that is the fruit, of active charity.[22] That is, we come to love a person as a result of acting as if we loved him; beneficence leads to benevolence.[23]

(3) The desire for God engendered by humility leads us to seek him, seeking leads us to find him, finding leads us to love him.

[17] *Ibid.* 3, 6. Cf. *Conversion* 7, 12 (*Opera* 1142).
[18] Sermon 47 on Canticles, 7: Consummationem profecto justitiae in humilitatis perfectione constituens (*Opera* 2954).
[19] Misc. Sermon 54: Justitia est in duobus: in innocentia et in beneficentia; innocentia justitiam inchoat, beneficentia consummat (XB 925). Cf. Misc. Sermon 18, 4 (XB 807); Misc. Sermon 125, 3 (XB 1022).
[20] Misc. Sermon 50, 3: Timor enim affectio est naturalis, quae nos conjungit superiori per inferiorem partem et habet se ad solum Deum; amor affectio est, quae nos conjungit superiori et inferiori et aequali, et habet se ad Deum et proximum. In his autem duobus perfecta consistit justitia, ut timeamus Deum propter potentiam, amemus propter bonitatem et proximum propter naturae societatem. (XB 920.) Only active charity is commanded; we are not commanded to be perfect.
[21] *Ibid.* 2: Est timor causa justitiae, amor fructus (XB 919).
[22] Sermon 50 on Canticles, 2: Illa mandatur ad meritum, ista in praemium datur (*Opera* 2967). Cf. *ibid.* 4 (*Opera* 2968).
[23] Cf. William James, *Principles of Psychology*, II, 463: "If we wish to conquer undesirable emotional tendencies in ourselves, we must assiduously, and in the first instance cold-bloodedly, go through the *outward movements* of those contrary dispositions which we prefer to cultivate."

But when, by reason of his own necessity, he has begun to worship him and to come to him again and again in thought, in reading, in prayer, in obedience; by a sort of familiarity of this kind, slowly and gradually, God becomes known and consequently becomes sweet. And thus by tasting how sweet the Lord is, he passes to the third step — to love God not for his own sake but for God's sake.[24]

Thus love of God is the fruit of desire for God.

Just as faith leads to full knowledge, so desire leads to perfect love. And just as it is said, *Unless ye have believed ye shall not understand*, so it may likewise be said without absurdity, "Unless ye have desired ye shall not perfectly love." Understanding is therefore the fruit of faith; perfect love, of desire.[25]

Not that love of God destroys desire for God; it perfects it; it consummates it.[26]

There will be no end of desire, nor therefore of seeking. Conceive if you can this fervor of seeking without want and desire without solicitude, for presence excludes the one, fullness the other.[27]

[24] *Loving God* 15, 39: At vero cum ipsum coeperit occasione propriae necessitatis colere et frequentare, cogitando, legendo, orando, obediendo; quadam hujuscemodi familiaritate paulatim sensimque Deus innotescit, consequenter et dulcescit: et sic gustato quam suavis est Dominus, transit ad tertium gradum, ut diligat Deum, non jam propter se, sed propter ipsum (*Opera* 1360).

[25] Letter 18, 2: Sicut autem fides ducit ad plenam cognitionem, sic desiderium ad perfectam dilectionem. Et sicut dicitur, *Nisi credideritis, non intelligetis* (Is. 7. 9 Vet. Lat.); sic dici aeque non absurde potest, Si non desideraveritis, non perfecte amabitis. Intellectus igitur est fructus fidei, perfecta charitas desiderii. (*Opera* 161.)

[26] Sermon 84 on Canticles, 1: Existimo quia nec cum inventus fuerit, cessabitur a quaerendo. Non pedum passibus, sed desideriis quaeritur Deus. Et utique non extundit desiderium sanctum felix inventio, sed extendit. Numquid consummatio gaudii, desiderii consumptio est? Oleum magis est illi: nam ipsum flamma. (*Opera* 3181.)

[27] *Ibid.* 1: Desiderii non erit finis, ac per hoc nec quaerendi. Tu vero cogita, si potes, quaeritandi hoc studium sine indigentia, et desiderium sine anxietate. Alterum profecto praesentia, alterum copia excludit. (*Opera* 3181.)

To conclude: Love, which is purely voluntary, is the fruit of humility, which is purely rational; but between them must be that intermediate step in which will and reason cooperate — that intermediate step which appears in its various aspects as self-knowledge, sorrow, penitence, conative humility, justice, active charity, works of mercy, desire for God. This intermediate step Bernard calls "love of love"; [28] it manifests itself in all good works; it is that "free counsel" in which merit consists.

4. Fruits of love

The desired product of love is love itself.

Love is sufficient in itself, it is pleasing [1] in itself and for its own sake. It is itself a merit, and is its own reward. Love seeks no reason or fruit beyond itself. Its use is its fruit. I love because I love; I love in order to love.[2]

If you love for the sake of some reward, it is that reward which you are really loving.

It is a bond of affection, not of law; it neither acquires nor is acquired by contract. It moves freely, and makes us free. True love is content with itself. It has a reward, but it is the beloved object. For whatever you pretend to love for the sake of something else, you are obviously loving that which is the end of your love, not that which is its means.[3]

Rousselot criticizes this doctrine, saying:

On pouvait donc, avec une égale vraisemblance, soutenir ou que l'auteur condamnait comme contraire à la pureté de l'amour,

---

[28] Sermon 50 on Canticles, 4 (*Opera* 2969).

[1] That is, to the beloved, according to the context; but also to the lover, according to the words following.

[2] Sermon 83 on Canticles, 4: Is per se sufficit, is per se placet, et propter se. Ipse meritum, ipse praemium est sibi. Amor praeter se non requirit causam, non fructum. Fructus ejus, usus ejus. Amo, quia amo; amo, ut amem. (*Opera* 3179.)

[3] *Loving God* 7, 17: Affectus est, non contractus: nec acquiritur pacto, nec acquirit. Sponte afficit, et spontaneum facit. Verus amor se ipso contentus est. Habet praemium, sed id quod amatur. Nam quidquid propter aliud amare videaris, id plane amas, quo amoris finis pertendit, non per quod tendit. (*Opera* 1343.) Cf. Sermon 11 on Canticles, 4 (*Opera* 2717); Sermon 83 on Canticles, 3 (*Opera* 3178).

le désir de posséder Dieu, ou qu'il exceptait ce désir de ses condamnations. La vérité est que la pensée n'est pas parfaitement conséquente avec elle-même. Si l'on accorde que le véritable amant désire la possession réelle de l'objet aimé, l'on ne peut plus écrire, en toute rigueur logique: *Verus amor se ipso contentus est.*[4]

Certainly, for Bernard, the true lover always does desire the real possession of the loved object. Perfect love is typified by the bride — who would hardly be content with her love alone, without the bridegroom. Even when the desire is satisfied, it does not cease to exist.[5] But Rousselot's dilemma vanishes when we realize that love, as Bernard understands it, *is* real possession. The lover desires the loved object in the sense of loving it but not in the sense of wanting it.

Love of God is an emotion, not a mere sentiment. The sentiment, found even in active charity, is "love of love," that is, rational desire to have emotional love.[6] The emotion is love of God, that is, emotional sympathy with him. It unites the soul and God, so that they become one spirit — although subject to degrees; to love God does not imply the perfect union of mystical contemplation. "Real possession" of God can have no meaning other than this spiritual union — whether in this life or the next. There is no question of spatial presence, for God is ever present;[7] nor of God's loving the soul in return, for his love always prevents ours.[8] To love God and to possess him are, therefore, identical.[9]

It is the same with love of neighbor. This is possible only among those who are close together, and so able to sympathize with each other. It unites lover and beloved even when space separates them.

[4] P. Rousselot, *Pour l'Histoire du Problème de l'Amour au Moyen Age* (Beiträge zur Geschichte der Philosophie des Mittelalters, 6, 6), p. 52.

[5] Sermon 84 on Canticles, 1 (*Opera* 3181).

[6] Sermon 50 on Canticles, 4 (*Opera* 2968).

[7] Sermon 3 in praise of the Virgin Mary, 4 (XB 55).

[8] *Loving God* 1, 1 (*Opera* 1330); Letter 107, 8 (*Opera* 294); Sermon 69 on Canticles, 7 (*Opera* 3092); Sermon 84 on Canticles, 5 (*Opera* 3183).

[9] Cf. *Loving God* 7, 22: Nemo te quaerere valet, nisi qui prius invenerit (*Opera* 1347).

Therefore let us be of good cheer, having with us God, in whom we are present to you also, no matter how great a space of land may seem to separate us from you. Whoever among you shows himself dutiful, humble, reverent, zealous in study, vigilant in prayers, solicitous of fraternal love — let him not think me absent from him. For how am I not present in spirit to him with whom I have one heart and one soul? [10]

Therefore the lover always does possess the loved object. It may be objected that there are still two ways in which love of neighbor may desire "real possession" of its object and so not be content with itself: it may desire that the love be returned, and it may desire the object's spatial presence.

Love is sympathy, a symmetrical relation; therefore it always is returned. It makes two souls one spirit just as marriage makes two bodies one flesh; you can no more love without being loved in return than you can marry without being married in return.[11] Both parts of the mutual love must exist, although both need not be equal.[12] The greatest love a man can have is willingness to lay down his life for his friends.[13] His enemies, who do not love him, he cannot love; Bernard rejects as absurd a literal interpretation of the commandment to love your enemies.[14]

The lover always desires the spatial presence of the beloved; if this is an impurity, Bernard's love is not pure.

I must be afflicted with anxieties equal in number to you; I grieve at the absence, I tremble at the danger of each one of you.

[10] Letter 143 (to his monks), 2: Propterea bono animo simus, Deum habentes nobiscum, in quo et vobis praesentes sumus, quantislibet terrarum spatiis divisi a vobis videamur. Quicumque in vobis bene officiosum se ipsum exhibet, humilem, timoratum, studiosum lectionis, orationibus vigilem, fraternae charitatis sollicitum; non me putet absentem sibi. Nam quomodo ei praesens spiritu non sum, cum quo est mihi cor unum, et anima una? (*Opera* 354.)

[11] Sermon 84 on Canticles, 6: Non timeo, quia amo; quod non amata omnino non facerem. Itaque etiam amor. (*Opera* 3184.) Cf. Letter 107, 8 (*Opera* 294).   [12] Letter 85 (*Opera* 248).

[13] *Ibid.* 3 (*Opera* 249). Joan. 15. 13.

[14] Sermon 50 on Canticles, 3 (*Opera* 2968); *ibid.* 7 (*Opera* 2970). Cf. Letter 143, 2 (*Opera* 354).

This twofold pang will not desert me until I am restored to my offspring; and I do not doubt that you feel the same for me.[15]

He laments their absence and their danger; that is, he desires their presence, because of sympathy, and their safety, because of benevolence. It is true that continued absence makes sympathy difficult and so causes love to decay, and therefore the presence of the object is necessary for the continuance of love;[16] but that is not why the lover desires the beloved's presence. The lover loves the beloved, not his love. *I love because I love; I love in order to love*, does not mean, "I love because I realize that loving is good for me." It means, "The emotion by which my beloved attracts me is sufficient to move me without any rationalization; will, not reason, provides the only motive."

Love, therefore, seeks no fruit or reward beyond itself, that is, beyond union with the beloved object. Nevertheless it obtains one.

True love seeks no reward; nevertheless it merits one. Those who do not yet love hear of this reward, those who love merit it, those who persevere attain it.[17]

This reward or fruit, which the lover does not seek but nevertheless obtains, is twofold — knowledge and purity.

(1) Just as the first step of truth, knowledge of yourself, is the fruit of humility; so the second step of truth, knowledge of your neighbors, is the fruit of love.[18]

And this is the second step of truth, when they seek it in their neighbors, when they learn others' wants from their own, when

[15] Letter 143, 1: Tot me necesse est affici curis, quot vos estis; et ad singulos quosque vestrum dolere absentiam, timere pericula. Duplex contritio ista non me deseret, quousque meis visceribus ego reddar: quod quidem et vos sentire pro me non ambigo. (*Opera* 353.)

[16] Sermon 51 on Canticles, 3: Cum praesto est quod amatur, viget amor; languet, cum abest (*Opera* 2973).

[17] *Loving God* 7, 17: Verus amor praemium non requirit, sed meretur. Praemium sane necdum amanti proponitur, amanti debetur, perseveranti redditur. (*Opera* 1343.) Cf. Sermon 11 on Canticles, 4 (*Opera* 2717).

[18] Knowledge of neighbor is the fruit of love of neighbor. Knowledge of God is the fruit of that perfect love of God called contemplation.

they know from their own miseries how to commiserate with others who are miserable.[19]

Rather, just as humility *is* knowledge of yourself, so love *is* knowledge of your neighbors.[20] No intellectual understanding can give us knowledge of other men. Like knows like; only the will can know another will. Love, uniting the lover's will with his beloved's by sympathy, gives him an intuitive knowledge of his beloved's soul. Only by love, therefore, can we know our neighbors as they are.

But those who do not unite themselves with their brethren in this way, but on the contrary either revile those who weep or disparage those who do rejoice, not feeling in themselves that which is in others, because they are not similarly affected — how can they grasp truth in their neighbors? For the popular proverb well applies to them: The healthy do not know how the sick feel, nor the full how the hungry suffer. But sick sympathize with sick, and hungry with hungry, the more closely the more they are alike.[21]

(2) Love purifies the will,[22] and so makes the mind's eye capable of contemplation.[23] Thus the perfect love of God called contemplation is made possible by the love of neighbor which is a fruit of humility.[24]

After the spiritual vision has been purified by this brotherly love, they enjoy the contemplation of truth in its own nature.[25]

[19] *Steps of Humility* 5, 18.

[20] Misc. Sermon 29, 1: Exponit beatus Gregorius, quia amor ipse notitia est (XB 849). Cf. Sermon 82 on Canticles, 8: Charitas illa visio, illa similitudo est (*Opera* 3176).

[21] *Steps of Humility* 3, 6. Cf. Augustinus, *De Anima et ejus Origine*, 4, 19, 30: Quis autem recte dicat, se aliquem hominem cognovisse, nisi in quantum potuit ejus vitam voluntatemque cognoscere, quae utique moles non habet vel colores? Sic enim et nos ipsos certius quam caeteros novimus, quia nobis conscientia nostra nota est et voluntas. (*Pat. Lat.* 44, 542.)

[22] Misc. Sermon 45, 4: Caritas vero purgavit voluntatem (XB 913).

[23] *Precept and Dispensation* 14, 36: Ego vero ut interior oculus vere simplex sit, duo illi esse arbitror necessaria, charitatem in intentione, et in electione veritatem (*Opera* 1199).

[24] Sententiae S. Bernardi, 21: Incipit enim homo diligere Deum, antequam proximum: sed quia illa dilectio non potest perfici, nisi nutriatur, et crescat per dilectionem proximi, oportet ut proximus diligatur (*Opera* 2588).

[25] *Steps of Humility* 3, 6.

Section 3. Contemplation

1. Definition of contemplation

Contemplation in general, as distinguished from consideration, is defined as the mind's true and certain intuition of any object, or as the indubitable apprehension of a truth.[1] Mystical contemplation is a form of ecstasy.[2] In the lower form of ecstasy the soul withdraws from sensations and sensuous desires.[3] In contemplation it withdraws even from sensuous images.

May my soul die the death, if I may call it that, of angels, so that, departing from the remembrance of things present, it may put away not only the desire but even the images of lower and material things, and have pure communion with those things in which is the image of purity. Such ecstasy, I think, is alone, or principally, what is called contemplation.[4]

2. Objects of contemplation

The supreme object of mystical contemplation is Truth in itself,[1] which is the Word of God.[2] But contemplation also reveals the saints and angels in heaven. This kind of contemplation is less difficult than the former. Bernard distinguishes

[1] *Consideration* 2, 2, 5: Potest contemplatio quidem definiri, verus certusque intuitus animi de quacumque re, sive apprehensio veri non dubia (*Opera* 1024).

[2] Sermon 52 on Canticles, 4: Non absurde sponsae ecstasim vocaverim mortem, quae tamen non vita, sed vitae eripiat laqueis (*Opera* 2979). Cf. Misc. Sermon 87, 2 (XB 962).

[3] *Ibid.* 4: Excedente quippe anima, etsi non vita, certe vitae sensu, necesse est etiam ut nec vitae tentatio sentiatur (*Opera* 2980).

[4] *Ibid.* 5: Sed moriatur anima mea morte etiam, si dici potest, Angelorum, ut praesentium memoria excedens, rerum se inferiorum corporearumque non modo cupiditatibus, sed et similitudinibus exuat, sitque ei pura cum illis conversatio, cum quibus est puritatis similitudo. Talis, ut opinor, excessus aut tantum aut maxime contemplatio dicitur. (*Opera* 2980.)

[1] *Steps of Humility* 3, 6; *ibid.* 6, 19.

[2] Sermon 80 on Canticles, 2 (*Opera* 3158). Cf. *Steps of Humility* 7, 20–21 (where the Father is called the object of contemplation; this is inconsistent with the sermons on Canticles).

them in one of his sermons on Canticles, of which the following is a summary:

"*My dove in the clefts of the rock, in the hollows of the wall.*[3] If we understand the wall to mean the communion of saints, the hollow places refer to the fallen angels, who left vacancies which have to be filled with men. For the present we occupy them only in anticipation; but the time will come when we shall fill all the hollows with our souls and bodies, and the wall will be made whole again.

"But if you prefer, we may say that these hollows are not found but rather made by zealous and pious minds, by means of thought and desire. The wall, as if made of some soft material, gives way to the soul's yearning, to pure contemplation, and to frequent prayer. The prayer of a just man penetrates the heavens — not the physical sky, but the holy, living, and rational heavens which declare the glory of God, and which freely incline themselves to our prayers and receive us into their interiors, whenever we knock at them with worthy intention. Each one of us is able, even in this life, to excavate hollows in the heavenly wall, wherever he wishes; now to see the patriarchs, now to greet the prophets, now to mingle with the senate of the apostles, now to join the choirs of martyrs; and even to wander with all the swiftness of the mind among the stations and mansions of the holy powers, from the lowliest angel up to the cherubim and seraphim, as each one's devotion may lead him. Wherever he is drawn (the Holy Ghost infusing himself by grace), if he stands and knocks, straightway it is opened to him, and a hollow is made among the holy minds, as they curve themselves around him, so that he may rest, if only for a moment, in their midst. To the soul who does this it is said, *Let me see thy countenance, let me hear thy voice.*[4]

"Happy is he who devotes himself to cutting hollows in this wall; but happier is he who does so in the rock. It is possible to cut into the rock also; but this requires a purer

[3] Cant. 2. 14.
[4] Cant. 2. 14, con.

eye of the mind and a more vehement intention, as well as more efficacious merits. John, Paul, and David were able to do this; and they have revealed to us what little can be said of their ineffable visions.

"It is clear, therefore, that there are two kinds of contemplation: one is of the condition and felicity and glory of the heavenly city, where that mighty multitude of celestial citizens is engaged either in activity or in leisure; the other is of the majesty, eternity, and divinity of the King himself. The former is in the wall, the latter in the rock. The latter is more difficult to carve out, but its product is sweeter. Fear not the scriptural warning to searchers of majesty.[5] Only bring a pure and simple eye; you will not be overwhelmed by glory, but admitted — unless you are seeking your own glory instead of God's. If all cupidity has been expelled, we shall search securely in the rock, *in which are hid the treasures of wisdom and knowledge*. There the gentle and simple soul finds rest, but the crafty or haughty or vain-glorious is overwhelmed. The Church is the dove, and rests there, that is, in the Word, which is the rock. The Church, therefore, rests in the clefts of the rock, through which she looks and sees the glory of her Bridegroom; she is not overwhelmed by the glory, for she does not usurp it to herself. She is not overwhelmed, because she is a searcher not of his majesty but of his will. But if she is rapt in ecstasy even to see that majesty, it is the finger of God condescending to raise man, not the insolence of man reaching up to God. They are called searchers of majesty, and are overwhelmed by glory, who rush upon it; not those who are rapt to it.

"Searching majesty, therefore, is dangerous; but searching will is both safe and pious. For *we, with open face beholding, are transformed into the same image from glory to glory, even as by the Spirit of the Lord*. We are transformed when we are conformed; for human conformity to God is in the will, not in the majesty.

"But since the Church cannot as yet, in all her members,

[5] Prov. 25. 27.

attain to boring in the rock (for it is not given to all Church members to examine the mysteries of the divine will or discover for themselves the secrets of God), she is said to have her dwelling not only in the clefts of the rock but also in the hollows of the wall. She dwells in the clefts of the rock in the persons of those perfect souls which both dare, by purity of conscience, and are able, by acuteness of intellect, to scrutinize and penetrate the hidden treasures of wisdom. In the hollows of the wall, on the other hand, are those who either are not able or do not presume to dig in the rock for themselves, but dig in the wall, content to intuit mentally the glory of the saints.[6] If anyone finds even this impossible, to him she presents Jesus crucified; so that even such a one, without any labor of his own, may dwell in those clefts of the rock on which he has not labored.[7] For it was the Jews who labored to make these clefts. The feeble and inactive soul (which says, *I cannot dig; to beg I am ashamed* [8]) is shown a place already excavated where it may lie until it grows strong enough to cut out its own clefts in the rock, by which to enter in to the heart of the Word by means of vigor and purity of mind.

"For what is so efficacious for curing the wounds of conscience and purifying the mind's eye, as meditation on the wounds of Christ? But until this curing and purifying are completed, I do not see how it can be said to such a one: *Let me see thy countenance, let me hear thy voice*. It will not be worthy to be seen until it is fit to see. The Bridegroom will desire to look upon this face only when it, itself pure, shall be able to intuit pure truth.

"To the impure, Truth does not reveal itself or Wisdom entrust itself. All who seek human praise, who will not preach the gospel without pay, who evangelize for a living, who reckon gain as godliness, who seek not fruits but gifts — all such are impure. They are unable to see the truth because of their impurity; yet they are able to preach it! Truth is

---

[6] Contenti vel gloriam sanctorum mente intueri.
[7] That is, in the wounds of Christ.
[8] Luc. 16. 3.

invisible to the proud eye, but obvious to the sincere one." [9]

In this sermon three kinds of religion are distinguished:

(1) For the so-called perfect souls, who have the capacity for mysticism, and who have made sufficient progress in humility and love, there is mystical contemplation of the Word of God.

(2) For monks less proficient, there is contemplation of the saints and angels in heaven. This is a sort of clairvoyance. On the one hand, it is very different from the spiritual union by which God is contemplated, for it is an external relation, not a direct infusion of the object in the soul.[10] On the other hand, it is not mere meditation on the Christian doctrine concerning heavenly things, but intuition of the things themselves. In this connection it is necessary to consider a curious passage in another sermon:

I am lying (and I say this for your consolation) if from the hands of this sinner there have not flown to the joys above the souls of monks, novices, and lay-brothers, without any hindrance once they were freed from the prison of our mortality. If you ask how I know this, know that absolutely certain evidence of it has been given and revealed to me.[11]

This passage and the sermon just summarized are (I believe) the only references to this kind of knowledge in Bernard's works.

[9] Sermon 62 on Canticles (*Opera* 3037).

[10] Sermon 5 on Canticles, 8: Illud autem scitote, nullum creatorum spirituum per se nostris mentibus applicari, ut videlicet, nullo mediante nostri suive corporis instrumento, ita nobis immisceatur vel infundatur, quo ejus participatione docti sive doctiores, vel boni sive meliores efficiamur. Nullus Angelorum, nulla animarum hoc modo mihi capabilis est, nullius ego capax. Nec ipsi Angeli ita se alterutrum capiunt. Sequestretur proinde praerogativa haec summo ac incircumscripto Spiritui, qui solus, cum docet Angelum sive hominem scientiam, instrumentum non quaerit nostrae corporeae auris, sicut nec sibi oris. Per se infunditur, per se innotescit, purus capitur a puris. (*Opera* 2686.) Cf. *Consideration* 5, 5, 12 (*Opera* 1080).

[11] Misc. Sermon 22, 2: Mentior (quod ad consolationem vestram dico), si non ex manibus hujus peccatoris monachorum, novitiorum et conversorum animae ad coelestia gaudia volaverunt, tam liberae quam liberatae de carcere nostrae mortalitatis! Si quaeritis, unde id sciam, scitote, quia certissima mihi signa inde facta sunt et ostensa. (XB 817.)

(3) For those incapable of contemplation, there is the assurance that meditation on Christ crucified will lead to the overcoming of their disabilities.[12]

The proficient mystic contemplates the Word under three aspects — as the natural law, as the moral law, and as the divine law.

(1) The contemplator is rapt in wonder and admiration to the vision of the law of nature.

There is a place in the house of the Bridegroom from which as governor of the universe he decrees his laws and disposes judgments, appointing rules and weight and measure and number for every creature. And this place is lofty and secret, but nowise quiet. For although he, as regards himself, *disposes all things sweetly*, yet he does dispose; and does not permit the contemplator who perchance has attained to that place to be at rest; but wearies him with marvelous, though delightful, wonder and admiration, and makes him restless.[13]

This vision gives knowledge.

(2) He is rapt in fear and trembling to the vision of the law of retribution.

There is another place from which the unalterable vengeance, most mysterious and most severe, of God the just judge, terrible in his judgments over the children of men, watches over the reprobate rational creature. In this place, I say, God is seen by the terrified contemplator in his just but inscrutable judgment, neither washing away the evil deeds nor accepting the good deeds of the reprobate; furthermore even hardening their hearts, lest

[12] The reference to the wounds of Christ might seem to mean that monks incapable of mysticism, if they cannot attain heaven in this life by contemplation, will attain it after death by the merit of Christ crucified. But this would be an interpretation not justified by Bernard's words. Cf. Sermon 5 on Canticles, 1: "What have I to do with a miracle of God when I am discussing the processes of nature?"

[13] Sermon 23 on Canticles, 11: Est locus apud sponsum, de quo sua jura decernit, et disponit consilia ipse universitatis gubernator, leges constituens omni creaturae, pondus, et mensuram, et numerum. Et locus iste altus et secretus, sed minime quietus. Nam etsi ipse, quantum in se est, *disponit omnia suaviter* (Sap. 8. 1), disponit tamen; et contemplantem, qui forte eo loci pervenerit, quiescere non permittit; sed mirabiliter, quamvis delectabiliter, rimantem et admirantem fatigat, redditque inquietum. (*Opera* 2800.)

perchance they should grieve and repent and be converted and he should heal them. And this is not without a fixed and eternal reason, which is surely the more fearful the more unalterably it stands fixed in eternity.[14]

This vision gives wisdom.[15]

(3) He is rapt in love and joy to the vision of the law of God, which is love.[16]

But there is a place where God is seen truly quiescent and quiet; a place not of the Judge, not of the Teacher, but only of the Bridegroom; and which for me at least (for I do not know about others) would be a bedchamber indeed, if ever I should happen to be admitted there. But, alas! a rare event of brief extent! Here is clearly seen the Lord's mercy from eternity to eternity toward those that fear him.[17]

This vision gives peace. It is the vision, by means of love (the sensitivity of the soul), of Love (Truth in itself in the aspect of the divine law by which God himself is ruled). It is the spiritual marriage, by love, of the soul with God, the ineffable consummation of perfect contemplation.

[14] *Ibid.* 12: Est item locus, de quo super rationalem reprobam quidem creaturam immobilis vigilat secretissima et severissima animadversio justi judicis Dei, terribilis in consiliis super filios hominum. Cernitur, inquam, a timorato contemplatore hoc loco Deus, justo, sed occulto judicio suo, reproborum nec diluens mala, nec acceptans bona; insuper et corda indurans, ne forte doleant, et resipiscant, et convertantur, et sanet eos. Et hoc non absque certa et aeterna ratione, quod tanto formidolosius constat esse, quanto immobilius fixum exstat in aeternitate. (*Opera* 2800.)

[15] *Ibid.* 14 (*Opera* 2801).

[16] *Loving God* 12, 35 (*Opera* 1356).

[17] Sermon 23 on Canticles, 15: Sed est locus, ubi vere quiescens et quietus cernitur Deus; locus omnino, non judicis, non magistri, sed sponsi: et qui mihi quidem (nam de aliis nescio) plane cubiculum sit, si quando in illum contigerit introduci. Sed, heu! rara hora, et parva mora! Clare ibi agnoscitur misericordia Domini ab aeterno et usque in aeternum super timentes eum. (*Opera* 2802.)

3. Cause of contemplation

Contemplation is brought about by the condescension of the Word of God to human nature through grace and the exaltation of human nature to the Word through divine love.[1]

Its efficient cause is God's consummating grace.[2] The condition of receptivity of this grace is the exaltation of human nature which makes it resemble the divine nature. Although in certain qualities — simplicity, immortality, freedom — the soul always resembles the Word,[3] contemplation requires that the organs of spiritual vision be purified from the sins which obscure their resemblance to that Truth which is the natural object of this vision.[4]

Pure truth is seen only with a pure heart.[5]

Knowledge of truth is attained not by discourse of reason but by sanctity of life.[6]

Spiritual vision consists of understanding and love.[7] Con-

---

[1] Misc. Sermon 87, 3: Fit autem contemplatio ex condescensione Verbi Dei ad humanam naturam per gratiam et exaltationem humanae naturae ad ipsum Verbum per divinum amorem (XB 963).

[2] Cf. *Grace and Free Choice* 14, 49 (*Opera* 1398).

[3] Sermon 81 on Canticles, 11: Animam pro ingenita atque ingenua similitudine, quae in his tam eximie claret, non parvam cum Verbo habere affinitatem (*Opera* 3171).

[4] Misc. Sermon 16, 2: Sicut autem corporis natura est sanitas, ita cordis natura est puritas, quia turbato oculo non videbitur Deus et cor humanum ad hoc factum est, ut suum videat Creatorem (XB 795).

[5] *Steps of Humility* 3, 6. Cf. Sermon 31 on Canticles, 4: Oportet namque ut sancti desiderii ardor praeveniat faciem ejus ad omnem animam, ad quam est ipse venturus, qui omnem consumat rubiginem vitiorum, et sic praeparet locum Domino. Et tunc scit anima quoniam juxta est Dominus, cum se senserit illo igne succensam. (*Opera* 2865.) Cf. Sermon 32 on Canticles, 3: Nec tamen vel in transitu praesto erit sic omni animae, nisi illi duntaxat, quam ingens devotio, et desiderium vehemens, et praedulcis affectus sponsam probat, et dignam, ad quam gratia visitandi accessurum Verbum decorem induat, formam sponsi accipiens (*Opera* 2870).

[6] *Consideration* 5, 14, 30: Non ea disputatio comprehendit, sed sanctitas (*Opera* 1093). Cf. *Conversion* 13, 25: Non illud eruditio, sed unctio docet: nec scientia, sed conscientia comprehendit (*Opera* 1152).

[7] Letter 18, 3 (*Opera* 161). Cf. Sermon 3 for Ascension, 1: Rediit ad regionem sapientiae Sapientia Dei, ubi omnes bonum et intelligunt et requirunt, intellectu perspicacissimi, affectu paratissimi ad audiendam vocem sermonum ejus (XB 370).

templation requires, therefore, that understanding and love be purified; [8] this double purification produces that undivided intention on the good which is religion,[9] and which makes contemplation possible.[10] The organ of understanding is the reason; the organ of love is the will. The reason is obscured by pride and curiosity; [11] the will is perverted by the temptations of the flesh.[12]

Just as our physical vision is obstructed either by an internal humor or by an intrusion of foreign matter; so also our spiritual intuition is disturbed sometimes by the lures of our own flesh, sometimes by worldly curiosity and ambition.[13]

The reason is purified by humility; the will is purified by love. Thus the soul becomes capable of contemplating Truth in itself.

Both faculties, reason and will, the one taught by the Word of Truth, the other inspired with the Spirit of Truth, the former sprinkled with the hyssop of humility, the latter kindled with the fire of love, now form a finally perfected soul, flawless through humility and unruffled through love, since neither the will resists reason, nor does reason dissemble truth. The Father unites this soul to himself as a glorious bride, so that neither the reason can think of itself nor the will of its neighbor, but that blessed soul delights only in saying, *The King hath brought me into his chamber*.[14]

[8] Sermon 3 for Ascension, 2: Duo ergo sunt, quae in nobis purganda sunt: intellectus et affectus; intellectus, ut noverit, affectus, ut velit (XB 371).
[9] *Ibid*. 4 (XB 372). Cf. *ibid*. 5: Quis est ergo spiritus iste duplex, qui quaeritur, nisi illuminatio intellectus et affectus purgatio? (XB 373.)
[10] *Ibid*. 9: Et intellectu clarificato et affectu purificato veniat ad nos et apud nos faciat mansionem (XB 375).
[11] *Ibid*. 1: Arbitror intellectum designari, qui tunc vere deprimitur, cum multa cogitat, cum non colligit se circa illam unam et unicam meditationem, quae concipitur de civitate illa (XB 370).
[12] *Ibid*. 1: Affectiones, quae corrupto corpore diversis passionibus afficiuntur, quae mitigari numquam possunt, ne dicam sanari, donec voluntas unum quaerat et tendat ad unum (XB 371).
[13] *Conversion* 17, 30: Ut enim corporeus nobis visus aut humore interiori, aut exterioris injectione pulveris impeditur: sic et intuitus spiritualis interdum quidem propriae carnis illecebris, interdum curiositate saeculari et ambitione turbatur (*Opera* 1156).
[14] *Steps of Humility* 7, 21. Cf. Sermon 3 for Ascension, 2 (XB 371).

As this passage shows, the purification of the reason must come first,[15] and the purification of the will consists essentially in its submission to the reason.[16] This reunion with God is the reversal of the process by which man was separated from God, losing first his love of God and afterwards his knowledge of God.

We too were able to be eternal and blessed by adhering to him who is eternal and blessed. But by adhering, I should say, not only by knowledge but also by love. For some of the children of Adam, *when they knew God, glorified him not as God, neither were thankful; but became vain in their imaginations.* Rightly therefore *their foolish heart was darkened;* because, when they knew the truth but despised it, they obtained the just punishment that they should not even know it. Alas! thus adhering to truth by knowledge but withdrawing from it in love, loving vanity instead, man became like unto vanity. And what is vainer than to love vanity? or what is more wicked than to despise truth? What is juster than to take away even knowledge of it from those who despise it? what, I ask, is juster than to stop him from glorying in knowledge who did not glorify the object of that knowledge? And thus desire for vanity is contempt of truth; and contempt of truth is the cause of our blindness.[17]

---

[15] Cf. Sermon 3 for Ascension, 6 (XB 373).

[16] Cf. *Grace and Free Choice* 2, 4: Ratio data voluntati ut instruat illam (*Opera* 1368).

[17] Letter 18, 1: Adhaerendo ei qui semper et beate est; semper et nos esse, et beate esse poteramus. Adhaerendo autem dixerim, non solum per cognitionem, sed per amorem. Nam quidam ex filiis Adam *cum cognovissent Deum, non sicut Deum glorificaverunt, aut gratias egerunt: sed evanuerunt in cogitationibus suis.* Merito proinde *obscuratum est insipiens cor eorum* (Rom. 1. 21): quia cum veritatem cognoscerent et contemnerent, jure receperunt in poenam ut nec cognoscerent. Heu! sic adhaerendo veritati per cognitionem, sed ab illa defluendo per amorem, amando pro illa scilicet vanitatem, homo vanitati similis factus est. Et quid vanius quam diligere vanitatem; et quid iniquius, quam contemnere veritatem? Quid vero justius quam contemptoribus subtrahi et ipsam cognitionem? quid, inquam, justius, quam ut jam de ejus cognitione gloriari non possit, qui cognitam non glorificavit? Itaque appetitus vanitatis est contemptus veritatis; contemptus veritatis, causa nostrae caecitatis. (*Opera* 160.) This last sentence contains the sum and substance of mysticism.

4. Nature of contemplation

The monk, thus purified by humility and love, who with strong desire, burning thirst, and constant meditation seeks to be united with the Word of God in mystical contemplation, will surely succeed.[1]

The experience of God's presence is not phenomenal (consisting of perceptions or images) or even noumenal (consisting of concepts), but is emotional.[2]

But be careful not to think that I find anything physical or imaginary in this mingling of the Word and the soul. I say what the Apostle says, that *he that is joined unto God is one spirit*. The rapture of the pure mind into God, or the loving descent of God into the soul, I express in our language, so far as possible, comparing spiritual things with spiritual. This union, then, is made in the spirit, because God is a spirit, and has a desire for the beauty of that soul which he has observed to be walking in the spirit and not fulfilling the lusts of the flesh, especially if he sees it burning with love for him. A soul thus loving and thus loved will not at all be satisfied, therefore, either with that manifestation of the Bridegroom which is made to many through his creatures, or that which is made to few through visions and dreams, unless, by a peculiar privilege, it may also receive him coming down from heaven, in the love and very marrow of its heart, and may have its beloved in its presence, not perceived but absorbed, not appearing but affecting; and no doubt the more delightfully for being inward, not outward. For it is the Word not speaking but entering, not loquacious but efficacious, not striking the ears but seducing the emotions. His appearance is not in any form, but rather formative; not affecting the eyes of the body, but rather rejoicing the face of the heart; pleasing because of the gift, rather than the blush, of love.[3]

[1] Sermon 32 on Canticles, 2 (*Opera* 2870). Cf. *Grace and Free Choice* 13, 43 (*Opera* 1394).

[2] Sermon 8 on Canticles, 6: Merito proinde sponsa, quem diligit anima sua inquirens, non se suae carnis sensibus credit, non curiositatis humanae inanibus ratiociniis acquiescit, sed petit osculum (*Opera* 2700).

[3] Sermon 31 on Canticles, 6: Vide autem tu ne quid nos in hac Verbi animaeque commixtione corporeum seu imaginatorium sentire existimes. Id loquimur quod Apostolus dicit, quoniam *qui adhaeret Deo, unus spiritus est*

The mystical experience may, however, be accompanied by likenesses of lower things, evoked in the contemplator not by God but by angels,[4] unlike any ordinary experience,[5] yet not ineffable; they are spiritual icons by which the visions of divine wisdom are introduced to the sight of the contemplating soul.[6]

When something more divine has suddenly and as if with the speed of lightning flashed upon a mind in spiritual ecstasy, whether for tempering the too great splendor or for the sake of teaching, there are present forthwith, I know not whence, certain likenesses of lower things, suitably adapted to the divinely infused visions, somehow shaded by which that most pure and most brilliant ray of truth is made both more endurable for the soul itself and more capable for those to whom she will communicate it. It is my opinion, however, that these are formed in us by the suggestions of holy angels, just as on the other hand contrary and bad instigations are no doubt insinuated by bad angels.[7]

(1 Cor. 6. 17). Excessum purae mentis in Deum, sive Dei pium descensum in animam, nostris quibus possumus exprimimus verbis, spiritualibus spiritualia comparantes. Itaque in spiritu fit ista conjunctio, quia spiritus est Deus, et concupiscit decorem animae illius, quam forte adverterit in spiritu ambulantem, et curam carnis non perficientem in desiderio, praesertim si sui amore flagrantem conspexerit. Non ergo sic affecta et sic dilecta, contenta erit omnino vel illa quae multis per ea quae facta sunt, vel illa quae paucis per visa et somnia facta est manifestatio sponsi, nisi et speciali praerogativa intimis illum affectibus atque ipsis medullis cordis coelitus illapsum suscipiat, habeatque praesto quem desiderat non figuratum sed infusum; non apparentem sed afficientem; nec dubium quin eo jucundiorem quo intus, non foris. Verbum nempe est, non sonans sed penetrans, non loquax sed efficax, non obstrepens auribus sed affectibus blandiens. Facies est non formata, sed formans; non perstringens oculos corporis, sed faciem cordis laetificans: grata quippe amoris munere, non colore. (*Opera* 2866.) Cf. Sermon 20 on Canticles, 8 (*Opera* 2776).

[4] Sermon 41 on Canticles, 4: Illi coelestes administratorii spiritus (*Opera* 2922).

[5] *Ibid.* 3: Divina sunt, et nisi expertis prorsus incognita (*Opera* 2921).

[6] *Ibid.* 3: Spirituales quasdam similitudines, et in ipsis purissima divinae sapientiae sensa animae contemplantis conspectibus importare (*Opera* 2921).

[7] *Ibid.* 3: Cum autem divinius aliquid raptim et veluti in velocitate corusci luminis interluxerit menti spiritu excedenti, sive ad temperamentum nimii splendoris, sive ad doctrinae usum: continuo, nescio unde, adsunt imaginatoriae quaedam rerum inferiorum similitudines, infusis divinitus sensis convenienter accommodatae, quibus quodam modo adumbratus purissimus ille

Contemplation is the absorption of a pure soul into God or the descent of God into the soul, so that God is in the soul and the soul is in God. Its essential feature is an identity of wills so perfect that the contemplating soul and the contemplated God become one spirit, although they remain substantially distinct.[8]

O chaste and holy love! [9] O sweet and tender passion! O pure and flawless intention of the will! surely the purer and more flawless as there now remains no admixture of its own, the sweeter and more tender as all which is felt is of God. Such an experience is deification. As a little drop of water, mixed with much wine, seems to vanish completely as it takes on the taste and color of the wine; and as fiery, glowing iron becomes indistinguishable from the fire, putting off its own former appearance; and as air flooded with sunlight is transformed into the same brilliant light, so that it seems to be no longer lighted but rather light itself; thus in the saints [10] every human emotion must finally melt away in some ineffable way and be wholly absorbed into the will of God. Otherwise how will God be all in all if anything of man survives in man? The substance indeed will remain, but in another form, another glory, another power.[11]

---

ac splendidissimus veritatis radius, et ipsi animae tolerabilior fiat, et quibus communicare illum voluerit, capabilior. Existimo tamen ipsas formari in nobis sanctorum suggestionibus Angelorum, sicut e contrario contrarias et malas ingeri immisiones per angelos malos non dubium est. (*Opera* 2922.)

[8] Sermon 8 on Canticles, 9 (*Opera* 2702). Cf. Sermon 74 on Canticles, 7: Etsi non pari, simili tamen vel ex parte desiderio feror (*Opera* 3126).

[9] Cf. Sermon 7 on Canticles, 3: Amat profecto caste, quae ipsum quem amat, quaerit; non aliud quidquam ipsius. Amat sancte, quia non in concupiscentia carnis, sed in puritate spiritus. (*Opera* 2693.)

[10] But the description applies equally to mystical contemplation in this life, the possibility of which is being considered in this chapter.

[11] *Loving God* 10, 28: O amor sanctus et castus! o dulcis et suavis affectio! o pura et defaecata intentio voluntatis! eo certe defaecatior et purior, quo in ea de proprio nil jam admixtum relinquitur: eo suavior et dulcior, quo totum divinum est quod sentitur. Sic affici, deificari est. Quomodo stilla aquae modica, multo infusa vino, deficere a se tota videtur, dum et saporem vini induit, et colorem; et quomodo ferrum ignitum et candens, igni simillimum fit, pristina propriaque forma exutum; et quomodo solis luce perfusus aer in eamdem transformatur luminis claritatem, adeo ut non tam illuminatus, quam ipsum lumen esse videatur: sic omnem tunc in sanctis humanam affectionem quodam ineffabili modo necesse erit a semetipsa

This is not a confusion of natures but an agreement of wills.[12]

By this consensus the two are in one spirit, nay, they are one spirit. Do you see the difference? Consubstantial is not the same as consentible. But the difference between the two kinds of oneness is sufficiently shown by the genders of *one person* [13] and *one thing*; for *one person* cannot be applied to Father and Son, nor *one thing* to man and God. Father and Son cannot be called one person, because one is the Father and one is the Son; nevertheless they are called and are one thing, because they have one substance together, not each his own. Man and God, on the contrary, not being of one substance or nature, cannot be called one thing, yet they are called one spirit with certain and absolute truth, provided they enter into each other by the bond of love. This unity is produced not so much by a coherence of essences as by an agreement of wills.[14]

In his doctrine of mysticism, as in his doctrine of creation,[15] Bernard uncompromisingly rejects pantheism. Far from being implied by mysticism, pantheism would make mysticism im-

---

liquescere, atque in Dei penitus transfundi voluntatem. Alioquin quomodo omnia in omnibus erit Deus, si in homine de homine quidquam supererit? Manebit quidem substantia, sed in alia forma, alia gloria, aliaque potentia. (*Opera* 1351.)

[12] Sermon 71 on Canticles, 7: Et tamen unus spiritus dicitur, et est cum Deo, anima adhaerens Deo; nec praejudicat rerum pluralitas unitati huic, quam facit non confusio naturarum sed voluntatum consensio (*Opera* 3104).

[13] Not, of course, one "person" in the theological sense. Cf. *Consideration* 5, 5, 12: Deus sic inest ut afficiat, ut infundat, vel potius ut infundatur et participetur, ita ut unum perinde cum nostro spiritum esse dicere quis non timuerit, etsi non unam personam, unamve substantiam (*Opera* 1080).

[14] Sermon 71 on Canticles, 8: Consensio quaedam haec, ut sint duo in uno spiritu, imo unus spiritus sint. Videsne diversitatem? Non est idem profecto consubstantiale et consentibile. Quanquam, si advertisti, satis tibi per *unus* et *unum* ipsarum quoque innuitur differentia unitatum: quoniam quidem nec Patri et Filio *unus*, nec homini et Deo *unum* poterit convenire. Non possunt dici unus Pater et Filius, quia ille Pater, et ille Filius est: unum tamen dicuntur et sunt, quod una omnino illis, et non cuique sua substantia est. Quo contra homo et Deus, quia unius non sunt substantiae vel naturae; unum quidem dici non possunt, unus tamen spiritus certa et absoluta veritate dicuntur, si sibi glutino amoris inhaereant. Quam quidem unitatem non tam essentiarum cohaerentia facit, quam conniventia voluntatum. (*Opera* 3104.)

[15] *Consideration* 5, 6, 14 (*Opera* 1081).

possible. Man can love God, and God can love man, only
because they are substantially distinct. The mystical union is
a union of love, and love is sympathy, that is, harmony of wills,
which requires two distinct wills.[16] In contemplation, as in
all love, the lover's will and the beloved's will are one in their
object, not in their substance. Perfect love, that is, perfect
harmony of will, is not identity; it is marriage.[17] Perfect love
of God is not identity with God; it is marriage with God.

> Such a conformity marries the soul to the Word, since to him
> to whom she is similar by nature she shows herself no less similar
> by will, loving as she is loved.[18]

Contemplation is both cognitive and erotic.[19]

> Let neither him who understands truth without loving nor him
> who loves it without understanding suppose that he has received
> the kiss. Certainly in that kiss neither error nor lukewarmness
> has any place. Therefore, for receiving the double grace of the
> all-holy kiss, let whoever is a bride make ready both her two lips,
> the reason for understanding, the will for wisdom.[20]

It is the "third step of truth," by which the monk comes to
know "Truth in itself"; [21] and it is the "fourth step of love,"
by which he loves "not even himself save for God's sake." [22]
By contemplation the monk embraces truth with "both arms

[16] Sermon 71 on Canticles, 9 (*Opera* 3105).

[17] Sermon 83 on Canticles, 3: Si perfecte diligit, nupsit (*Opera* 3178).

[18] *Ibid.* 3: Talis conformitas maritat animam Verbo, cum cui videlicet
similis est per naturam, similem nihilominus ipsi se exhibet per voluntatem,
diligens sicut dilecta est (*Opera* 3178). Cf. Sermon 68 on Canticles, 1 (*Opera*
3083); Sermon 85 on Canticles, 12 (*Opera* 3193).

[19] Sermon 49 on Canticles, 4: Duo sint beatae contemplationis excessus,
in intellectu unus, et alter in affectu (*Opera* 2963).

[20] Sermon 8 on Canticles, 6: Neuter ergo se osculum percepisse putet,
sive qui veritatem intelligit, nec diligit; sive qui diligit, nec intelligit. Sane in
osculo isto nec error locum habet, nec tepor. Quamobrem geminae gratiae
sacrosancti osculi suscipiendae paret e regione duo labia sua quae sponsa est,
intelligentiae rationem, sapientiae voluntatem. (*Opera* 2700.)

[21] *Steps of Humility* 6, 19.

[22] *Loving God* 10, 27 (*Opera* 1350).

of the soul, understanding and love," [23] and it is in this that his beatitude consists.[24]

When the iniquity which causes that unlikeness which is in part has been put away, there will be a union of spirit, there will be a mutual vision and a mutual love. When that which is perfect is come, then that which is in part shall be done away; and there will be a chaste and consummate love between them, a full comprehension, a clear vision, a firm union, an inseparable association, a perfect likeness. Then the soul will know even as also it is known; then it will love even as also it is loved; and the Bridegroom will rejoice over the bride, being himself both knower and known, lover and beloved.[25]

This mystical experience is ineffable.[26] And in this life it is always imperfect because always transient,[27] being interrupted by the physical requirements of the body, or by the sting of some care, or by the pang of some sin. Above all it is disturbed by the flood of sensory images which rush into the mind and which the mystic finds very difficult to banish from his consciousness.[28] Even the perfect mystic, who has banished all perceptions and all images, and has succeeded in concentrating all his consciousness on the non-phenomenal

[23] Letter 18, 3: His igitur fortassis quasi duobus animae brachiis, intellectu videlicet et amore, id est cognitione et dilectione veritatis, amplectitur et comprehenditur cum omnibus sanctis longitudo, latitudo, sublimitas et profundum (Opera 161).

[24] Sermon 37 on Canticles, 1: Noveris proinde te, ut Deum timeas: noveris ipsum, ut aeque ipsum diligas. In altero initiaris ad sapientiam, in altero et consummaris. (Opera 2902.)

[25] Sermon 82 on Canticles, 8: Facta igitur de medio iniquitate, quae eam quae ex parte est dissimilitudinem facit, erit unio spiritus, erit mutua visio, mutuaque dilectio. Siquidem veniente quod perfectum est, evacuabitur quod ex parte est; eritque ad alterutrum casta et consummata dilectio, agnitio plena, visio manifesta, conjunctio firma, societas individua, similitudo perfecta. Tunc cognoscet anima, sicut cognita est (1 Cor. 13. 10, 12); tunc amabit, sicut amata est; et gaudebit sponsus super sponsam, cognoscens et cognitus, diligens et dilectus. (Opera 3176.)

[26] Steps of Humility 7, 21; Sermon 3 on Canticles, 1 (Opera 2676); Sermon 51 on Canticles, 7 (Opera 2976); Sermon 79 on Canticles, 1 (Opera 3153); Sermon 85 on Canticles, 14 (Opera 3194).

[27] Sermon 32 on Canticles, 2 (Opera 2870).

[28] Sermon 23 on Canticles, 16 (Opera 2803).

and non-imaginary object of contemplation, is recalled, if by
nothing else, by the requirements of fraternal charity.[29] When
the death of the body has freed him from some of these distractions, he finds himself plunged in the boundless ocean of
eternal light,[30] and is united in spirit with God in eternal contemplation.[31] But even the saints in heaven are distracted both
by the call of the flesh and by the call of charity. In the first
place, they desire to recover their bodies, and this desire is a
flaw in the purity of their intention; until it is satisfied, they
cannot pass over into God absolutely, by that perfect self-
abandonment which is the soul's highest state.[32] In the second
place, they devote themselves to works of charity even more
fervently than when on earth.[33] They are freed from misery
but not from desire; they rest in peace but not in glory.[34]

[29] *Loving God* 10, 27 (*Opera* 1351).

[30] *Ibid.* 11, 30: Immersas ex toto credimus immenso illi pelago aeterni
luminis, et luminosae aeternitatis (*Opera* 1352). Cf. Sermon 4 for All Saints',
1: In luce multa (XB 630).

[31] Sermon 2 on St Malachy, 6: Exsultet in Domino spiritus Malachiae,
quod levatus pondere corporeae molis nulla jam faeculenta vel terrena
materia praegravatur, quominus tota alacritate et vivacitate corpoream
omnem et incorpoream transiens creaturam pergat totus in Deum et adhaerens illi unus sit cum eo spiritus in aeternum (XB 652). This applies, of
course, only to mystics. In heaven no less than on earth, individuals differ
from each other in their degree of spiritual advancement. One person may
be more advanced spiritually during this life than another person is even in
heaven. Ordinary saints in heaven, before the resurrection, enjoy no higher
vision than that of Christ's humanity (Sermon 4 for All Saints', 2, XB 630).
Mystics enjoy the vision of Christ's deity even in this life (Sermon 20 on
Canticles, 8, *Opera* 2776). It is fallacious to detect an inconsistency (as does,
e.g., Vacandard, *Dictionnaire de Théologie Catholique*, article *Bernard*,
p. 781) between the sermons for All Saints' and those on St Malachy or
St Victor. In the former Bernard is discussing the condition of ordinary
saints; in the latter, that of great mystics.

[32] *Loving God* 11, 30 (*Opera* 1352). Cf. Sermon 3 for All Saints', 2 (XB
626); Misc. Sermon 41, 12 (XB 902).

[33] Sermon 2 on St Victor, 3: Latitudo coeli dilatat corda, non arctat;
exhilarat mentes, non alienat; affectiones non contrahit, sed extendit. In
lumine Dei serenatur memoria, non obscuratur; in lumine Dei discitur, quod
nescitur, non, quod scitur, dediscitur. (XB 501.) Cf. Sermon 5 for All
Saints', 11 (XB 642).

[34] *Grace and Free Choice* 4, 9 (*Opera* 1372). Cf. Sermon 3 for Palm Sunday, 5: Non erit nobis requies, ne in requie quidem ipsa, a desiderio gloriae,

Only after the resurrection will the saints finally be freed from
every interest either selfish or fraternal.[35] Only after the
resurrection, therefore, will they contemplate Truth in itself
with perfect intention and so attain the beatific vision of God
not as he appears but as he is.[36] Perfect likeness will make
perfect vision; they will see him as he is because they will be
as he is.[37] This is beatitude, when Wisdom itself is the object
of our wisdom.[38]

For in that eternal and perfect beatitude we shall enjoy God
in triple fashion: seeing him in all creatures, possessing him in
ourselves, and also (what is ineffably more joyful and blessed than
all these) knowing the Trinity itself in itself and contemplating
that glory without any veil with the pure eye of the heart; for
eternal and perfect life will consist in this, that we shall know the
Father and the Son with the Holy Ghost and shall see God as he
is, that is, not only as he is in us or in other creatures, but as he
is in himself.[39]

a desiderio resurrectionis (XB 314). Cf. Sermon 3 for All Saints', 3 (XB
627); Sermon 4 for the Dedication of a Church, 5 (XB 706).

[35] Misc. Sermon 18, 1 (XB 805). Cf. *Loving God* 10, 29 (*Opera* 1352).
They will not be concerned for the damned. *Ibid.* 15, 40 (*Opera* 1362).

[36] Sermon 31 on Canticles, 2: Non sapiens, non sanctus, non propheta
videre illum, sicuti est, potest aut potuit in corpore hoc mortali; poterit
autem in immortali, qui dignus habebitur (*Opera* 2863). Cf. Sermon 38 on
Canticles, 5 (*Opera* 2909); Misc. Sermon 41, 12 (XB 902).

[37] *Ibid.* 3: Porro jam praesentibus non aliud est videre sicuti est, quam esse
sicuti est, et aliqua dissimilitudine non confundi (*Opera* 2864). Cf. *Consideration* 5, 13, 27: Nec enim jam tunc fragilis acies mentis nostrae, quantumlibet
vehementer intendens, aliquatenus resiliet, dissilietve in suam pluralitatem.
Colliget sese magis, adunabit, conformabitque unitati illius, vel potius unitati
illi, ut una uni facies respondeat faciei. Nempe *similes ei erimus, quia vide-
bimus eum sicuti est* (1 Joan. 3. 2). (*Opera* 1092.)

[38] Misc. Sermon 18, 1: Est enim sapiens, cui quaeque res sapiunt, prout
sunt; cui vero ipsa jam in se, prout est, sapientia sapit, is non modo sapiens
sed etiam beatus est; nempe hoc est videre Deum, sicuti est (XB 805).

[39] Sermon 4 for All Saints', 3: Tripliciter enim, fratres! in aeterna illa et
perfecta beatitudine fruemur Deo: videntes eum in omnibus creaturis,
habentes eum in nobis ipsis et (quod his omnibus ineffabiliter jucundius sit
atque beatius) ipsam quoque cognoscentes in semet ipsa Trinitatem et
gloriam illam sine ullo aenigmate mundo cordis oculo contemplantes; in hoc
enim erit vita aeterna et perfecta, ut cognoscamus Patrem et Filium cum
sancto Spiritu et videamus Deum, sicuti est, id est, non modo sicut inest nobis
videlicet aut ceteris creaturis, sed sicut est in semet ipso (XB 631).

There are, therefore, three stages of contemplation: in this life, in heaven after death, and in eternity after resurrection.[40]

5. Bernard's own experience

Bernard himself had never had the experience of mystical contemplation when he wrote the letter to the Carthusians in 1125, for in this letter he denied the possibility of it.[1] In *Loving God*, written probably in 1127,[2] he repeated this letter without change; but in the new part of the essay he expressed his doubt of the possibility of mystical experience with more hesitation.[3] In *Grace and Free Choice*, written in 1128, he asserted the possibility of it, but with an explicit emphasis which seems to indicate that he considered it a strange proposition which the reader would not naturally assume.[4] In the *Steps of Humility*, written probably between 1129 and 1135, the possibility of mystical experience was taken for granted.[5] In the 23rd sermon on Canticles, preached in 1137,[6] he spoke of his own mystical experiences.[7]

Toward the end of his life, in the 74th sermon on Canticles, he described his own experience in the following words:

I confess that the Word has come to me too (*I speak foolishly*), and many times. And although it has often entered me, I have never felt when it entered. I have felt that it was present, I remember that it was present, sometimes I could even anticipate its coming, but never feel it, nor its going either. For whence it

[40] Misc. Sermon 87, 4 (XB 964). Cf. Sermon 3 for All Saints', 1 (XB 625).

[1] Letter 11, 8: Asserant hoc si qui experti sunt: mihi, fateor, impossibile videtur (*Opera* 153).

[2] Soon after the letter to the Carthusians (*Loving God* 12, 34, *Opera* 1355), but not before Letter 18, written in 1127 (Letter 18, 5, *Opera* 163).

[3] *Loving God* 10, 27: Beatum dixerim et sanctum, cui tale aliquid in hac mortali vita raro interdum, aut vel semel, et hoc ipsum raptim, atque unius vix momenti spatio experiri donatum est (*Opera* 1351).

[4] *Grace and Free Choice* 5, 15: Hi plane (quod negandum non est) etiam in hac carne, raro licet raptimque, complaciti libertate fruuntur (*Opera* 1376).

[5] *Steps of Humility* 7, 21.

[6] Cf. Sermon 24 on Canticles, 1 (*Opera* 2804) and Mabillon's note (*Opera* 3210).

[7] Sermon 23 on Canticles, 15 (*Opera* 2803).

came into my soul, or whither it went on leaving it again, even by what way it either came or went, I confess I know not even now; as it is said, *Thou canst not tell whence it cometh and whither it goeth*. And no wonder, for it is he to whom it was said, *Thy footsteps are not known*. Surely it came not through the eyes, for it is colorless; nor through the ears, for it made no sound; nor through the nostrils, for it is not dissolved in the air, but in the mind — it created, rather than permeated, the air; nor through the mouth, for it is not chewed or swallowed; nor have I discovered it by touch, for it is not palpable. By what way, then, has it entered? Or perhaps it did not enter at all, not having come from without? For it is not any of those things which are external. But neither has it come from within me, for it is good, and I know there is nothing good in me. I have ascended to that which is highest in me; and lo the Word rising above this. I have also descended through curiosity to explore what is lowest in me; and nevertheless it is found deeper still. If I have looked without, I have found it to be outside everything which is outside me; but if within, it was even more inward. And I have learned that it is true which I have read, that *in him we live and move and have our being*; but blessed is he in whom it is, who lives for it, who is moved by it.

Do you ask, then, since *his ways* are thus *past finding out*, how I know it is present? It *is quick and powerful*; and as soon as it entered, it awakened my sleeping soul; it moved, and softened, and wounded my heart, which was hard and stony and sick. It began also to root out and to pull down, to build and to plant, to water what was dry, enlighten what was dark, unlock what was closed, inflame what was cold, at the same time making *the crooked straight and the rough ways smooth*, so that *my soul* might *bless the Lord, and all that is within me bless his holy name*. And so it is that the Bridegroom Word, entering me at different times, has not made its entrance known by any signs, or voice, or appearance, or footstep. By no movement of its own is it manifested to me, by none of my senses does it penetrate within me; I have known its presence only by the beating of my heart, as I have just said, and I have discovered the power of its virtue by the expulsion of vices and the suppression of carnal emotions; and from the examination or reproof of my secret thoughts I have wondered at the profundity of its wisdom; and by any little improvement in my behavior I have experienced the goodness of its mercy; and by the renewal and reformation of the spirit of my mind, that is, of my inner man, I have perceived to some extent *the perfection of his beauty*; and from the contemplation of all these things together I have greatly feared *his excellent greatness*.

But when the Word has departed, just as if you should take away the fire from beneath a boiling pot, all these things immediately begin to lie torpid and cold, in a sort of languor; and this is the sign of its withdrawal. Therefore my soul must be sad until it comes again, and my heart is warmed again within me, as it is wont; and this is the sign of the return.[8]

---

[8] Sermon 74 on Canticles, 5: Fateor et mihi adventasse Verbum, *in insipientia dico* (2 Cor. 11. 21), et pluries. Cumque saepius intraverit ad me, non sensi aliquoties cum intravit. Adesse sensi, adfuisse recordor, interdum et praesentire potui introitum ejus, sentire nunquam, sed ne exitum quidem. Nam unde in animam meam venerit, quove abierit denuo eam dimittens; sed et qua vel introierit vel exierit; etiam nunc ignorare me fateor, secundum illud: *Nescis unde veniat, aut quo vadat* (Joan. 3. 8). Nec mirum tamen, quia ipse est, cui dictum est: *Et vestigia tua non cognoscentur* (Ps. 76. 20). Sane per oculos non intravit, quia non est coloratum: sed neque per aures, quia non sonuit: sed neque per nares, quia non aeri miscetur, sed menti; nec infecit aerem, sed fecit: neque vero per fauces, quia non est mansum vel haustum: nec tactu comperi illud, quia palpabile non est. Qua igitur introivit? An forte nec introivit quidem, quia non deforis venit? Neque enim est unum aliquid ex iis quae foris sunt. Porro nec deintra me venit quoniam bonum est, et scio quoniam non est in me bonum. Ascendi etiam superius meum: et ecce supra hoc Verbum eminens. Ad inferius quoque meum curiosus explorator descendi: et nihilominus infra inventum est. Si foras aspexi, extra omne exterius meum comperi illud esse: si vero intus, et ipsum interius erat. Et cognovi verum quidem esse quod legeram, quia *in ipso vivimus, movemur et sumus* (Act. 17. 28): sed ille beatus est, in quo est ipsum, qui illi vivit, qui eo movetur.

6. Quaeris igitur, cum ita sint omnino *investigabiles viae ejus* (Rom. 11. 33), unde adesse norim? *Vivum et efficax est* (Heb. 4. 12): moxque ut intus venit, expergefecit dormitantem animam meam; movit, et mollivit, et vulneravit cor meum, quoniam durum lapideumque erat, et male sanum. Coepit quoque evellere et destruere, aedificare et plantare (Jer. 1. 10), rigare arida, tenebrosa illuminare, clausa reserare, frigida inflammare, nec non et mittere *prava in directa, et aspera in vias planas* (Is. 40. 4; Luc. 3. 5); ita ut *benediceret anima mea Domino, et omnia quae intra me sunt nomini sancto ejus* (Ps. 102. 1). Ita igitur intrans ad me aliquoties Verbum sponsus, nullis unquam introitum suum indiciis innotescere fecit, non voce, non specie, non incessu. Nullis denique suis motibus compertum est mihi, nullis meis sensibus illapsum penetralibus meis: tantum ex motu cordis, sicut praefatus sum, intellexi praesentiam ejus; et ex fuga vitiorum, carnaliumque compressione

6. Fruit of contemplation

The fruit of contemplation is beatitude.[1]

Man alone among animals is capable of beatitude because he alone has a rational soul with its unique faculties of will and reason and the free choice which is a union of the two.[2] Pure reason, pure will, and the joint faculty of reason and will are called in Platonic language the rational, irascible, and concupiscible forces respectively.[3] The function of the pure reason is understanding.[4] The function of the pure will is joy and sadness.[5] The function of the joint faculty is voluntary choice, that is, desire or aversion.[6] The perfection of the

affectuum adverti potentiam virtutis ejus; et ex discussione sive redargutione occultorum meorum admiratus sum profunditatem sapientiae ejus; et ex quantulacumque emendatione morum meorum expertus sum bonitatem mansuetudinis ejus; et ex renovatione ac reformatione spiritus mentis meae, id est interioris hominis mei, percepi utcumque *speciem decoris ejus* (Ps. 49. 2); et ex contuitu horum omnium simul expavi *multitudinem magnitudinis ejus* (Ps. 150. 2).

7. Verum quia haec omnia, ubi abscesserit Verbum, perinde ac si ollae bullienti subtraxeris ignem, quodam illico languore torpentia et frigida jacere incipiunt; atque hoc mihi signum abscessionis ejus: tristis sit necesse est anima mea, donec iterum revertatur, et solito recalescat cor meum intra me; idque sit reversionis indicium. (*Opera* 3125.)

[1] Cf. Sermon 23 on Canticles, 15: Subito tanta mihi quoque de me suborta fiducia et infusa laetitia est, quantus certe in loco horroris, id est in loco secundae visionis, non praecesserat timor, ita ut mihi visus sim tanquam unus ex illis beatis esse (*Opera* 2803).

[2] *Grace and Free Choice* 3, 6 (*Opera* 1370); Sermon 81 on Canticles, 6 (*Opera* 3167).

[3] Sermon 4 for All Saints', 5 (XB 632). Cf. Misc. Sermon 74 (XB 950).

[4] Intention on the expedient, intention on the good, dispensative consideration, estimative consideration of invisible things by opinion and by faith, and speculative consideration require the cooperation of the will; estimative consideration of visible things requires the cooperation of the body.

[5] The *objective* emotions (love and fear) and all *actions* of the will, since they involve choosing, require the cooperation of the reason.

[6] Sermon 4 for All Saints', 5: Quemadmodum circa rationale nostrum et scientia et ignorantia constat tamquam habitus et privatio, sic et circa concupiscibile desiderium et contemptus, et circa id, quod dicitur irascibile, et laetitia pariter et ira versatur (XB 632). (For the equivalence of *ira* and *tristitia*, cf. Letter 69, 1, *Opera* 219.)

reason is perfect understanding.[7] The perfection of the will is perfect joy and tranquillity (the opposites of sadness and wrath), that is, perfect freedom of enjoyment.[8] The perfection of the free choice is perfect justice, that is, perfect freedom of counsel.[9] Understanding,[10] joy,[11] and justice [12] are ends in themselves. Together they constitute the beatitude of the rational soul.[13]

Contemplation gives perfect understanding,[14] because it reveals Truth not merely as it is in yourself or in other creatures but as it is in itself.[15] Contemplation gives perfect joy,[16] as Bernard testifies from his own experience.[17] Contemplation gives perfect justice,[18] because it harmonizes the will with God's will.[19] By contemplation, therefore, the rational soul attains to beatitude, even in this life.[20] By it man is deified,

[7] *Consideration* 5, 3, 6: Nil supererit ad beatitudinem, cum quae jam certa sunt nobis fide, erunt aeque et nuda (*Opera* 1075). Cf. *ibid.* 5, 13, 27: Non in cognitione est fructus, sed in comprehensione (*Opera* 1092). Cf. Letter 18, 2: Interim justus ex fide vivit; nam beatus ex intellectu (*Opera* 161). Cf. Sermon 33 on Canticles, 3: Numquid vero par sapor intellectui fideique, cum sit in meritum ista, ille in praemium? (*Opera* 2878.)

[8] *Grace and Free Choice* 3, 7 (*Opera* 1370). Cf. *ibid.* 4, 11 (*Opera* 1373); *ibid.* 6, 19 (*Opera* 1378).

[9] Sermon 4 for All Saints', 5: Nulla enim alia res implere potest desiderium animae, nulla alia praeter justitiam beatificare animam potest (XB 633).

[10] *Consideration* 5, 3, 6: Quod intellexisti, non est de eo quod ultra quaeras (*Opera* 1075).

[11] Misc. Sermon 1, 8: *Justorum exspectatio* non aliquid laetum sed ipsa *laetitia* (Prov. 10. 28) est (XB 742).

[12] Misc. Sermon 72, 2: Justitia est perfectio animae rationalis. Aliae virtutes sunt ad ejus acquisitionem vel conservationem. (XB 947.)

[13] Sermon 4 for All Saints', 5 (XB 633).

[14] *Consideration* 5, 14, 30 (*Opera* 1093).

[15] *Steps of Humility* 3, 6. Cf. Sermon 50 on Canticles, 6 (*Opera* 2970).

[16] *Grace and Free Choice* 5, 15 (*Opera* 1376). Cf. *Steps of Humility* 2, 4; Sermon for the Octave of Epiphany, 5 (XB 168); Misc. Sermon 18, 1 (XB 805); Sermon 41 on Canticles, 2 (*Opera* 2921); Sermon 83 on Canticles, 3 (*Opera* 3178).

[17] Sermon 23 on Canticles, 15 (*Opera* 2803); Sermon 74 on Canticles, 7 (*Opera* 3127).

[18] *Grace and Free Choice* 6, 19 (*Opera* 1379).

[19] Sermon 71 on Canticles, 7 (*Opera* 3104).

[20] *Grace and Free Choice* 5, 15: Attamen fatendum est eos, qui per excessum contemplationis rapti quandoque in spiritu, quantulumcumque de

so that nothing of the natural man, except the substance, remains in him.[21]

These fruits of contemplation — perfect understanding, joy, and justice — are the beatitude of the rational soul, that is, of the reason and will; nevertheless they are not the perfect beatitude of the whole human soul, because that soul has also a third faculty, the memory. It is the memory, and only the memory, which remains unsatisfied by even the most perfect contemplation in this life. The transient mystical experience cannot be retained. In heaven, however, in spite of the distractions which make it imperfect before the resurrection, contemplation may be eternal. This difference of time, which is a matter of memory, not of reason or will, is the difference between contemplation in this life and in the future life before the resurrection. The security of eternal contemplation is the perfection of the memory. Perfect understanding, joy, and security (together with the perfect justice which has led to them) are therefore the beatitude of the whole human soul, possible only in heaven.

All error will recede from the reason, grief from the will, and fear from the memory; and be succeeded by that hoped for marvelous clarity, complete sweetness, eternal security. God supreme truth will accomplish the first; God supreme love, the second; God supreme power, the third — so that God may be all in all, the reason receiving an inextinguishable light, the will attaining an imperturbable peace, the memory plunged eternally in the never failing font.[22]

---

supernae felicitatis dulcedine degustare sufficiunt, toties esse liberos a miseria, quoties sic excedunt (*Opera* 1376).

[21] *Loving God* 10, 28 (*Opera* 1351).

[22] Sermon 11 on Canticles, 6: Error videlicet a ratione, a voluntate dolor, atque a memoria timor omnis recesserit; et successerit illa quam speramus mira serenitas, plena suavitas, aeterna securitas. Primum illud faciet veritas Deus; secundum, charitas Deus; tertium, summa potestas Deus: ut sit Deus omnia in omnibus, ratione recipiente lucem inexstinguibilem, voluntate pacem imperturbabilem consequente, memoria fonti indeficienti aeternaliter inhaerente. (*Opera* 2718.) Cf. Sermon 4 for Christmas Eve, 9: Lux enim est propter serenitatem, pax propter tranquillitatem, fons propter affluentiam et aeternitatem (XB 99).

The perfect beatitude of the whole man, possible only after the resurrection, is the beatitude of the soul together with the beatitude of the body (immortality, impassibility, lightness, and beauty).[23]

These fruits of contemplation — perfect understanding, joy, and justice — are the rational soul's beatitude — insofar as it is effable. But what is effable is a very small part of the whole; it is only its subjective aspect. Mystics are always speaking of the ineffable! It is the subjective experience which they speak of; it is the object of that experience which is ineffable. God is beatitude. Understanding, joy, and justice are God in us; to possess them is to have God in us.[24] There is also God in other creatures; and this vision also is not ineffable, because ordinary experience gives some knowledge of other creatures.[25] But there is also God in himself. The objective knowledge of God in himself in the ineffable union of perfect contemplation is the summit of felicity, is supereminent glory, is supereffluent beatitude.[26] Both subjective beatitude (having God in us) and objective beatitude (knowing God in himself) are fruits of contemplation. The subjective experience is deification;[27] the object of that experience is God.

7. *The anagogic path*

These, then, are the three steps of the anagogic path: humility, love, and contemplation. They lead respectively to knowledge of truth in yourself, knowledge of truth in your neighbor, and knowledge of Truth in itself.

Since there are therefore three steps or states of truth, we ascend to the first by the toil of humility, to the second by the

[23] Sermon 4 for All Saints', 6 (XB 633).

[24] *Ibid*. 5 (XB 632). Not to be confused with the mere knowledge of truth in yourself given by humility.

[25] *Ibid*. 4 (XB 632).

[26] *Ibid*. 3 (XB 631). The statement here that even partial knowledge of God in himself is impossible in this life is not Bernard's definitive doctrine. This sermon, like all his works in which the possibility of mystical contemplation is denied, is an early work — as is shown by the use of the Platonic terms *rational*, *irascible*, *concupiscible*, unknown in his later works.

[27] *Loving God* 10, 28: Sic affici, deificari est (*Opera* 1351).

emotion of compassion, to the third by the ecstasy of contemplation. In the first truth is found harsh; in the second, loving; in
the third, pure. Reason, by which we examine ourselves, leads
us to the first; love, by which we sympathize with others, entices
us to the second; purity, by which we are lifted to invisible
heights, snatches us up to the third.[1]

The path is exhibited by the diagram on the opposite page.
It follows the order of the Beatitudes: [2] blessed are the poor
in spirit (*humilitas*),[3] the meek (*humilitas voluntaria*),[4] they
that mourn (*luctus poenitentiae*),[5] they which do hunger and
thirst after righteousness (*fervor justitiae*),[6] the merciful
(*compassio*),[7] the pure in heart (*puritas*) [8] — for they shall see
God (*contemplatio*).

Bernard gives three other accounts of the steps of the
anagogic path. In *Loving God* they are loving yourself for
your own sake, loving God for your own sake, loving God
for his sake, and loving yourself only for God's sake.[9] In
Grace and Free Choice they are free choice, free counsel, and
free enjoyment.[10] In the sermons on Canticles they are the
feelings of the slave, the hireling, the disciple, the son, and the
bride.[11] Different as these accounts seem at first sight, both

---

[1] *Steps of Humility* 6, 19. Cf. *ibid*. 2, 5; Misc. Sermon 87, 1 (XB 962);
Sermon 3 on Canticles, 6 (*Opera* 2679); Sermon 4 on Canticles, 1 (*Opera*
2680).

[2] *Ibid*. 3, 6.

[3] Beati pauperes spiritu, id est quem spiritus vel ratio facit pauperem,
ostendens illum sibi. (*Les Inédits Bernardins du MS d'Anchin*, "S. Bernard
et Son Temps," Tome II, Dijon, 1929, p. 271.)

[4] Beati mites qui semper volunt subesse (*ibid*., p. 273).

[5] Beati qui lugent suavitates veteris vitae (*ibid*., p. 273).

[6] Beati qui esuriunt et sitiunt justitiam novae vitae (*ibid*., p. 274).

[7] Beati mites (*read* misericordes): jam beatus iste discit misereri animae
suae placens Deo, jam debet misereri et proximo. Didicit bene amare seipsum, jam debet amare proximum sicut seipsum. (*Ibid*., p. 274.)

[8] Postquam vero flagitia destruxit in se, facinora in aliis, incipit oculum
mundare et attollere ad visionem Dei (*ibid*., p. 274).

[9] *Loving God* 15, 39 (*Opera* 1360). Cf. *ibid*. 8, 23 ff. (*Opera* 1347);
Letter 11, 8 (*Opera* 153).

[10] *Grace and Free Choice* 4, 11 (*Opera* 1373).

[11] Sermon 7 on Canticles, 2 (*Opera* 2693). Cf. Misc. Sermon 8, 6–9
(XB 771).

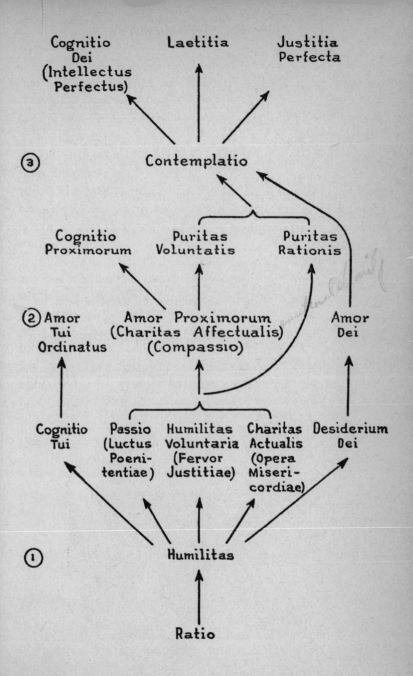

in the nature of the steps and even in their number, a comparison of each with the account in the *Steps of Humility* shows that the doctrine is the same in all.

Loving yourself for your own sake is self-love, that is, pride,[12] which is the natural condition of man before he begins the ascent of the anagogic path.[13] Loving God for your own sake is the realization of your dependence on God,[14] that is, self-knowledge or cognitive humility. Loving God for his sake is love in the strict sense of the word.[15] "Loving yourself only for God's sake" [16] or "loving not even yourself save for God's sake" [17] means the consummation of love in mystical contemplation.[18]

Free choice, without the other kinds of freedom, is the natural condition of man.[19] Free counsel is charity [20] — but only in the sense of active charity [21] and zeal for justice.[22] Free enjoyment is found, in this life, only in mystical contemplation.[23] While humility is not included as a kind of freedom, it is stated in this essay that non-voluntary "good thought" (i.e. cognitive humility) is preliminary to good will.[24]

The slave respects his master through fear, not benevo-

---

[12] *Steps of Humility* 4, 14.

[13] *Loving God* 8, 23 (*Opera* 1347).

[14] *Ibid.* 15, 39 (*Opera* 1360).

[15] Cf. *ibid.* 7, 17 (*Opera* 1343).

[16] *Ibid.* 15, 39: Ut se scilicet diligat homo tantum propter Deum (*Opera* 1360).

[17] *Ibid.* 10, 27: Quatenus nec se ipsum diligat homo nisi propter Deum (*Opera* 1350). Cf. Misc. Sermon 16, 5: In Deum tota affectio dirigenda, ut diligamus nos propter ipsum (XB 797). Cf. Letter 85, 3 (*Opera* 249).

[18] *Ibid.* 15, 39: Quasi enim miro quodam modo oblitus sui, et a se penitus velut deficiens, totus perget in Deum: et deinceps adhaerens ei, unus cum eo spiritus erit (1 Cor. 6. 17) (*Opera* 1360). Cf. *ibid.* 10, 27 (*Opera* 1350).

[19] *Grace and Free Choice* 3, 7 (*Opera* 1370).

[20] Good will. *Ibid.* 4, 9 (*Opera* 1372).

[21] *Ibid.* 4, 11: Non omnia, quae tanquam recta et commoda consulte observamus, etiam ut beneplacita libenter amplectimur, sed insuper quasi dura ac molesta vix aequanimiter ferre perduramus (*Opera* 1373).

[22] *Ibid.* 5, 15: Libertate consilii fruuntur etiam quilibet justi (*Opera* 1376).

[23] *Ibid.* 5, 15: Itaque in hac vita soli contemplativi possunt utcumque frui libertate complaciti (*Opera* 1376).

[24] *Ibid.* 14, 46 (*Opera* 1396).

lence.[25] He loves only himself for his own sake. The hireling
has a benevolent feeling toward his employer, but it is based
on cupidity; he is interested in his employer as the source of
his wages.[26] This is not love, because it has an ulterior object;
it is recognition of dependence, that is, humility. The disciple
obeys his teacher.[27] He therefore performs works of active
charity, for this alone is commanded.[28] The son honors his
father [29] for his father's sake, and this is love.

There is one who acknowledges a lord because he is powerful,
and there is one who acknowledges him because he is good to
him, and finally one who acknowledges him because he is good
simpliciter. The first is a slave, and fears for himself; the second,
a hireling, and desires for himself; the third, a son, and defers to
his father. And so both he who fears and he who desires are
acting for themselves. Only the love which is in the son *seeketh
not her own.*[30]

The bride loves the bridegroom so perfectly that her love for
him is her whole being, excluding all other desires.[31]

Love is the bride's only dowry and only expectation. With
this the bride is filled, with this the bridegroom is satisfied. He
seeks nothing else, and she has nothing else. And that is just why
he is bridegroom and she is bride. No other love, not even filial,
is like this; it is found only in brides.[32]

[25] Sermon 7 on Canticles, 2: Si servus est, timet a facie Domini (*Opera*
2693).
[26] *Ibid.* 2: Si mercenarius, sperat de manu Domini (*Opera* 2693).
[27] *Ibid.* 2: Si discipulus, aurem parat magistro (*Opera* 2693).
[28] Sermon 50 on Canticles, 2 (*Opera* 2967).
[29] Sermon 7 on Canticles, 2: Si filius, honorat patrem (*Opera* 2693).
[30] *Loving God* 12, 34: Est qui confitetur Domino quoniam potens est, et
est qui confitetur quoniam sibi bonus est, et item qui confitetur quoniam
simpliciter bonus est. Primus servus est, et timet sibi; secundus, mercenarius,
et cupit sibi; tertius, filius, et defert patri. Itaque et qui timet, et cupit,
utrique pro se agunt. Sola quae in filio est charitas, *non quaerit quae sua
sunt* (1 Cor. 13. 5). (*Opera* 1356.) Cf. Sermon 83 on Canticles, 5: Purus amor
mercenarius non est (*Opera* 3180). Cf. Misc. Sermon 8, 8: Numquid enim
mercenarium eum quis aestimet, qui paternae inhiat haereditati? (XB 773.)
[31] Sermon 7 on Canticles, 2: Non petit libertatem, non mercedem, non
haereditatem, non denique vel doctrinam, sed osculum (*Opera* 2693).
[32] Sermon 83 on Canticles, 5: Sponsae res et spes unus est amor. Hoc

Such perfect love is spiritual union, and when God is its object it is mystical contemplation.[33]

All steps of the anagogic path are gifts of grace.[34] Man's natural endowment is a gift of creating grace.[35] Humility is a gift of preventing grace.[36] The free counsel by which good works are performed is a gift of saving or provecting grace.[37] Love is a gift of vivifying grace.[38] Contemplation is a gift of consummating grace.[39] Humility is neither merit nor reward; [40] good works are merits; [41] love is both merit and reward; [42] contemplation is reward.[43]

The equivalent phrases used in the various essays are shown by the chart on the next page.

There is still one significant difference between the doctrine of the essay on *Loving God* and that of the essay on the *Steps of Humility*. In both, the fundamental doctrine is the same, that love is the mean by which the monk passes from humility to contemplation. But in the former essay it is love of God, while in the latter it is love of neighbor. This difference is not an inconsistency in Bernard's teaching. The reason for the difference is clear when we consider the readers for whom

---

sponsa abundat, hoc contentus est sponsus. Nec is aliud quaerit, nec illa aliud habet. Hinc ille sponsus, et sponsa illa est. Is sponsis proprius est, quem alter nemo attingat, nec filius quidem. (*Opera* 3180.)

[33] *Ibid*. 3 (*Opera* 3178).

[34] *Grace and Free Choice* 14, 49 (*Opera* 1398).

[35] *Ibid*. 6, 16 (*Opera* 1377). Pride, considered as a vice, that is, as the absence of humility, is not a gift of grace; but natural self-love is part of created human nature. Cf. *Loving God* 8, 23 (*Opera* 1347).

[36] *Ibid*. 14, 46 (*Opera* 1396). Cf. *Steps of Humility* 9, 26.

[37] *Ibid*. 6, 16 (*Opera* 1377). Cf. *ibid*. 1, 1 (*Opera* 1365).

[38] Letter 107, 9 (*Opera* 294). Cf. *Precept and Dispensation* 20, 60 (*Opera* 1212); Misc. Sermon 10, 1 (XB 777).

[39] *Grace and Free Choice* 14, 49: Prima, creatio; secunda, reformatio; tertia est consummatio (*Opera* 1398). Creation, reformation, and consummation make man a creature, God's creature (*ibid*. 6, 17, *Opera* 1377), and God (*deificari, Loving God* 10, 28, *Opera* 1351) respectively.

[40] Cf. Sermon 42 on Canticles, 6 (*Opera* 2927).

[41] *Grace and Free Choice* 14, 49 (*Opera* 1399).

[42] Sermon 83 on Canticles, 4 (*Opera* 3179). Cf. Sermon 50 on Canticles, 2 (*Opera* 2967).

[43] Sermon 46 on Canticles, 5 (*Opera* 2947).

3	contem-platio	nec seipsum diligere nisi propter Deum	liberum complaci-tum	sponsa	consummans gratia	praemium
2	charitas	diligere Deum propter ipsum		filius	vivificans gratia	meritum
	opera		liberum consilium	discipulus	provehens vel salvans gratia	
1	humilitas	diligere Deum propter se	bona cogitatio	mercena-rius	prae-veniens gratia	
	superbia	diligere seipsum propter seipsum	liberum arbitrium	servus	creans gratia	

the two essays were written.[44] *Loving God* (especially the part concerning the four steps of love) is an expansion of what was originally a letter to the monks of Chartreuse.[45] The *Steps of Humility* was written for his own monks at Clairvaux.[46] The former was for Carthusians, that is, hermits. The latter was for Cistercians, that is, Benedictines. Seeking God through direct love of God is the hermit's way. Seeking God through love of neighbor is the Benedictine way.

8. *The descent into the cave*

There is a fourth step of the path beyond contemplation — not a step upward, for contemplation is the summit of human

[44] Bernard never wrote a book (except, perhaps, *Grace and Free Choice*). His works consist of letters and sermons. Each of his so-called essays is a long letter or sermon written at a particular time for a particular person or group.

[45] Letter 11 (*Opera* 147).

[46] Or, as some believe, for the monks of Fontenay — but for Cistercians in any case.

knowledge, but a step downward. Following the tradition which has its classical expression in Plato's allegory of the cave. Bernard teaches the duty of the enlightened man to descend again into the world to help his fellow men.[1] The mystic, whether in this life [2] or in heaven,[3] must descend into the world, not merely to do the sort of good works which were a necessary part of his upward path, but to do those things which only the mystic can do — preach the Truth he has intuited [4] and perform miracles of charity.[5] This is the fecundity of the spiritual marriage of contemplation.[6]

9. Summary

Bernard, when his life was approaching its close, delivered to his assembled monks a summary of the doctrine he had been teaching them. This, the 85th sermon on Canticles, was his last work.[1] Preaching from the text, *By night on my bed I sought him whom my soul loveth*,[2] he summarized his whole

---

[1] Sermon 41 on Canticles, 6: Nec cuiquam sibi, sed omnibus esse vivendum (*Opera* 2923). Sermon 57 on Canticles, 9: Hoc siquidem vera et casta contemplatio habet, ut mentem, quam divino igne vehementer succenderit, tanto interdum repleat zelo et desiderio acquirendi Deo qui eum similiter diligant, ut otium contemplationis pro studio praedicationis libentissime intermittat: et rursum potita votis, aliquatenus in hac parte tanto ardentius redeat in idipsum, quanto se fructuosius intermisisse meminerit; et item sumpto contemplationis gustu, valentius ad conquirenda lucra solita alacritate recurrat (*Opera* 3010). Cf. Sermon 11 on *Qui Habitat*, 11 (XB 270); Sermon 50 on Canticles, 5 (*Opera* 2969); Sermon 52 on Canticles, 7 (*Opera* 2982).

[2] *Loving God* 10, 27 (*Opera* 1351).

[3] Sermon 2 on St Victor, 3 (XB 501).

[4] Only mystics are competent to preach. Sermon 62 on Canticles, 8 (*Opera* 3043). Cf. Sermon 18 on Canticles, 6: Charitatem nondum adeptus periculosissime promovetur (*Opera* 2764). Cf. *ibid.* 1-3 (*Opera* 2760).

[5] Sermon 18 on Canticles, 6 (*Opera* 2764). Bernard refers to his own miracles in Letter 242, 1 (*Opera* 509) and *Consideration* 2, 1, 3 (*Opera* 1023).

[6] Sermon 58 on Canticles, 1 (*Opera* 3013). Cf. Richard of St Victor, *The Four Steps of Passionate Love*: In primo gradu fit desponsatio, in secundo nuptiae, in tertio copula, in quarto puerperium (*Pat. Lat.* 196, 1216). For a further discussion of this subject, see Butler, *Western Mysticism*, pp. 245-254.

---

[1] Not counting the unfinished 86th.

[2] Cant. 3. 1

philosophy in three words: *The soul seeks the Word*, and then described seven reasons why the soul seeks the Word.

The soul seeks the Word in order to yield to it for correction, to be enlightened by it for knowledge, to rely upon it for virtue, to be reformed by it for wisdom, to be conformed to it for beauty, to be married to it for fecundity, to enjoy it for bliss.[3]

(1) The fear of God first leads the soul to flee the wrath to come by turning away from its innate lusts and established habits and submitting its will to the will of God. But since it cannot do this by its own efforts, it must seek the Word, not only that it may yield to the Word but that the Word may cause it to yield. This is the first step of humility.[4]

(2) Secondly it is necessary that the reason be illumined by the light of the Word in order that the soul may have true knowledge of the way it is to follow. This is cognitive humility.[5]

(3) Virtue, the moral strength which subjects all activity to reason, must be acquired from the Word in order that the soul, overcoming the devil, the world, and itself, may actually perform the good which it has come to will and to know. This is good works.[6]

(4) Wisdom, which is the love of virtue or delight in the good, reforms the soul. The virtuous man who is not also wise does good, but it is hard work and requires all his effort. The wise man does good because he loves to, and this is not work but leisure and delight. Virtue is active charity; wisdom is love.[7]

(5) The beauty of the soul is honor, which consists inwardly in purity of conscience and is manifested outwardly

[3] Sermon 85 on Canticles, 1: Quaerit anima Verbum, cui consentiat ad correptionem, quo illuminetur ad cognitionem, cui innitatur ad virtutem, quo reformetur ad sapientiam, cui conformetur ad decorem, cui maritetur ad fecunditatem, quo fruatur ad jucunditatem (*Opera* 3185).

[4] *Ibid.* 1 (*Opera* 3186). Cf. Benedictus, *Regula*, 7.

[5] *Ibid.* 2 (*Opera* 3186).

[6] *Ibid.* 4 (*Opera* 3188).

[7] *Ibid.* 8 (*Opera* 3190). Cf. Sermon 23 on Canticles, 14 (*Opera* 2801).

by dignity in behavior. It is defined as nobility of mind, solicitous to preserve integrity of reputation along with a good conscience, to provide good things in the sight of God and man. This is the resemblance of God which man has lost but can regain, the beauty which attracts the divine Bridegroom (for spiritual beauty plays the same role in spiritual marriage which physical beauty plays in physical marriage), the purity of reason and will which makes contemplation possible.[8]

(6) Last in order of causality, but next to last in order of exaltation, is the fecundity which results from the spiritual marriage, the generation of new spiritual lives by the soul which has already enjoyed fertilizing union with the Word. This is the descent into the cave of the mystic who, having already experienced contemplation, now seeks to win other men by his preaching.[9]

(7) The consummation of bliss is union with the Word in the ecstasy of mystical contemplation.

But observe that spiritual marriage has two kinds of fecundity and consequently dissimilar offsprings, though not discordant; since the mystic mothers bear either souls by preaching or spiritual intelligences by meditating. In this last kind there is a rapture and a withdrawal from even the bodily senses, so that the soul which is conscious of the Word is not conscious of itself. This occurs when the mind, seduced by the sweetness of the ineffable Word, somehow steals itself away, or rather is rapt away and escapes from itself, in order to enjoy the Word. The mind is moved in one way when it is rearing offspring to the Word, in another way when it is enjoying the Word. To the former it is compelled by the necessity of its neighbor; to the latter it is drawn by the loveliness of the Word. The mother rejoices indeed in her offspring; but the wife rejoices more in her husband's embraces. Darling children are dear; but kisses give greater delight. It is good to save many; but to be in ecstasy and with the Word is more blissful. But when is this, or for how long? It is a sweet

---

[8] *Ibid.* 10–12 (*Opera* 3191). Cf. Sermon 31 on Canticles, 6 (*Opera* 2866); Sermon 62 on Canticles, 5 (*Opera* 3041).
[9] *Ibid.* 13 (*Opera* 3193).

intercourse, but a brief moment, and a rare experience. This is what I remember saying above, after the other reasons, that the soul seeks the Word to enjoy it for bliss.[10]

At the conclusion of this sermon Bernard asks what remains after all the most important question: what is meant by "enjoying the Word"? Much has been said about the preparation for the mystical experience and about some of its psychological manifestations; but just what is the nature of the mystical experience itself? The only answer to this question is: it is ineffable.

Some one may proceed to ask me perhaps: What is it to enjoy the Word? I answer: Let him rather seek somebody who has experienced it to inquire of. Or if it has been granted to me also to experience it, do you suppose I can speak that which is ineffable? Listen to one who has experienced it. *Whether we be beside ourselves, it is to God: or whether we be sober, it is for your cause.* That is: it is one thing for me to be with God, with God as sole witness; another to be with you. It is permitted to have that experience, but not to speak of it: in doing so I am coming down to your level, so that I may be able to speak and you to understand. O thou who art curious to know what it is to enjoy the Word, do not prepare your ear for this but your mind. The tongue does not teach this, but grace does. It is hid from the wise and prudent, and revealed unto babes. Great, my brethren, great and sublime is the virtue of humility, which can reach what none can teach, worthy to obtain what none can explain, worthy

[10] *Ibid.* 13: Sed attende in spirituali matrimonio duo esse genera pariendi, et ex hoc etiam diversas soboles, sed non adversas: cum sanctae matres aut praedicando animas, aut meditando intelligentias pariunt spirituales. In hoc ultimo genere interdum exceditur, et seceditur etiam a corporeis sensibus, ut sese non sentiat quae Verbum sentit. Hoc fit, cum mens ineffabilis Verbi illecta dulcedine, quodam modo se sibi furatur, imo rapitur atque elabitur a se ipsa, ut Verbo fruatur. Aliter sane afficitur mens fructificans Verbo, aliter fruens Verbo. Illic sollicitat necessitas proximi, hic invitat suavitas Verbi. Et quidem laeta in prole mater: sed in amplexibus sponsa laetior. Chara pignora filiorum: sed oscula plus delectant. Bonum est salvare multos: excedere autem et cum Verbo esse, multo jucundius. At quando hoc, aut quamdiu hoc? Dulce commercium: sed breve momentum, et experimentum rarum. Hoc est quod supra post alia memini me dixisse, quaerere utique animam Verbum, quo fruatur ad jucunditatem. (*Opera* 3193.)

to conceive by the Word and of the Word that which it cannot set forth in its own words. And why? Not because this is merited but because it is pleasing in the sight of the Father of the Word, Bridegroom of the soul, Jesus Christ our Lord, who is above all things God blessed for ever. Amen.[11]

[11] *Ibid.* 14: Pergat quis forsitan quaerere a me etiam, Verbo frui quid sit? Respondeo: Quaerat potius expertum a quo id quaerat. Aut si et mihi experiri daretur, putas me posse eloqui quod ineffabile est? Audi expertum: *Sive*, inquit, *mente excedimus, Deo*; *sive sobrii sumus, vobis* (2 Cor. 5. 13). Hoc est: Aliud mihi cum Deo, solo arbitro Deo; aliud vobiscum mihi. Illud licuit experiri, sed minime loqui: in hoc ita condescendo vobis, ut et ego dicere, et vos capere valeatis. O quisquis curiosus es scire quid sit hoc, Verbo frui; para illi non aurem, sed mentem. Non docet hoc lingua, sed docet gratia. Absconditur a sapientibus et prudentibus, et revelatur parvulis (Luc. 10. 21). Magna, fratres, magna et sublimis virtus humilitas, quae promeretur quod non docetur, digna adipisci quod non valet addisci, digna a Verbo, et de Verbo concipere, quod suis ipsa verbis explicare non potest. Cur hoc? Non quia sic meritum, sed quia sic placitum coram Patre Verbi sponsi animae, Jesu Christi Domini nostri, qui est super omnia Deus benedictus in saecula. Amen.

DE GRADIBUS HUMILITATIS

THE STEPS OF HUMILITY

ADMONITIO

1. Primus Bernardi fetus est libellus sequens, inscriptus "de Gradibus Humilitatis," primusque nominatur tum a Bernardo ipso, tum a Gaufrido monacho, ejus Vitae scriptore. Bernardi haec verba sunt in epistola decima octava, ad Petrum cardinalem: "Et ut sciatis quid petatis, scio me scripsisse libellum, qui inscribitur de Humilitate, et quatuor Homilias," etc. Haec epistola sub annum 1127 exarata est. Gaufridus vero in libro tertio de ejus Vita, cap. 8, "Si quis," inquit, "nosse desiderat, quam sollicitus ab initio sui ipsius dijudicator et scrutator exstiterit, primum opus illius de Gradibus Humilitatis inspiciat." Rationem hujusce tituli reddit Vir sanctus in Censura seu Retractatione libri, quam in fronte operis praefigi voluit. Cum enim quoddam verbum, quasi e Scriptura sacra prolatum, ipsi excidisset, et quamdam de Seraphim expositionem, quam in Patribus non legerat, adduxisset; hoc comperto, incunctanter sententiam ipse suam emendare non dubitavit. Tantus erat in sancto Doctore veritatis amor! tanta in Patres reverentia! Hic Manricus graviter monet exemplo Bernardi auctores mysticos ac theologicos nonnullos, "qui vel in litteralibus, vel in altissimis theologiae sacrae sensibus novitates non solum inducunt, sed etiam profitentur: dum Bernardus, theologia divinitus infusa praeditus, in sensu mystico quod a Patribus non acceperat, suspectum habet, nec satis credit suae conscientiae factum, donec rem a se excogitatam retractaret." Quanquam alio in loco quiddam amplius sibi licere permisit, nempe in fine homiliarum super *Missus est*, ubi ita ait, "Si quid dictum est praeter Patres, quod non sit contra Patres; nec Patribus arbitror, nec cuiquam displicere debere": et in epistola septuagesima septima, "Sane ibi unusquisque in suo sensu securus abundet, ubi aut certae rationi, aut non contemnendae auctoritati quod sentitur non obviat." Haec sanctus Doctor, priorem sententiam temperans, nec tam novos

MABILLON'S PREFACE TO THE BENEDICTINE EDITION

1. The following little book, entitled "On the Steps of Humility," [1] is Bernard's first production,[2] and is named first both by Bernard himself and by the monk Geoffrey, his biographer. These are Bernard's words in Letter 18 to Cardinal Peter: "And in order that you may know what you are asking for, I may say I have written a little book, entitled On Humility, and four homilies," etc. This letter was written about the year 1127. Geoffrey, moreover, in the third book of the biography, chapter eight, says: "If anyone wants to know how thoroughly he searched himself and passed judgment on himself from the very beginning, let him examine his first work, on the Steps of Humility." The Saint gives the reason for this title in the criticism or retractation of the book, which he wished to have prefixed to it. For, having misquoted a certain word from scripture and having set forth a certain opinion about seraphim which he had not read in the Fathers, upon realizing this he did not hesitate to correct his own statement immediately. So great was the holy doctor's love of truth! so great his reverence for the Fathers! By this example of Bernard Manriquez solemnly admonishes those mystical and theological writers "who not only introduce novelties in interpretations, either literal or recondite, of sacred theology but even boast of them; while Bernard, although endowed with wisdom inspired by heaven, mistrusts an allegorical meaning not taken from the Fathers and cannot satisfy his conscience until he retracts [3] his original statement." Yet in another place he allows himself more liberty, namely at the end of the homilies on *Missus est*, where he says, "If anything is said in addition to the Fathers which is not contrary to the Fathers, I do not think it should give offence to the Fathers or to anyone." And in Letter 77, "Each person may hold safely to his own opinion, when it does not contradict

sensus, si ratione ducantur, quam affectatum eorum studium reprehendens.

2. Tempus scripti libri de Gradibus Humilitatis colligimus ex praelaudata epistola decima octava sub annum 1127 scripta. Tunc enim Bernardus quatuor tantum opuscula dictaverat cum aliquot epistolis, quorum opusculorum cum primum fuerit de Humilitate, ante annum 1125 scriptum dici debet. Certe ad Godefridum Clarae-Vallis Priorem ac consanguineum suum, postea Lingonensem episcopum, ad quem epistola tre-centesima vigesima. Hunc "filium, fratrem, socium, et pro-fectus sui participem" vocat hic n. 24. In codice Colbertino, notato 3964, haec inscriptio libri legitur post libros de Con-sideratione: "Incipit liber ejusdem de Gradibus Humilitatis, ad Godefridum tunc in Clara-Valle Priorem, postea Lingo-nicae civitatis episcopum." Deest in hoc codice Retractatio, quae in quatuor aliis manuscriptis libro praemittitur. Unde eam in hunc locum restituere visum est, quam Horstius ad calcem rejecerat.

either sound reason or unimpeachable authority." Thus did the Saint modify his earlier statement, not censuring new interpretations, if they are reasonable, so much as affected delight in them.

2. The time of composition of the book on the Steps of Humility we gather from the aforesaid Letter 18 written about 1127. For at that time Bernard had composed only four works,[4] besides several letters. As this was the first of the works, it can be said to have been written before 1125. It is addressed to Godfrey, prior of Clairvaux, his kinsman, later bishop of Langres, to whom Letter 320 [5] was written. In section 24 of the present work he calls him son, brother, comrade, and partner of his progress. In the Colbertine codex, number 3964, the following title comes after the books on Consideration: "Here begins his book on the Steps of Humility, to Godfrey then prior at Clairvaux, later bishop of Langres." The retractation is lacking in this codex, but in four other manuscripts it is prefixed to the book. We have accordingly restored it to this place, although Horstius put it at the end.

RETRACTATIO

In hoc Opusculo, cum illud de Evangelio, quod Dominus ait, diem ultimi judicii se nescire, ad aliquam sententiam confirmandam atque corroborandam proferrem in medium,[1] improvide quiddam apposui, quod in Evangelio scriptum non esse postea deprehendi. Nam cum textus habeat tantummodo, *Neque Filius scit*; ego deceptus magis, quam fallere volens, litterae quippe immemor, sed non sensus, "Nec ipse," inquam, "Filius hominis scit." Unde etiam totam ordiens sequentem disputationem, ex eo quod non veraciter posui, veram conatus sum approbare assertionem. Sed quia talem errorem meum multo post, quam a me idem libellus editus, et a pluribus jam transcriptus fuit, deprehendi; cum non potui per tot jam libellos sparsum persequi mendacium, necessarium credidi confugere ad confessionis remedium. Alio quoque in loco[2] quamdam de Seraphim opinionem posui, quam nunquam audivi, nusquam legi. Ubi sane lector meus attendat, quod proinde temperanter, "puto," dixerim: volens videlicet non aliud, quam putari, quod certum reddere de Scripturis non valui. Titulus quoque ipse qui de Gradibus Humilitatis inscribitur, pro eo forsitan quod non humilitatis, sed superbiae potius hic distingui describique videntur gradus, calumniam patietur, sed hoc a minus vel intelligentibus, vel attendentibus ejusdem tituli rationem, quam tamen in fine opusculi ipse ᵃ breviter intimare curavi.

ᵃ *ipse*, Mab.; *ipsa*, Ed. Cant. sine nota.
[1] Infra, sec. 11.
[2] Infra, sec. 35.

RETRACTATION

In the course of this essay, in order to confirm and strengthen some statement, I quoted from the gospel the Lord's saying that he did not know the day of the last judgment. But I carelessly wrote what, as I found later, is not in the gospel. For while the text has simply, *Neither does the Son know*; I, not deceitfully but myself deceived, forgetting the words but not the meaning, say, "Nor does the Son of Man himself know." This became my premise, and I tried to prove the truth of my thesis from this false quotation. I discovered this error of mine long after the book had been published. Since I could not overtake a falsehood now scattered through so many copies, I have thought it necessary to take refuge in confession. Moreover, in another passage, I stated a certain opinion about seraphim which I have read nowhere, nor ever heard. Let the reader notice the qualifying "I think," for I wished to give only as an opinion what I could not prove from scripture. Moreover, because the book appears to distinguish and describe the steps of pride rather than of humility, the title "On the Steps of Humility" might be objected to, but only by those who have ignored or misunderstood the reason for this title, which I have myself briefly pointed out at the end of the essay.

PRAEFATIO

Rogasti me, frater Godefride, quatinus ea quae de gradibus humilitatis coram fratribus locutus fueram, pleniori tibi tractatu dissererem. Cui tuae petitioni digne, ut dignum erat, et volens satisfacere, et timens non posse; evangelici consilii memor, non prius, fateor, incipere ausus sum, quam sedens computavi, si sufficerent sumptus ad perficiendum.[1] Cum autem charitas foras hunc misisset timorem,[2] quo mihi timebam illudi de opere non consummando; subintravit alius timor de contrario, quo coepi timere gravius periculum de gloria si perfecissem, quam de ignominia si defecissem. Unde inter hunc timorem et charitatem, velut in quodam bivio positus, diu haesitavi, cui viarum tuto me crederem; metuens aut loquendo utiliter de humilitate, ipse humilis non inveniri; aut tacendo humiliter, inutilis fieri. Cumque neutram tutam, alterutram tamen mihi tenendam esse conspicerem; elegi potius tibi, si quem possem, communicare fructum sermonis, quam tutari me solum portu silentii: simul fiduciam habens, si quid forte, quod approbes, dixerim, tuis precibus posse me non superbire; sin autem (quod magis puto) nihil tuo studio dignum effecerim, de nihilo superbire non posse.

[1] Luc. 14. 28.
[2] 1 Joan. 4. 18.

AUTHOR'S PREFACE

You have asked me, Brother Godfrey,[6] to set forth for you in more extended form that which I said to the brethren about the steps of humility. While my eagerness to grant your wish urged me on, the meagerness of my ability held me back, and, mindful of our Lord's warning, I did not dare begin until I had sat down and counted the cost, whether I had sufficient to finish it. But when love had cast out the fear of being mocked on account of an unfinished work, there arose another fear, that the fame of success might be more perilous than the shame of failure. Being thus placed in a dilemma between this fear and love,[7] I hesitated a long time, wondering which path would be safe to follow, and fearing that a useful discourse would violate what humility I have, while humble silence would nullify what utility I have. Since I saw neither was safe, yet one or the other must be chosen, I have decided to share the fruit of my discourse with you, so far as possible, rather than seek my own safety in the haven of silence. And I am confident that, if by chance I say anything which you approve, I shall be able to keep from being proud by the help of your prayers; while if, as is more likely, I do not accomplish anything worthy of your consideration, I shall then have nothing to be proud of.

CAPUT 1

CHRISTUM ESSE VIAM HUMILITATIS, QUA PERVENITUR AD VERITATEM

1. Locuturus ergo de gradibus humilitatis, quos beatus Benedictus non numerandos, sed ascendendos proponit; [1] prius ostendo, si possum, quo per illos perveniendum sit, ut audito fructu perventionis, minus gravet labor ascensionis. Proponat itaque Dominus nobis viae laborem, laboris mercedem: *Ego sum*, inquit, *via, veritas, et vita*.[2] Viam dicit humilitatem, quae ducit ad veritatem. Altera labor, altera fructus laboris est. Unde sciam, inquis, quod ibi de humilitate locutus sit, cum indeterminate dixerit, *Ego sum via*? Audi apertius: *Discite a me quia mitis sum et humilis corde*.[3] Se ergo proponit humilitatis exemplum, mansuetudinis formam. Si imitaris eum, non ambulas in tenebris, sed habebis lumen vitae.[4] Quid est lumen vitae, nisi veritas; quae illuminans omnem hominem venientem in hunc mundum,[5] ostendit ubi sit vera vita? Ideo cum dixisset, *Ego sum via et veritas*, subdidit, *et vita*: ac si diceret, Ego sum via, quae ad veritatem duco: ego sum veritas, quae vitam promitto: ego sum vita, quam do. *Haec est enim*, ait, *vita aeterna, ut cognoscant te verum Deum; et quem misisti Jesum Christum*.[6] Vel sic, quasi tu dicas: Viam considero, id est humilitatem: fructum desidero, veritatem. Sed quid si tantus est labor viae, ut ad optatum lucrum non possim pervenire? Respondet, *Ego sum vita*, id est viaticum, quo sustenteris in via. Clamat igitur errantibus, et viam ignorantibus, *Ego sum via*: dubitantibus, et non credentibus, *Ego sum veritas*: jam ascendentibus, sed lassescentibus, *Ego sum vita*. Satis, ut reor, ostensum est[a] ex proposito capitulo Evan-

---

[a] *ut reor, ostensum est*, Mab. et omnia MSS praeter unum; *ostensum est ut reor*, Ed. Cant.

[1] Benedictus, *Regula*, cap. 7.
[2] Joan. 14. 6.
[3] Matth. 11. 29.
[4] Joan. 8. 12.
[5] Joan. 1. 9.
[6] Joan. 17. 3.

CHAPTER 1

HUMILITY, THE WAY TO TRUTH

1. I am going to speak, therefore, about the steps of humility, which St Benedict proposes, not to count but to mount; first I will show, if possible, whither they lead, so that knowledge of the goal may make the toil of the ascent seem less wearisome. So let the Lord tell us of the toil of the way and of the reward of that toil. He says, *I am the way, the truth, and the life*. He calls humility the way which leads to truth. The former is the toil; the latter, the fruit of the toil. How am I to know, you ask, that he was speaking of humility when he said simply, *I am the way*? But hear this, which is clearer: *Learn of me, for I am meek and lowly in heart*. He offers himself as an example of humility, as the type of gentleness. If you follow him, you shall not walk in darkness, but shall have the light of life. What is the light of life but truth, which lighteth every man that cometh into the world and showeth where true life is? Likewise when he said, *I am the way and the truth*, he added, *and the life*; as if to say, I am the way, leading to truth; I am the truth, promising life; [8] I am the life, and give it. *And this*, he says, *is life eternal, that they might know thee the only true God, and Jesus Christ, whom thou hast sent*. Or it is as if you should say: I know the way, humility; I want the reward, truth. But what if the toil of the way is so great that I cannot attain the desired goal? He answers, *I am the life*, that is, the means of support on the way. Thus he cries to wanderers, who have lost the way, *I am the way*; to sceptics and unbelievers, *I am the truth*; to those already mounting, but growing weary, *I am the life*. It is clear enough, I think, from the verse cited that knowledge of the truth is the fruit of humility. But hear also another: *I thank thee, O Father, Lord of heaven and earth, because thou hast hid these things*, no doubt the secrets of truth, *from*

gelii, cognitionem veritatis fructum esse humilitatis. Accipe
et aliud. *Confiteor tibi, Pater, Domine* ᵇ *coeli et terrae, quia
abscondisti haec*, haud dubium quin veritatis secreta, *a sapientibus et prudentibus*, id est a superbis, *et revelasti ea parvulis*,⁷
hoc est humilibus. Et in hoc apparet quod veritas, quae superbis absconditur, humilibus revelatur.

2. Humilitatis vero talis potest esse definitio: Humilitas est
virtus, qua homo verissima sui cognitione sibi ipse vilescit.
Haec autem convenit his, qui ascensionibus in corde suo dis-
positis,¹ de virtute in virtutem, id est de gradu in gradum
proficiunt, donec ad culmen humilitatis perveniant, in quo
velut in Sion, id est in speculatione, positi, veritatem prospi-
ciant. *Etenim*, inquit, *benedictionem dabit legislator*: ² quia
qui dedit legem, dabit et benedictionem; hoc est, qui jussit
humilitatem, perducet ad veritatem. Quis vero est hic legislator, nisi dulcis et rectus Dominus, qui legem dedit delinquentibus in via? ³ In via quippe delinquunt, qui veritatem
derelinquunt. Sed numquid vel sic a dulci Domino derelin-
quuntur? Ipsis ergo dulcis et rectus Dominus legem dat viam
humilitatis, per quam redeant ad cognitionem veritatis. Dat
occasionem recuperandae salutis, quia dulcis est; non tamen
absque disciplina legis, quia rectus est. Dulcis, quia perire
non patitur; rectus, quia punire non obliviscitur.

ᵇ *Domine*, deest in Ed. Cant.   ⁷ Matth. 11. 25.

¹ Ps. 83. 6.   ² Ps. 83. 8.   ³ Ps. 24. 8.

the wise and prudent, that is, from the proud, *and hast revealed them unto babes*, that is, to the humble. Here too it appears that the truth is concealed from the proud and revealed to the humble.

2. Humility may be defined thus: Humility is that thorough self-examination which makes a man contemptible in his own sight. It is acquired by those who set up a ladder in their hearts whereby to ascend from virtue to virtue, that is, from step to step, until they attain the summit of humility, from where, as from the Zion of speculation,[9] they can see the truth. *For the lawgiver*, it is said, *shall give a blessing*, because he who has given the law will give a blessing too, that is, he who has commanded humility will lead to truth. Now who is this lawgiver but the gracious and righteous Lord, who teaches the abandoned in the way? For they are surely abandoned who have abandoned truth. But are they thus abandoned by the gracious Lord? Nay, for they are the very ones whom the gracious and righteous Lord commands to follow the way of humility by which they may return to knowledge of the truth. He gives an opportunity to recover salvation, because he is gracious; yet not without due discipline, because he is righteous. Gracious, because he does not allow to perish; righteous, because he does not neglect to punish.

CAPUT 2

QUO FRUCTU ASCENDANTUR GRADUS HUMILITATIS

3. Hanc itaque legem, qua reditur ad veritatem, beatus Benedictus per duodecim gradus disponit: ut sicut post decem praecepta legis ac geminam circumcisionem (in quo duodenarius numerus impletur) ad Christum venitur; ita his duodecim gradibus ascensis, veritas apprehendatur. Illud quoque quod in scala illa, quae in typo Jacob humilitatis monstrata est, Dominus desuper innixus apparuit,[1] quid nobis aliud innuit, nisi quod in culmine humilitatis cognitio constituitur veritatis? Dominus quippe de summitate scalae prospiciebat super filios hominum tanquam Veritas, cujus oculi sicut fallere nolunt, ita falli non norunt; ut videret si sit intelligens, aut requirens Deum.[2] An non tibi de alto videtur clamare ac dicere requirentibus se (novit enim qui sunt ejus[3]), *Transite ad me, omnes qui concupiscitis* * *me, et a generationibus meis implemini?* [4] et illud, *Venite ad me, qui laboratis et onerati estis, et ego vos reficiam.*[5] Venite, inquit. Quo? Ad me veritatem. Qua? Per humilitatem. Quo fructu? Ego vos reficiam. Sed quae est refectio, quam Veritas ascendentibus promittit, pervenientibus reddit? An forte ipsa est charitas? Ad hanc quippe, ut ait beatus Benedictus, ascensis omnibus humilitatis gradibus monachus mox perveniet.[6] Vere dulcis et suavis cibus charitas, quae fessos allevat, debiles roborat, moestos laetificat. Jugum denique Veritatis facit suave, et onus leve.

4. Bonus cibus charitas, quae media in ferculo Salomonis consistens,[1] diversarum odore virtutum, velut diversi generis

---

* *ad me, omnes qui concupiscitis,* Mab. et Vulg. l. c.; *ad me, qui cupiscitis,* Ed. Cant. sine nota.

[1] Gen. 28. 13. [3] 2 Tim. 2. 19. [5] Matth. 11. 28.
[2] Ps. 13. 2.   [4] Ecclus. 24. 26. [6] Benedictus, *Regula,* cap. 7.

[1] Cant. 3. 9, 10.

CHAPTER 2

THE BANQUETS OF WISDOM

3. This law, therefore, which leads to truth, St Benedict arranges in twelve steps, in order that, just as we come to Christ after the ten commandments and the double circumcision [10] (which make twelve), so we may apprehend truth by the ascent of these twelve steps. Moreover, what else is signified to us by the fact that the Lord was seen standing above the ladder which appeared to Jacob as a symbol of humility, but the fact that knowledge of truth is established at the summit of humility? For the Lord looked down from the top of the ladder upon the children of men, like Truth whose eyes neither deceive nor are deceived, to see if there were any that did understand, and seek God. Does he not seem to you to be crying from above and saying to those who seek him (for the Lord knoweth them that are his), *Come over to me, all ye that desire me, and be filled with my fruits*; and also, *Come unto me, all ye that labor and are heavy laden, and I will refresh you*? Come, he says. Whither? Unto me, Truth. How? Through humility. Why? I will refresh you. But what is the refreshment which Truth promises to those who are climbing and gives to those who reach the top? Is it love, perhaps? To this, as St Benedict says, the monk will soon attain when he has mounted all the steps of humility. A truly sweet and pleasant food is love, which sustains the weary, strengthens the weak, rejoices the sad. It makes the yoke of Truth easy, and its burden light. [11]

4. Love is a good food. Placed in the midst of Solomon's palanquin, it both refreshes the hungry and gives pleasure to those who serve the refreshment, with its odor of various virtues, like the fragrance of different kinds of spices. Peace, patience, kindness, long-suffering, joy in the Holy Ghost are served with it; and all other fruits of truth and wisdom are

fragrantia pigmentorum, esurientes reficit, jucundat reficientes. Ibi siquidem apponitur pax, patientia, benignitas, longanimitas, gaudium in Spiritu sancto: [2] et si quae sunt aliae veritatis seu sapientiae generationes, apponuntur in illa. Habet et humilitas in eodem ferculo suas epulas, panem scilicet doloris et vinum compunctionis, quas primo Veritas incipientibus offert, quibus utique dicitur: *Surgite postquam sederitis, qui manducatis panem doloris.*[3] Habet ibidem contemplatio ex adipe frumenti solidum cibum sapientiae, cum vino quod laetificat cor homi-nis,[4] ad quem Veritas perfectos invitat, dicens: *Comedite, amici mei, et bibite; et inebriamini, charissimi.*[5] *Media*, inquit, *charitate constravit propter filias Jerusalem*;[6] propter imper-fectas videlicet animas, quae dum adhuc solidum illum cibum minus capere possunt, lacte interim charitatis pro pane, oleo pro vino nutriendae sunt. Quae recte *media* describitur, quia ejus suavitas nec incipientibus praesto est, prohibente timore; nec perfectis satis est, pro abundantiori contemplationis dulce-dine. Hi adhuc a noxiis carnalium delectationum humoribus, timoris amarissima potione purgandi, nondum lactis dulce-dinem experiuntur: illi jam avulsi a lacte, epulari ab introitu gloriae gloriosius delectantur: solis mediis, id est proficientibus, ita jam melleas quasdam sorbitiunculas charitatis expertis, ut illis interim pro sui teneritudine contenti sint.

5. Primus ergo cibus est humilitatis, purgatorius cum amari-tudine: secundus charitatis, consolatorius cum dulcedine: ter-tius contemplationis, solidus cum fortitudine. Heu mihi, *Domine Deus virtutum! quousque irasceris super orationem servi tui, cibabis me pane lacrymarum, et potum dabis mihi in lacrymis?*[1] Quis me invitabit ad illud vel medium ac dulce charitatis convivium: ubi justi epulantur in conspectu Dei, et delectantur in laetitia, ut jam non *loquens in amaritudine animae meae, dicam Deo, Noli me condemnare:*[2] sed * epu-lando in azymis sinceritatis et veritatis,*[3] laetus cantem in viis

[2] Gal. 5. 22.   [4] Ps. 103. 15.
[3] Ps. 126. 2.   [5] Cant. 5. 1.   [6] Cant. 3. 10.
_____
* *sed*, deest in Ed. Cant. et uno MS.
[1] Ps. 79. 5, 6.   [2] Job 10. 2.   [3] 1 Cor. 5. 8.

included in the banquet of love. Humility too has its banquet in the same palanquin, the bread of sorrow, namely, and the wine of remorse, which Truth offers first to the beginners, to whom it is said, *Rise ye after you have sitten, you that eat the bread of sorrow.* And there too contemplation has the solid food of wisdom, made from the fat of the grain, with wine that maketh glad the heart of man, to which Truth bids the perfect, saying, *Eat, O friends; drink, yea, drink abundantly, O beloved. The midst thereof,* he says, *is spread with love, for the daughters of Jerusalem,* that is to say, for the imperfect souls which, not yet able to take that solid food, must meanwhile be nourished with the milk of love instead of bread, oil instead of wine. It is rightly said to be in the *midst,* because its sweetness is not given to the beginners, whose fear prevents them, and does not satisfy the perfect, who have the more abundant sweetness of contemplation. The former, still to be purged of the noxious humors of carnal pleasures by the bitter potion of fear, have not yet tasted the sweetness of the milk; the latter, already weaned from the milk, as soon as they enter into glory, enjoy more glorious feasting. Only those in the midst, that is, those who are on the way, taste those honey-sweet sips of love, with which they must be satisfied for the present, because of their weakness.

5. The first food, therefore, is that of humility, bitter and purging; second, that of love, sweet and consoling; third, that of contemplation, solid and strengthening. Ah me, *Lord God of hosts, how long wilt thou be angry against the prayer of thy servant? Thou feedest me with the bread of tears, and givest me tears to drink.* Who will bid me even to that halfway but sweet banquet of love,[12] where the just are feasted in the sight of God and gladdened with pleasure, so that no longer *speaking in the bitterness of my soul will I say unto God, Do not condemn me;* but keeping the feast with the unleavened bread of sincerity and truth, I may sing joyfully in the ways of the Lord, that great is the glory of the Lord? Nevertheless the way of humility is good, by which we turn to truth, learn to love, and partake of the fruits of wisdom.[13]

Domini, quoniam magna est gloria Domini? [4] Bona tamen via
humilitatis, qua veritas inquiritur, charitas acquiritur, generationes sapientiae participantur. Denique sicut finis legis
Christus, sic perfectio humilitatis, cognitio veritatis. Christus
cum venit attulit gratiam: Veritas quibus innotuerit, dat
charitatem. Innotescit autem humilibus: humilibus ergo dat
charitatem.[b]

[b] *charitatem*, conjicio legendum; *gratiam*, omnia MSS et Edd.
[4] Ps. 137. 5.

Therefore, just as Christ is the end of the law,[14] so knowledge of truth is the perfection of humility. Christ brought grace when he came; Truth gives love to those to whom it is revealed. But it is revealed to the humble, and so it gives love [15] to the humble.

CAPUT 3

QUO ORDINE GRADUS HUMILITATIS AD PROPO-
SITUM BRAVIUM VERITATIS PERDUCANT: ET
QUOMODO CHRISTUS PER PASSIONEM
DIDICIT MISERICORDIAM

6. Dixi, ut potui, quo fructu humilitatis gradus ascendi
debeant: dicam, ut potero, quo ordine ad propositum bravium
veritatis perducant. Sed quia ipsa quoque veritatis agnitio in
tribus gradibus consistit; ipsos breviter distinguo, si possum:
quatenus ex hoc clarius innotescat, ad quem trium veritatis,
duodecimus humilitatis pertingat. Inquirimus namque veritatem in nobis, in proximis, in sui natura. In nobis, nosmetip-
sos dijudicando: in proximis, eorum malis compatiendo: in sui
natura, mundo corde contemplando. Observa sicut numerum,
ita et ª ordinem. Primo te doceat Veritas ipsa, quod prius
in proximis, quam in sui debeat inquiri natura. Post haec
accipies, cur prius in te, quam in proximis inquirere debeas.
In numero siquidem beatitudinum, quas suo sermone distinxit,
prius misericordes, quam mundicordes posuit.[1] Misericordes
quippe cito in proximis veritatem deprehendunt, dum suos
affectus in illos extendunt: dum sic per charitatem se illis con-
formant, ut illorum vel bona, vel mala, tanquam propria sen-
tiant. Cum infirmis infirmantur, cum scandalizatis uruntur.[2]
Gaudere cum gaudentibus, flere cum flentibus [3] consueverunt.
Hac charitate fraterna cordis acie mundata, veritatem delect-
tantur in sui contemplari natura, pro cujus amore mala tolerant
aliena. Qui vero se ita fratribus non consociant, sed e contrario aut flentibus insultant, aut gaudentibus derogant; dum
quod in illis est, in se non sentiunt, quia similiter affecti non
sunt, veritatem in proximis qualiter deprehendere possunt?
Bene namque convenit illis illud vulgare proverbium: Nescit

ª *et ita*, Ed. Cant. et unum MS.   [2] 2 Cor. 11. 29.
[1] Matth. 5. 7, 8.   [3] Rom. 12. 15.

CHAPTER 3

THE STEPS OF TRUTH

6. I have shown, so far as I could, to what end the steps of humility should be ascended; I will show, so far as I can, in what order they lead to the promised prize of truth. But since the knowledge of truth consists itself of three steps, I will briefly distinguish them, if I can, that it may thus appear more clearly to which of the three of truth the twelfth of humility leads. For we seek truth in ourselves, in our neighbors, and in its own nature: in ourselves, judging ourselves; in our neighbors, sympathizing with their ills; in its own nature, contemplating with pure heart. Observe not only the number but the order. First let Truth itself teach you that you should seek it in your neighbors before seeking it in its own nature. Later you will see why you should seek it in yourself before seeking it in your neighbors. For in the list of Beatitudes which he distinguished in his sermon, he placed the merciful before the pure in heart. The merciful quickly grasp truth in their neighbors, extending their own feelings to them and conforming themselves to them through love, so that they feel *their* joys or troubles as their own. They are weak with the weak; they burn with the offended. They *rejoice with them that do rejoice, and weep with them that weep*. After the spiritual vision has been purified by this brotherly love, they enjoy the contemplation of truth in its own nature, and then bear others' ills for love of it. But those who do not unite themselves with their brethren in this way, but on the contrary either revile those who weep or disparage those who do rejoice, not feeling in themselves that which is in others, because they are not similarly affected — how can they grasp truth in their neighbors? For the popular proverb well applies to them: The healthy do not know how the sick feel, nor the full how the hungry suffer. But sick sympathize with

sanus quid sentiat aeger, aut plenus quid patiatur jejunus. Et
aeger aegro, et jejunus jejuno quanto propinquius, tanto
familiarius compatiuntur. Sicut enim pura veritas non nisi
puro corde videtur: sic miseria fratris verius misero corde
sentitur. Sed ut ob alienam miseriam cor miserum habeas,
oportet tuam prius agnoscas: ut proximi mentem in tua invenias, et ex te noveris, qualiter illi subvenias, exemplo scilicet
Salvatoris nostri, qui pati voluit, ut compati sciret; miser fieri,
ut misereri disceret, ut quomodo de ipso scriptum est, *Et didicit
ex his quae passus est obedientiam*,[4] ita disceret et misericordiam.
Non quod ante misereri nesciret, cujus misericordia ab aeterno,
et usque in aeternum:[5] sed quod natura sciebat ab aeterno,
temporali didicit experimento.

7. Sed forte durum tibi videtur, quod dixi Dei sapientiam
Christum didicisse misericordiam; quasi is per quem omnia
facta sunt, aliquid aliquando ignorasset ex iis[a] quae sunt:
maxime cum illud quod ex Epistola ad Hebraeos ad id com-
probandum commemoravi, alio sensu, qui non ita videatur
absurdus, possit intelligi; ut hoc quod dictum est, *didicit*, non
ad ipsum caput referatur in sui persona, sed ad corpus ejus,
quod est Ecclesia; et sit ita sensus, *Et didicit ex his quae passus
est obedientiam*, hoc est, obedientiam didicit in suo corpore ex
his quae passus est in capite. Nam illa mors, illa crux, oppro-
bria, sputa, flagella, quae omnia caput nostrum Christus pertransiit, quid aliud corpori ejus, id est nobis, quam praeclara
obedientiae documenta fuerunt? *Christus* enim, ait Paulus,
factus est obediens Patri usque ad mortem.[1] Qua necessitate?
Respondeat apostolus Petrus: *Christus passus est pro nobis,
vobis relinquens exemplum, ut sequamini*, inquit, *vestigia ejus*,[2]
id est, ut imitemini obedientiam ejus. Ex his ergo quae passus
est, discimus quanta nos, qui puri homines sumus, oporteat pro
obedientia perpeti, pro qua is, qui et Deus erat, non dubitaverit
mori. Et hoc modo, inquis, inconveniens non erit, si dicitur
Christus vel obedientiam, vel misericordiam, seu aliquid aliud

---

[4] Heb. 5. 8.   [5] Ps. 102. 17.

[a] *iis*, Mab.; *his*, Ed. Cant. sine nota.
[1] Phil. 2. 8.   [2] 1 Petr. 2. 21.

sick, and hungry with hungry,[16] the more closely the more they are alike. For just as pure truth is seen only with a pure heart, so a brother's misery is truly felt with a miserable heart.[17] But in order to have a miserable heart because of another's misery, you must first know your own; so that you may find your neighbor's mind in your own and know from yourself how to help him, by the example of our Savior, who willed his passion in order to learn compassion; [18] his misery, to learn commiseration. For, just as it is written of him, *Yet learned he obedience by the things which he suffered*, so also he learned mercy in the same way. Not that he did not know how to be merciful before, he whose mercy is from everlasting to everlasting; he knew it by nature from eternity, but learned it in time by experience.

7. But perhaps you object to my saying that Christ, the wisdom of God, learned mercy, as if he through whom all things are made should ever be ignorant of anything that is, especially since that which I cited from the Epistle to the Hebrews in proof of this can be understood in another sense which does not seem so absurd. Perhaps the phrase *Yet learned he* refers not to the head in his own person but to his body, which is the Church, and so the meaning would be, *It learned obedience by the things which he suffered*, that is, the body learned obedience from the things which the head suffered. For that death, that cross, the mocking, spitting, flagellation, all that Christ, our head, went through — what else were they to his body, that is, ourselves, but magnificent examples of obedience? For *Christ*, says Paul, *became obedient to the Father*, *even unto death*. What was the necessity? Let the apostle Peter answer. *Christ also suffered for us*, he says, *leaving us an example*, *that ye should follow his steps*, that is, that ye should imitate his obedience. From the things which he suffered, therefore, we learn how we who are mere men ought to suffer patiently for the sake of obedience, for which he who was also God did not hesitate to die. And in this way, you think, it will not be unfitting to say that Christ learned obedience or mercy or anything else in his body, while at

in suo corpore didicisse: dum tamen sibi in sua persona nil, quod se ante latuerit, credatur ex tempore potuisse accedere. Sicque ipse sit qui misereri aut obedire doceat, ipse qui discat: quia caput et corpus unus est Christus.

8. Non nego hunc intellectum, quin rectus sit: sed ex alio loco ipsius Epistolae, superior interpretatio videtur approbari, ubi dicitur: *Nusquam enim Angelos apprehendit, sed semen Abrahae apprehendit: unde debuit fratribus per omnia similari, ut misericors fieret.*[1] Puto quod haec verba sic ad caput referenda sint, ut corpori penitus aptari non possint. De Verbo utique Dei dictum est quod *non Angelos apprehendit*, hoc est, non in unam sibi personam assumpsit, *sed semen Abrahae*. Neque enim legitur, Verbum angelus factum * est, sed *Verbum caro factum est*,[2] et caro de carne Abrahae, juxta promissionem, quae illi primum ᵇ facta est. *Unde*, id est ex qua seminis assumptione, *debuit per omnia fratribus similari*; id est, oportuit ac necesse fuit, ut similis nobis passibilis,[3] nostrarum omnia, excepto peccato, genera miseriarum percurreret. Si quaeris, qua necessitate? *Ut misericors*, inquit, *fieret*. Et hoc, ais, cur non recte ad corpus referri potest? Sed audi quod paulo post sequitur: *In eo enim, in quo passus est ipse et tentatus, potens est et eis qui tentantur auxiliari.*[4] In quibus verbis quid melius intelligi possit non video; nisi quod ideo pati ac tentari, omnibusque, absque peccato, humanis voluit communicare miseriis (quod est per omnia fratribus similari), ut similiter passis ac tentatis misereri ac ᶜ compati ipso disceret experimento.

9. Quo quidem experimento non dico ut sapientior efficeretur, sed propinquior videretur: quatenus infirmi filii Adam, quos suos fieri et appellari fratres non dedignatus est, suas illi

* *factum*, Mab.; *factus*, Ed. Cant. cum nota, *This is the unaltered reading of one of the primary manuscripts and the correction to "factum" in the other was made by a later hand. The reading is supported by the nearly contemporary manuscript at Montpellier. If it is really what Bernard wrote, it is explained by the fact that "verbum" is the personal Word, and therefore masculine. Cf. Leon. Magn.* Serm. XXI. c. 2 ad init.: *"Verbum igitur Dei Deus, Filius Dei . . . factus est homo."*

ᵇ *primum*, deest in Ed. Cant. et duobus MSS.

ᶜ *ac*, Mab.; *et*, Ed. Cant. sine nota.

[1] Heb. 2. 16, 17.   [2] Joan. 1. 14.   [3] Jac. 5. 17.   [4] Heb. 2. 18.

the same time we believe that nothing formerly hidden could be revealed in time to him in his own person. And thus he who teaches mercy or obedience may be the same as he who learns it, for the head and the body are one same Christ.

8. I do not deny that this sense is right; but the former interpretation seems to be approved by another passage of that very epistle, where it is said: *For verily he took not on him the nature of angels; but he took on him the seed of Abraham. Wherefore in all things it behoved him to be made like unto his brethren, that he might be merciful.* I think that these words refer to the head so peculiarly that they cannot apply to the body. It is concerning the Word of God that it is said that *he took not on him the nature of angels*, that is, did not assume that nature in one person with himself, *but the seed of Abraham.* For we do not read that the Word was made angel, but that *the Word was made flesh*, and flesh of the flesh of Abraham, according to the promise originally made to him. *Wherefore*, that is, from this assumption of the seed, *in all things it behoved him to be made like unto his brethren*; that is, it was fitting and necessary that, subject to like passions as we are, he should experience all the kinds of our miseries, except sin. If you ask what was the necessity, it is answered, *That he might be merciful.* And why, you ask, cannot this rightly refer to the body? But hear what follows directly: *For in that he himself hath suffered being tempted, he is able to succour them that are tempted.* I do not see what can better be understood from these words, than that he wished to partake of the same suffering and temptation and all human miseries except sin (which is being made like unto his brethren), in order to learn by his own experience how to commiserate and sympathize with those who are similarly suffering and tempted.

9. I do not say he became any wiser through this experience, but he seemed to be nearer, so that the feeble sons of Adam, whom he was not ashamed to make and call his brethren, should not hesitate to commit their infirmities to him who could cure them, being God; wanted to cure them, being their

infirmitates committere non dubitarent, qui sanare illas et posset ut Deus, et vellet ut proximus, et cognosceret ut eadem passus. Unde Isaias *virum* eum appellat *dolorum, et scientem infirmitatem*: [1] et Apostolus, *Non enim habemus*, inquit, *Pontificem, qui non possit compati infirmitatibus nostris*. Unde autem possit, indicans adjungit: *Tentatum autem per omnia pro similitudine, absque peccato*.[2] Beatus quippe Deus, beati Dei Filius, in ea forma, qua non rapinam arbitratus est esse se aequalem Patri, procul dubio impassibilis, priusquam se exinanisset formam servi accipiens,[3] sicut miseriam vel subjectionem expertus non erat, sic misericordiam vel obedientiam experimento non noverat. Sciebat quidem per naturam, non autem sciebat per experientiam. At ubi minoratus est non solum a se ipso, sed etiam paulo minus ab Angelis, qui et ipsi impassibiles sunt per gratiam, non per naturam, usque ad illam formam, in qua pati et subjici posset, quod utique (sicut dictum est) in sua non posset; et in passione expertus est misericordiam, et in subjectione obedientiam. Per quam tamen experientiam, non illi (ut dixi) scientia, sed nobis fiducia crevit, dum ex hoc misero genere cognitionis, is a quo longe erraveramus, factus est propior nobis. Quando enim illi appropinquare auderemus, in sua impassibilitate manenti? Nunc autem, Apostolo suadente, monemur cum fiducia adire thronum gratiae ipsius,[4] quem nimirum, sicut alibi scriptum est, languores nostros tulisse, et dolores portasse [5] cognoscimus, et in eo quo passus est ipse,[6] nobis compati posse non dubitamus.

10. Non ergo debet absurdum videri, si dicitur, Christum non quidem aliquid scire coepisse, quod aliquando nescierit; scire tamen alio modo misericordiam ab aeterno per divinitatem, et aliter in tempore didicisse per carnem. Vide ne et simili locutionis modo illud dictum sit, quod Dominus requirentibus discipulis de die ultimo se nescire respondit. Nam quomodo diem illum ille nesciebat, *in quo omnes thesauri sapientiae et scientiae absconditi sunt?* [1] Cur ergo se scire

---

[1] Is. 53. 3.   [3] Phil. 2. 6, 7.   [5] Is. 53. 4.
[2] Heb. 4. 15.   [4] Heb. 4. 16.   [6] Heb. 2. 18.

[1] Col. 2. 3.

neighbor; and understood them, having suffered the same things. Wherefore Isaiah calls him *a man of sorrows, and acquainted with grief*. And the apostle says, *For we have not an high priest which cannot be touched with the feeling of our infirmities*, and explains this by adding, *But was in all points tempted like as we are, yet without sin*. For the blessed God, Son of the blessed God, in that form in which he thought it not robbery to be equal with the Father, that is, passionless, before he had made himself of no reputation and taken upon him the form of a servant, as he had not undergone misery or submission, did not know mercy or obedience by experience. He knew them intuitively, but not empirically. But when he had made himself not only lower than his own dignity but even a little lower than the angels, who are themselves passionless by grace, not nature, even to that form in which he could undergo suffering and submission, which he could not do in his own form, as was said; then he learned mercy in suffering and obedience in submission. Through this experience, however, not his knowledge, as I said, but our boldness was increased, when he from whom we had long been astray was brought nearer to us by this sort of worldly wisdom. For when should we dare to approach him, remaining in his impassivity? But now we are urged by the apostle to *come boldly unto the throne of grace* of him who, we know from another verse, *hath borne our griefs and carried our sorrows*; and because of his own passion we are sure of his compassion for us.

10. Therefore it should not seem absurd to say, not that Christ began to know anything which he did not know before, but that he knows mercy eternally in one way through his divinity, and learned it temporally in another way through the flesh. Observe whether the Lord did not use a similar figure of speech when he replied, to the disciples asking about the last day, that he did not know. For how could he, *in whom are hid all the treasures of wisdom and knowledge*, not know the last day? Why then did he say he did not know that which he certainly must have known? Did he perhaps wish to conceal from them, by lying, that which it was not

negabat, quod certum est quia nescire non poterat? Numquid forte mendaciter eis voluit celare, quod utiliter non valuit innotescere? Absit. Sicut nil ignorare poterat, cum sapientia sit: sic nec mentiri, cum veritas sit. Sed volens discipulos ab inutilis inquisitionis curiositate compescere, quod inquirebant, se scire negavit: non omnimodo quidem, sed tali quodam modo, quo negare veraciter potuit. Nam etsi suae divinitatis intuitu aeque omnia, praeterita scilicet, praesentia atque futura perlustrando, diem quoque illum palam habebat; non tamen ullis carnis suae sensibus experiendo agnoverat.ᵃ Alioquin jam spiritu oris sui Antichristum interfecerat, jam auribus sui corporis archangelum vociferantem, et tubam sonantem, in quo strepitu mortui suscitandi sunt, audierat: jam oculis suae carnis oves haedosque, qui ab invicem segregandi sunt, perspexerat.

11. Denique ut intelligas, quod illa tantum cognitione, quae per carnem fit, se illum diem nescire perhibuerit, vigilanter respondens, non ait, Nec ego scio, sed *nec ipse*, inquit, *Filius hominis scit*.¹ Quid est Filius hominis, nisi nomen assumptae carnis? Quo siquidem nomine intelligi datur, quia dicens se aliquid nescire, non juxta quod Deus est, sed secundum hominem loquitur. Alias quippe loquens de se secundum suam deitatem, non Filius, vel Filium hominis; sed Ego, vel Me, saepius ponere consuevit, ut ibi: *Amen, amen dico vobis, antequam Abraham fieret, ego sum*.² Ego sum, ait: non, Filius hominis est. Nec dubium, quin de illa essentia diceret, qua ante Abraham et sine initio est, non qua post Abraham et ex Abraham factus est. Alibi quoque hominum de se opinionem a discipulis inquirens, *Quem dicunt*, inquit, *homines esse*, non me, sed *Filium hominis?* Rursus eosdem, quid de se ipsi quoque sentirent, interrogans: *Vos autem*, non quem Filium hominis; sed *quem me*, ait, *esse dicitis?* Carnalis videlicet populi sententiam de carne inquirens, nomen carnis, quod proprie est *Filius hominis*, posuit: spirituales vero discipulos de sua deitate interrogans, non Filium hominis, sed signanter *me* dixit. Quod

---

ᵃ *agnoverat*, Mab.; *noverat*, Ed. Cant. sine nota.

¹ Marc. 13. 32.   ² Joan. 8. 58.

expedient to reveal? Hardly. Just as he could not be ignorant, being wisdom, so neither could he lie, being truth. But wishing to check the disciples' curiosity and useless questions, he said he did not know what they asked; not absolutely, but in such a way that he could say so truthfully. For although in his divine intuition he apprehended clearly and completely all things past, present, and future, and that day as well; still he did not know it by any sensible experience of the flesh. Otherwise he would already have killed Antichrist by the breath of his mouth, and already have heard with the ears of his body the thundering archangel and the sounding trumpet by which the dead are to be aroused, and already have seen with the eyes of the flesh the sheep and goats which are to be separated from each other.

11. And, that you may see it was only by that knowledge which is acquired through the body that he claimed not to know the day, he replies carefully, not saying, Nor do I know, but, *Nor does the Son of Man himself know*. What is the "Son of Man" but the name of the assumed flesh? By this name it is given to understand that, in saying he does not know anything, he is speaking not as God but as man. In speaking elsewhere about himself according to his deity he was accustomed to say, not Son of Man, but I or me. For example, *Verily, verily, I say unto you, before Abraham was, I am. I am*, he says; not, The Son of Man is. He was undoubtedly speaking of that essence by which he is, before Abraham and without beginning; not of that by which he was made after Abraham and from Abraham. In another place also, inquiring the opinion of men about himself, he asks his disciples, *Whom do men say*, not, that I am? but, *that the Son of Man is?* Asking the same persons again how they themselves feel about him, he says, *But whom say ye*, not, that the Son of Man is? but, *that I am?* In seeking the opinion of a carnal people about his body he used the name of his body, which is rightly *the Son of Man*; but in questioning his spiritual disciples about his deity he expressly said, not Son of Man, but *I*. Peter understood this and showed by his reply what they had been

denique Petrus intelligens, quid per hoc quod dixerat, *me*, requisiti fuissent, sua responsione aperuit: *Tu es*, inquiens, non Jesus filius Virginis, sed *Christus Filius Dei.*[3] Quod utique si respondisset, nihilo minus veritatem dixisset: sed in verbis interrogationis sensum interrogantis prudenter advertens, competenter proprieque ad interrogata respondit, dicens, *Tu es Christus Filius Dei.*

12. Cum igitur videas Christum in una quidem persona duas habere naturas, unam qua semper fuit, alteram qua esse coepit; et secundum sempiternum quidem suum esse, semper omnia nosse; secundum temporale vero, multa temporaliter expertum fuisse: cur fateri dubitas, ut esse ex tempore coepit in carne, sic carnis quoque miserias scire coepisse, illo duntaxat modo cognitionis, quem docet defectio carnis? Quod utique genus scientiae protoplasti sapientius feliciusque nescirent, quando id attingere nisi stulte misereque non poterant. Sed plasmator eorum Deus requirens quod perierat, opus suum miseratus prosecutus est, descendens et ipse misericorditer, quo illi ceciderant miserabiliter. Voluit experiri in se, quod illi faciendo contra se merito paterentur, non simili quidem curiositate, sed mirabili charitate: non ut miser cum miseris remaneret, sed ut misericors factus miseros liberaret. Factus, inquam, misericors, non illa misericordia, quam felix manens habuit ab aeterno: sed quam mediante miseria reperit in habitu nostro. Porro pietatis opus, quod per illam coepit, in ista perfecit: non quod sola illa non posset perficere; sed quia nobis non potuit absque ista sufficere. Utraque siquidem necessaria; sed nobis haec magis congrua fuit. O ineffabilis pietatis excogitatio! Quando nos illam miram misericordiam cogitaremus, quam praecedens miseria non informat? Quando illam adverteremus incognitam nobis compassionem, quae non passione praeventa, cum impassibilitate perdurat? Attamen si illa, quae miseriam nescit misericordia non praecessisset, ad hanc, cujus miseria mater est, non accessisset. Si non accessisset, non attraxisset: si non attraxisset, non extraxisset. Unde autem ex-

[3] Matth. 16. 13–16.

asked by his saying *I. Thou art*, he said, not Jesus the son of the Virgin, but *the Christ, the Son of God*. Had he given the other answer, he would still have spoken the truth; but shrewdly interpreting the questioner's meaning from the wording of the question, he answered the question suitably and properly, saying, *Thou art the Christ, the Son of God*.

12. Since, then, you see that Christ in one person has two natures, one by which he always was, the other by which he began to be, and always knew everything in his eternal essence but temporally experienced many things in his temporal essence; why do you hesitate to grant that, as he began in time to be in the flesh, so also he began to know the ills of the flesh by that kind of knowledge which the weakness of the flesh teaches? Our first parents would have been wiser and happier to have remained ignorant of that kind of knowledge, since they could only attain it by folly and misery. But God their maker, seeking again what had perished, accompanied his creatures in pity. There whither they had fallen so pathetically, he also came down sympathetically, willing to experience in himself what they justly suffered for defying him, not because of a similar curiosity but because of marvelous love, not to remain miserable with the miserable but to become pitiful and free the pitiable. Become pitiful, I say, not with that pity which he, ever blessed, had from eternity, but with that which he learned through sorrow when in our form. And the labor of love which he began through the former, he consummated in the latter, not because he could not consummate it in the one, but because he could not fulfill our needs without the other.[19] Each was necessary, but the latter was more human. Device of ineffable love! How could we conceive that marvelous pity produced by no previous pain? How could we imagine that superhuman compassion [20] not preceded by passion but coexisting with impassivity? Yet if that pity free from pain had not come first,[21] he would never have thought of this pity which is born of pain. Had he not thought of it, he would not have sought it; had he not

traxit, nisi *de lacu miseriae, et de luto faecis*? [1] Nec illam tamen
misericordiam deseruit, sed hanc inseruit: non mutavit, sed
multiplicavit, sicut scriptum est, *Homines et jumenta salvabis,
Domine, quemadmodum multiplicasti misericordiam tuam,
Deus.*[2]

[1] Ps. 39. 3.   [2] Ps. 35. 7, 8.

sought it out, he would not have brought it out. And has he not brought it *out of an horrible pit, out of the miry clay*? Yet he nowise departed from the older mercy when he imparted the newer; not exchanging but excelling, as it is written, *O Lord, thou preservest man and beast. How excellent is thy loving-kindness, O God!*

CAPUT 4

PRIMUS VERITATIS GRADUS EST, PRIMUM SE IPSUM ATTENDERE, SEU PROPRIAM MISERIAM AGNOSCERE

13. Sed jam ad propositum redeamus. Si ergo se miserum fecit, qui miser non erat, ut experiretur quod et ante sciebat: quanto magis tu, non dico ut te facias quod non es, sed ut attendas quod es, quia vere miser es, et sic discas misereri, qui hoc aliter scire non potes? ne forte si proximi malum consideres, et tuum non attendas; movearis non ad miserationem sed ad indignationem; non ad juvandum, sed ad judicandum: denique non ad instruendum in spiritu lenitatis, sed ad destruendum in spiritu furoris. *Vos qui spirituales estis*, ait Apostolus, *hujusmodi instruite in spiritu lenitatis*. Apostoli consilium sive etiam praeceptum est, ut mansueto, id est eo spiritu fratri aegrotanti subvenias, quo tibi vis subveniri cum aegrotas. Et ut scias qualiter erga delinquentem mansuescere possis, *Considerans*, inquit, *te ipsum, ne et tu tenteris*.[1]

14. Considerare libet, quam bene discipulus Veritatis ordinem sequatur Magistri. In beatitudinibus, quas supra memoravi, sicut prius misericordes quam mundicordes, sic prius mites quam misericordes pronuntiati sunt.[1] Et Apostolus cum spirituales hortaretur ad instruendum carnales, adjunxit, *in spiritu lenitatis*. Instructio quippe fratrum pertinet ad misericordes; spiritus lenitatis, ad mites. Ac si diceret: Inter misericordes deputari non potest, qui in semetipso mitis non est. Ecce Apostolus aperte ostendit, quod superius me ostensurum promisi, prius videlicet veritatem inquirendam esse in nobis, quam in proximis; *considerans*, inquiens, *te ipsum*, hoc est, quam facilis ad tentandum, quam pronus ad peccandum: qua-

[1] Gal. 6. 1.

[1] Matth. 5. 4, 7, 8.

CHAPTER 4

THE FIRST STEP OF TRUTH, KNOWING YOURSELF

13. But now let us return to our thesis. If he made himself wretched who was not wretched before, in order to learn what he already knew; how much more should you, I do not say make yourself what you are not, but observe what you are,[22] that you are wretched indeed, and so learn to be merciful, a thing you cannot know in any other way. For if you regard your neighbor's faults but do not observe your own, you are likely to be moved not to ruth but to wrath, not to condole but to condemn, not to restore in the spirit of meekness but to destroy in the spirit of anger. *Ye which are spiritual*, says the apostle, *restore such an one in the spirit of meekness.* The apostle's counsel or rather command is to assist the weak brother in a gentle spirit, the spirit in which you wish to be assisted when you are weak. And that you may know how to act gently toward a trespasser, he adds, *Considering thyself, lest thou also be tempted.*

14. Let us see how well the disciple of Truth follows the Master's order. In the Beatitudes, which I referred to above, just as the merciful are mentioned before the pure in heart, so are the meek before the merciful. And when the apostle exhorted the spiritual to restore the carnal, he added, *In the spirit of meekness.* Restoring your brethren is the work of the merciful; the spirit is that of the meek; as if he had said, none can be considered merciful who is not meek in himself. See how the apostle clearly shows what I promised to show above, that truth is to be sought in ourselves before we seek it in our neighbors; *considering thyself*, he says, that is, how easily tempted, how liable to sin. For by considering yourself you grow meek, and thus you come to succour others in the spirit of meekness. But if you will not observe what the disciple commends, heed what the Master commands: *Thou*

tenus ex tui consideratione mitescas; sicque ad succurrendum
aliis in spiritu lenitatis accedas. Alioquin si monentem non
audis Discipulum, arguentem time Magistrum: *Hypocrita, ejice
primum trabem de oculo tuo; et sic videbis festucam ejicere de
oculo fratris tui.*[2] Trabes in oculo grandis et grossa, superbia
in mente est: quae quadam corpulentia sui vana, non sana;
tumida, non solida, oculum mentis obscurat, veritatem obum-
brat: ita ut si tuam occupaverit mentem, jam tu te videre, jam
te talem, qualis es, vel qualis esse potes, non possis sentire: sed
qualem te amas, talem * te vel putes esse, vel speres fore. Quid
enim aliud est superbia, quam (ut quidam sanctus definit)
amor propriae excellentiae? Unde et nos possumus dicere per
contrarium, humilitatem propriae excellentiae esse contemptum. Amor vero, sicut nec odium, veritatis judicium nescit.
Vis judicium Veritatis audire? *Sicut audio, sic judico.*[3] Non
sicut odi, non sicut amo, non sicut timeo. Est judicium odii, ut
illud: *Nos legem habemus, et secundum legem nostram debet
mori.*[4] Est et timoris, ut illud: *Si dimittimus eum sic, venient
Romani et tollent nostrum locum et gentem.*[5] Judicium vero
amoris, ut David de filio parricida: *Parcite,* inquit, *puero Ab-
salon.*[6] Et legibus humanis statutum, et in causis, tam ecclesias-
ticis, quam saecularibus servatum scio, speciales amicos causan-
tium non debere admitti ad judicium: ne vel fallant, vel fallan-
tur amore suorum. Quod si culpam amici tuo judicio amor
illius aut minuit, aut prorsus abscondit: quanto magis amor
tui tuum contra te judicium fallit?

15. Qui ergo plene veritatem in se cognoscere curat, necesse
est ut semota trabe superbiae, quae oculum arcet a luce, ascensiones in corde suo disponat,[1] per quas in se ipso se ipsum
inquirat; et sic post duodecimum humilitatis ad primum veritatis gradum pertingat. Cum autem veritate inventa in se,
imo se invento in veritate, dicere potuerit, *Credidi, propter*

---

* *te amas, talem* desunt in Ed. Cant. sine nota.
[2] Matth. 7. 5.   [4] Joan. 19. 7.
[3] Joan. 5. 30.   [5] Joan. 11. 48.   [6] 2 Reg. 18. 5 (Vet. Lat.).
[1] Ps. 83. 6.

hypocrite, first cast out the beam out of thine own eye; and then shalt thou see clearly to cast out the mote out of thy brother's eye. The great thick beam in the eye is pride in the mind. By its great size, although empty, not sound, swollen, not solid, it dims the mind's eye and overshadows truth in such a way that, when pride fills your mind, you can no longer see yourself, you can no longer feel yourself such as you are actually or potentially; but you either fancy that you are or hope you will become such as you would love to be. For what is pride but love of your own excellence, as some saint [23] has defined it? We may say likewise, on the other hand, that humility is contempt of your own excellence. Love, like hate, is a stranger to true judgment. Will you hear a true judgment? *As I hear, I judge;* not as I hate, not as I love, not as I fear. There is a judgment of hate, for example, *We have a law, and by our law he ought to die.* Also of fear, for example, *If we let him thus alone, the Romans shall come and take away both our place and nation.* And there is a judgment of love, as David's command concerning his parricide son, *Deal gently with the young man, even with Absalom.* And I know it is a rule in human law observed in both ecclesiastical and secular cases that personal friends of the litigants cannot be admitted as judges, lest they either defraud or be defrauded by their love for their friends. Now if your love for a friend either lessens or completely conceals his guilt in your judgment, how much more will your love of yourself deceive you in judging yourself!

15. He, therefore, who wants to know truth in himself fully must first get rid of the beam of pride, which prevents him from seeing the light, and then erect a way of ascent in his heart [24] by which to seek himself in himself; and thus after the twelfth step of humility he will come to the first step of truth. When he has found truth in himself, or rather has found himself in truth, and is able to say, *I believed, and therefore have I spoken; but I was greatly humbled*; let him ascend to the heights of his heart, that truth may be exalted, and passing to the second step let him say in his passage, *All men*

quod locutus sum; ego autem humiliatus sum nimis: ascendat homo ad cor altum, ut exaltetur veritas, et ad gradum secundum perveniens dicat in excessu suo, *Omnis homo mendax*.[2] Putas, hunc ordinem David non tenuit? Putas, hoc Propheta non sensit, quod Dominus, quod Apostolus, quod et nos post ipsos, et per ipsos sentimus? *Credidi*, inquit, Veritati dicenti: *Qui sequitur me, non ambulat in tenebris*.[3] *Credidi* ergo sequendo, *propter quod locutus sum* confitendo. Quid confitendo? Veritatem quam cognovi credendo. Postquam autem et credidi ad justitiam, et locutus sum ad salutem,[4] *humiliatus sum nimis*, hoc est perfecte. Tanquam diceret: Quia veritatem cognitam in me confiteri contra me non erubui, ad perfectionem humilitatis profeci. *Nimis* enim pro Perfecte potest intelligi; ut ibi *In mandatis ejus volet nimis*.[5] Quod si quis contendat, *nimis* hic pro Valde positum esse, non pro Perfecte, quia et expositores id ipsum videntur astruere; neque hoc discordat a sensu Prophetae, ut sic sentiamus eum dixisse: Ego quidem, cum adhuc veritatem non nossem, aliquid me putabam esse, cum nihil essem.[6] At postquam in Christum credendo, id est ejus humilitatem imitando, veritatem agnovi; ipsa quidem exaltata est in me ex mea confessione: sed ego *humiliatus sum nimis*, id est, valde vilui mihi ex mei consideratione.

[2] Ps. 115. 10, 11.
[3] Joan. 8. 12.
[4] Rom. 10. 10.
[5] Ps. 111. 1.
[6] Gal. 6. 3.

are false. Pray, did not David follow this order? Pray, did not the prophet feel this which the Lord felt, and the apostle, and even we feel after them and through them? *I believed*, he says, in the Truth which declares, *He that followeth me shall not walk in darkness. I believed*, following; *and therefore have I spoken*, confessing. Confessing what? The truth which I have learned in believing. But after I both believed unto righteousness and spoke unto salvation, *I was greatly*, that is perfectly, *humbled*. As if he had said: Because I was not ashamed to confess against myself truth found in myself, I attained to perfect humility. For *greatly* can be understood to mean "perfectly," as in the phrase, *That delighteth greatly in his commandments*. If anyone should contend that *greatly* here means "extremely" rather than "perfectly," because the commentators seem to say so, that is also consistent with the prophet's meaning, and we may consider him to have said as follows: When I did not yet know truth, I thought myself to be something, whereas I was nothing; but after I learned the truth by believing in Christ, that is, imitating his humility, it was itself exalted in me by my confession; *but I was greatly humbled*, that is, I became in my own sight extremely contemptible as a result of my self-examination.

CAPUT 5

SECUNDUS GRADUS VERITATIS EST, EX AGNITIONE PROPRIAE INFIRMITATIS, COMPATI MISERIAE PROXIMI

16. Humiliatus ergo Propheta in hoc primo gradu veritatis, ut ait in alio psalmo, *Et in veritate tua humiliasti me*;[1] semetipsum attendat, et ex propria miseria generalem perpendat: sicque ad secundum transiens dicat in excessu suo, *Omnis homo mendax*. In quo excessu suo? In illo procul dubio, quo sese excedens, ac veritati adhaerens, se ipsum dijudicat. In illo ergo excessu suo[a] dicat, non indignando aut insultando, sed miserando et compatiendo: *Omnis homo mendax*. Quid est, *Omnis homo mendax*? Omnis homo infirmus, omnis homo miser et impotens, qui nec se, nec alium possit salvare.[b] Sicut dicitur, *Fallax equus ad salutem*,[2] non quod equus aliquem fallat, sed quia is se ipsum fallit, qui in fortitudine ejus confidit: sic omnis homo dicitur mendax, id est fragilis, mutabilis, a quo salus non possit vel sua, vel aliena sperari: quin potius maledictionem incurrat, qui spem suam in homine ponit.[3] Proficiens itaque humilis Propheta per ducatum veritatis, quodque in se lugebat videns in aliis, dum *apponit scientiam, apponat et dolorem*,[4] ac generaliter, sed veraciter dicat: *Omnis homo mendax*.

17. Vide quam longe aliud senserit de se Pharisaeus ille superbus. Quid deprompsit in excessu suo? *Deus, gratias ago tibi, quia non sum sicut caeteri hominum*.[1] Dum in se singulariter exsultat, aliis arroganter insultat. David aliter. Ait enim, *Omnis homo mendax*. Neminem excipit, ne quem decipiat: sciens quia omnes peccaverunt, et omnes egent gloria Dei.[2]

---

[a] *suo*, Mab.; deest in Ed. Cant. sine nota.
[b] *salvare*, Mab.; *salvari*, Ed. Cant.

[1] Ps. 118. 75.
[2] Ps. 32. 17.

[3] Jer. 17. 5.
[4] Eccl. 1. 18 (Vet. Lat.).

[1] Luc. 18. 11.

[2] Rom. 3. 23.

CHAPTER 5

THE SECOND STEP OF TRUTH, KNOWING YOUR NEIGHBOR

16. And so the prophet is humbled in this first step of truth, as he says in another psalm, *And in thy truth thou hast humbled me.* Let him observe himself and judge the common wretchedness from his own. And thus proceeding to the second step, let him say in his passage, *All men are false.* In what passage? In that doubtless in which, passing outside himself and cleaving to truth, he judges himself. Let him say, then, in that passage, not angrily or insolently, but pitifully and sympathetically, *All men are false.* What does this mean, *All men are false?* All men are weak, all men are wretched and impotent who can save neither themselves nor others. Just as it is said, *An horse is a vain thing for safety*, not because a horse deceives anyone, but because he deceives himself who trusts in its strength; so all men are called false, that is, frail and fickle, who can hope to achieve neither their own nor another's salvation. Rather does he incur a curse that trusteth in man. And so the prophet humbly advances under the leadership of truth, seeing in others what he deplores in himself; *and he that increaseth knowledge increaseth sorrow*, so as to say, broadly but truthfully, *All men are false.*

17. See how differently the proud Pharisee felt about himself. What did he exclaim in his passage? *God, I thank thee that I am not as other men are.* He exults in himself exceedingly; he insults all others arrogantly. David is otherwise. For he says, *All men are false.* He excludes none, and so deludes none, knowing that all have sinned and come short of the glory of God. The Pharisee deludes only himself when he excludes only himself and condemns all others. The prophet does not exclude himself from the common passion, lest he be excluded from the compassion; the Pharisee disdains mercy when he disclaims misery. The prophet maintains of all, as

Pharisaeus se solum decipit, quem solum * excipit, dum caeteros damnat. Propheta se non excipit a communi miseria, ne excipiatur a misericordia: Pharisaeus exsufflat misericordiam, dum dissimulat miseriam. Propheta affirmat tam de omnibus, quam de se, *Omnis homo mendax*: Pharisaeus confirmat de omnibus praeter se, *Non sum*, inquiens, *sicut caeteri hominum*. Et gratias agit, non quia bonus, sed quia solus: non tam de bonis quae habet, quam de malis quae in aliis videt. Nondum de suo trabem ejecerat, et festucas in oculis fratrum enumerat. Nam subdit, *Injusti, raptores*. Non frustra, ut arbitror, excessum a proposito feci, si utriusque excessus differentiam intellexisti.

18. Jam ad propositum redeundum est. Quos itaque veritas sibi jam innotescere, ac per hoc vilescere fecit; necesse est, ut cuncta, quae amare solebant, et ipsi sibi amarescant. Statuentes nimirum se ante se, tales se videre cogunt, quales vel a se videri erubescunt. Dumque sibi displicet quod sunt, et ad id suspirant quod non sunt, quod utique per se fore diffidunt; vehementer sese lugentes, id solum consolationis inveniunt, ut severi judices sui, qui scilicet amore veri esuriant et sitiant justitiam, usque ad contemptum sui districtissimam de se exigant satisfactionem, et de caetero emendationem. Sed cum se ad id sufficere non posse conspiciunt (cum enim fecerint omnia quae mandata fuerint sibi, servos se inutiles dicunt [1]), de justitia ad misericordiam fugiunt. Ut autem illam consequantur, consilium Veritatis sequuntur: *Beati misericordes, quoniam ipsi misericordiam consequentur.* [2] Et hic est secundus gradus veritatis, quo eam in proximis inquirunt; dum de suis aliorum necessitates exquirunt; dum ex his quae patiuntur, patientibus compati sciunt.

---

* *decipit, quem solum*, Mab.; desunt in Ed. Cant. sine nota.

---

[1] Luc. 17. 10. [2] Matth. 5. 7.

of himself, *All men are false*; the Pharisee complains of all, except himself, saying, *I am not as other men are*. And he gives thanks, not that he is good, but that he is different; not so much because of his own virtues as because of the vices which he sees in others. He has not yet cast out the beam out of his own eye, yet he points out the motes in his brothers' eyes. For he adds, *Unjust, extortioners*. This digressing passage is not in vain, I think, if you have learned to distinguish the different kinds of passage.

18. Now to return to the thesis. Those whom truth has caused to know, and so contemn, themselves must now find distasteful those things they used to love, even their own selves. Standing before themselves, they are forced to see that they are such as they blush to appear, even to themselves. Displeased with what they are, they aspire to what they are not and have no hope of becoming through themselves. Loudly mourning their lot, they find only this comfort, that, severe judges of themselves, who love truth and hunger and thirst after justice, contemptuous even of themselves, they require of themselves the strictest expiation and, what is more, emendation. But when they see that they are not sufficient for this (for when they have done all those things which are commanded them, they say, We are unprofitable servants), they flee from justice to mercy.[25] In order to obtain this they follow the precept of Truth: *Blessed are the merciful, for they shall obtain mercy*. And this is the second step of truth, when they seek it in their neighbors, when they learn others' wants from their own, when they know from their own miseries how to commiserate with others who are miserable.

CAPUT 6

TERTIUS GRADUS VERITATIS, MUNDARE OCULUM CORDIS AD CONTEMPLANDA COELESTIA ET DIVINA

19. In his ergo tribus quae dicta sunt, id est in luctu poenitentiae, in desiderio justitiae, in operibus misericordiae si perseverant, a tribus impedimentis, quae aut ignorantia, aut infirmitate, aut studio contraxerunt, cordis aciem mundant, quo per contemplationem ad tertium veritatis gradum pertranseant. Hae sunt viae, quae videntur hominibus bonae, illis duntaxat *qui laetantur cum male fecerint, et exsultant in rebus pessimis,*[1] ac se de infirmitate vel ignorantia tegunt ad excusandas excusationes in peccatis.[2] Sed frustra sibi de infirmitate, vel ignorantia blandiuntur, qui ut liberius peccent, libenter ignorant, vel infirmantur. Putas, primo homini profuit, licet ipse non libenter peccavit, quod se * per uxorem, tanquam per carnis infirmitatem, defendit? aut primi Martyris lapidatores, quoniam aures suas continuerunt, per ignorantiam excusabiles erunt? Qui igitur studio et amore peccandi a veritate se sentiunt alienatos, et infirmitate et ignorantia pressos; studium in gemitum, amorem in moerorem convertant, infirmitatem carnis fervore justitiae vincant, ignorantiam liberalitate repellant: ne si nunc egentem, nudam, infirmam veritatem ignorant; cum potestate magna et virtute 'venientem, terrentem, arguentem, sero cum rubore cognoscant, frustra cum tremore respondeant, *Quando te vidimus egere, et non ministravimus tibi?*[3] *Cognoscetur* certe *Dominus judicia faciens,*[4] qui nunc ignoratur misericordiam quaerens. Denique *videbunt in quem transfixerunt:*[5] similiter et avari quem contempserunt. Ab omni ergo labe, infirmitate, ignorantia, studiove contracta, flendo,

---

* *se,* Mab.; *in se,* Ed. Cant. sine nota.
[1] Prov. 2. 14.
[2] Ps. 140. 4.
[3] Matth. 25. 44.
[4] Ps. 9. 17.
[5] Joan. 19. 37.

CHAPTER 6

THE THIRD STEP OF TRUTH, KNOWING GOD

19. Those who persevere, therefore, in these three things,[26] the remorse of repentance, desire of justice, and works of mercy, may then pass through contemplation to the third step, having purged the spiritual vision of the three obstacles arising from ignorance and weakness and willfulness.[27] For these are the ways which seem good to men, to those at least *who rejoice to do evil and delight in the frowardness of the wicked*, and cover themselves with weakness or ignorance to plead as excuses in sinning. But they plead weakness or ignorance without avail who choose to be ignorant or weak in order to sin more freely. Do you suppose it availed the first man, or was it allowed that he did not sin willingly, because he pleaded his wife, that is, the weakness of the flesh, in defence? or will the stoners of the first martyr, because they stopped their ears, be excusable [28] through ignorance? Those who feel themselves alienated from truth by delight and gladness in sinning and overcome by weakness and ignorance, must change their delight to despite, their gladness to sadness, conquer the weakness of the flesh with the zeal of justice, and resist ignorance with philanthropy. Otherwise, if they do not know truth needy, naked, and weak [29] as it is now; they may shamefacedly recognize it too late when it comes with great power and strength, terrifying and accusing, and may in vain answer tremblingly, *When saw we thee in need and did not minister unto thee? The Lord shall be known when he executeth judgments*, if he is not known now when he seeketh mercy. Then *they shall look on him whom they pierced*, and likewise the avaricious on him whom they despised. From every blemish, therefore, arising from weakness or ignorance or willfulness [30] the eye of the heart is purified by weeping, hungering for justice, and devotion to works of mercy. To

justitiam esuriendo, operibus misericordiae insistendo, munda-
tur oculus cordis, cui se in sui puritate videndam Veritas
promittit: *Beati* enim *mundo corde, quoniam ipsi Deum videbunt.*[6] Cum sint itaque tres gradus seu status veritatis, ad
primum ascendimus per laborem humilitatis, ad secundum per
affectum compassionis, ad tertium per excessum contemplationis. In primo veritas reperitur severa; in secundo, pia; in
tertio, pura. Ad primum ratio ducit, qua nos discutimus; ad
secundum affectus perducit, quo aliis miseremur; ad tertium
puritas rapit, qua ad invisibilia sublevamur.

[6] Matth. 5. 8.

such a heart Truth promises to appear in his splendor: [31] *Blessed are the pure in heart: for they shall see God.* Since there are therefore three steps or states of truth,[32] we ascend to the first by the toil of humility, to the second by the emotion of compassion, to the third by the ecstasy of contemplation. In the first, truth is found harsh; in the second, loving; in the third, pure. Reason, by which we examine ourselves, leads us to the first; [33] love, by which we sympathize with others, entices us to the second; [34] purity, by which we are lifted to invisible heights, snatches us up to the third.[35]

CAPUT 7

QUOMODO SANCTA TRINITAS HOS TRES VERITATIS GRADUS IN NOBIS OPERETUR

20. Interlucet hic mihi mira quaedam ac divisa individuae Trinitatis operatio, si quo modo tamen ab homine sedente in tenebris ineffabilis illa possit capi cooperantium sibi personarum divisio. In primo siquidem gradu Filius, in secundo Spiritus sanctus, in tertio Pater operari videtur. Vis audire Filii operationem? *Si ego*, inquit, *lavi vobis pedes Dominus et magister, quanto magis vos debetis alter alterius lavare pedes?*[1] Tradebat discipulis humilitatis formam veritatis Magister, qua in primo gradu primum eis veritas innotesceret. Attende et opus Spiritus sancti: *Charitas diffusa est in cordibus nostris per Spiritum sanctum qui datus est nobis.*[2] Charitas quippe donum Spiritus sancti est, qua fit ut qui sub disciplina Filii per humilitatem ad primum usque gradum veritatis jam profecerunt, ad secundum per compassionem proximi, sub magisterio Spiritus sancti perveniant. Audi et de Patre, *Beatus es, Simon Bar Jona, quia caro et sanguis non revelavit tibi, sed Pater meus qui in coelis est:*[3] et illud, *Pater filiis notam faciet veritatem suam:*[a][4] et, *Confiteor tibi, Pater, quia abscondisti haec a sapientibus, et revelasti ea parvulis.*[5] Vides quia quos verbo et exemplo prius Filius humiliavit, super quos deinde Spiritus charitatem effudit, hos tandem in gloria Pater recepit. Filius facit discipulos, Paraclitus consolatur amicos, Pater exaltat filios. Quia vero non solum Filius, sed et Pater et Spiritus sanctus veraciter Veritas appellantur; constat quod una eademque Veritas, servata proprietate personarum, tria haec in tribus

---

[a] *suam*, Mab. et ratio; *tuam*, Ed. Cant. et MSS et Vulg. *Pater* hic significat Deum Patrem, non Ezechiae sed Bernardo, qui versiculum falso intellexit. *Tuam* Editionis Cant. significat nescio quid.   [1] Joan. 13. 14.

[2] Rom. 5. 5.   [3] Matth. 16. 17.   [4] Is. 38. 19.   [5] Matth. 11. 25.

CHAPTER 7

THE ANAGOGIC PATH

20. Here I see clearly a strangely divided operation of the indivisible Trinity, if indeed that ineffable division of mutually cooperating persons can in any way be apprehended by a man sitting in darkness. On the first step the Son, on the second the Holy Ghost, on the third the Father seems to be acting. Will you hear how the Son acts? He says, *If I then, your Lord and Master, have washed your feet; how much more ought ye to wash one another's feet.* The teacher of truth was giving his disciples an example of humility, by which truth should first be known to them on the first step. Observe likewise the work of the Holy Ghost: *Love is shed abroad in our hearts by the Holy Ghost which is given unto us.* Love is a gift of the Holy Ghost by which those who have already attained the first step of truth through humility under the Son's training may advance to the second through sympathy for neighbor under the Holy Ghost's teaching. And it is said of the Father, *Blessed art thou, Simon Bar-jona: for flesh and blood hath not revealed it unto thee, but my Father which is in heaven.* Also, *The Father to the children shall make known his truth.* And, *I thank thee, O Father, because thou hast hid these things from the wise, and hast revealed them unto babes.* You see that those whom the Son first humbled by precept and example, and over whom the Spirit then shed love, have finally been received in glory by the Father. The Son makes disciples, the Paraclete consoles friends, the Father exalts his children. But because not only the Son but also the Father and the Holy Ghost are truly called Truth, it follows that one and the same Truth, without violating the distinction of persons, performs these three things on the three steps. On the first it instructs, as a teacher; on the second it consoles, as a friend or brother; on the third it draws close, as a father his children.

gradibus operatur. Primo scilicet instruit, ut magister: secundo consolatur, ut amicus vel frater: tertio astringit, ut filios pater.

21. Dei quippe Filius, Verbum scilicet ac sapientia Patris, primum quidem illam animae nostrae potentiam, quae ratio dicitur, cum reperit carne depressam, peccato captivam, ignorantia caecam, exterioribus deditam; clementer assumens, potenter erigens, prudenter instruens, introrsum trahens, ac mirabiliter utens tanquam pro se vicaria, ipsam ᵃ sibi judicem statuit, ita ut pro reverentia Verbi cui conjungitur, ipsa sui accusatrix, testis, et judex, contra se Veritatis fungatur officio. Ex qua prima conjunctione Verbi et rationis, humilitas nascitur. Aliam deinde partem, quae dicitur voluntas, veneno quidem carnis infectam, sed jam ratione discussam, Spiritus sanctus dignanter visitans, suaviter purgans, ardenter afficiens, misericordem facit: ita ut more pellis, quae uncta extenditur; ipsa quoque unctione perfusa coelesti, usque ad inimicos per affectum dilatetur. Et sic ex hac secunda conjunctione Spiritus Dei et voluntatis humanae, charitas efficitur. Utramque vero partem, rationem scilicet ac voluntatem, alteram verbo veritatis instructam, alteram spiritu veritatis afflatam; illam hyssopo humilitatis aspersam, hanc igne charitatis succensam; tandem jam perfectam animam, propter humilitatem sine macula, propter charitatem sine ruga; ¹ cum nec voluntas rationi repugnat, nec ratio veritatem dissimulat, gloriosam sibi sponsam Pater conglutinat: ita ut nec ratio de se, nec voluntas de proximo cogitare sinatur, sed hoc solum beata illa anima dicere delectetur, *Introduxit me Rex in cubiculum suum*.² Digna certe, quae de schola humilitatis, in qua primum sub magistro Filio ad se ipsam ᵇ intrare didicit, juxta comminationem ad se factam, *Si ignoras te, egredere et pasce ᶜ haedos tuos*: ³ digna ergo, quae de schola illa humilitatis duce Spiritu sancto in cellaria charitatis (quae nimirum proximorum pectora intelligenda sunt) per affectionem introduceretur; unde suffulta floribus, ac stipata malis, bonis scilicet moribus et

---

ᵃ *ipsam*, Mab.; *ipsum*, Ed. Cant. sine nota.
ᵇ *ipsam*, Mab.; *ipsum*, Ed. Cant. sine nota.
ᶜ *pasce*, Mab.; *pascere*, Ed. Cant. sine nota.

¹ Eph. 5. 27.
² Cant. 1. 3 (Vet. Lat.).
³ Cant. 1. 7.

21. First, when the Son of God, who is the Word and wisdom of the Father,[36] finds that faculty of our soul called reason weighed down by the flesh, captive to sin, blinded by ignorance, and given over to external things; [37] he gently lifts it up, powerfully strengthens it, prudently instructs it, and turns it to internal things. Miraculously making the reason his vicar, as it were, he appoints it judge of itself, so that, out of reverence for the Word to which it is joined, prosecutor and witness and judge of itself, it performs the office of Truth against itself. From this first conjunction of the Word and the reason is born humility. Another faculty, called the will, infected to be sure with the poison of the flesh but now under the control of the reason, is graciously visited, gently purged, ardently energized, and made merciful [38] by the Holy Ghost; so that, like a skin which is anointed and stretched, it, divinely anointed, is extended in affection even to its enemies. And thus, by this second conjunction of the Spirit of God and the human will, love is created.[39] Both faculties, reason and will, the one taught by the Word of Truth, the other inspired with the Spirit of Truth, the former sprinkled with the hyssop of humility, the latter kindled with the fire of love, now form a finally perfected soul,[40] flawless through humility and unruffled through love, since neither the will resists reason, nor does reason dissemble truth. The Father unites this soul to himself as a glorious bride,[41] so that neither the reason can think of itself nor the will of its neighbor, but that blessed soul delights only in saying, *The King hath brought me into his chamber*. And it is worthy, coming from the school of humility, where it first learned from the Son's teaching to enter into itself, taking heed of the warning, *If thou know not thyself, go feed thy kids*.[42] It is worthy to be led by the Holy Ghost from that school of humility and brought by affection into the storerooms of love, by which are meant the hearts of its neighbors.[43] Thence, stayed with flagons and comforted with apples, namely good habits and holy virtues, it is finally admitted to the chamber of the King,[44] of love for whom it is sick. There for a little while,

virtutibus sanctis, ad Regis demum cubiculum, cujus amore languet,[4] admitteretur. Ibi modicum, hora videlicet quasi dimidia, silentio facto in coelo,[5] inter desideratos amplexus suaviter quiescens, ipsa quidem dormit, sed cor ejus vigilat,[6] quo utique interim veritatis arcana rimatur: quorum postmodum memoria statim ad se reditura pascatur. Ibi videt invisibilia, audit ineffabilia, quae non licet homini loqui.[7] Excedunt quippe omnem illam, quam nox nocti indicat, scientiam: dies tamen diei eructat verbum,[8] et inter sapientes sapientiam loqui, et spiritualibus spiritualia licet conferri.[9]

⁴ Cant. 2. 5.   ⁶ Cant. 5. 2.   ⁸ Ps. 18. 3.
⁵ Apoc. 8. 1.   ⁷ 2 Cor. 12. 4.   ⁹ 1 Cor. 2. 13.

about half an hour,[45] there being silence in heaven, it rests sweetly in the longed for embrace, and sleeps itself; but its heart waketh, with which it searches out the secrets of truth,[46] that it may feed on the memory of them when it returns to itself.[47] There it sees invisible things, hears unspeakable words,[48] which it is not lawful for a man to utter. They surpass all that knowledge which night sheweth unto night; but day unto day uttereth speech, and it is lawful to speak wisdom among the wise, and to compare spiritual things with spiritual.

CAPUT 8

GRADUS IIDEM IN RAPTU SANCTI PAULI DECLARANTUR

22. Putas, hos gradus Paulus non transierat, qui usque ad tertium coelum se raptum fuisse dicebat? [1] Sed quare raptum, et non potius ductum? Ut videlicet si tantus Apostolus raptum se dicit fuisse, quo nec doctus scivit, nec ductus potuit ire; me, qui procul dubio minor sum Paulo, ad tertium coelum nulla mea virtute, nullo meo labore pervenire posse praesumam: ne vel de virtute confidam, vel pro labore diffidam. Qui enim docetur aut ducitur, ex hoc ipso quod docentem vel ducentem sequitur, laborare convincitur, et aliquid de se agit, ut ad destinatum vel locum vel sensum pertrahatur, ita ut dicere possit: *Non autem ego, sed gratia Dei mecum.* [2] Qui vero rapitur, non suis viribus, sed alienis innixus, tanquam nescius quocumque portatur, nec de toto in se, nec de parte gloriatur, ubi nec per se, nec cum alio aliquid operatur. Ad primum itaque sive ad medium coelum ductus vel adjutus Apostolus ascendere potuit: ad tertium autem ut perveniret, rapi oportuit. Nam et Filius ad hoc legitur descendisse, ut juvaret ascensuros ad primum: et Spiritus sanctus missus fuisse, qui perduceret ad secundum. Pater vero, licet Filio et Spiritui sancto semper cooperetur, nunquam tamen aut de coelo descendisse, aut ad terras legitur missus fuisse. Lego certe, quod *misericordia Domini plena est terra;* [3] et, *Pleni sunt coeli et terra gloria tua,* [4] et multa hujusmodi. Lego et de Filio, *Postquam venit plenitudo temporis, misit Deus Filium suum.* [5] Et ipse Filius loquitur de se, *Spiritus Domini* [a] *misit me.* [6] Et per eundem prophetam: *Et nunc,* inquit, *Dominus misit me et Spiritus ejus.* [7] Lego et de Spiritu sancto, *Paraclitus autem*

---

[a] *Spiritus Domini*, Mab. et Vulg.; *spiritus*, Ed. Cant. sine nota.

[1] 2 Cor. 12. 2.

[2] 1 Cor. 15. 10.　　　[4] Praefatio missae.　　　[6] Is. 61. 1; Luc. 4. 18.

[3] Ps. 32. 5.　　　[5] Gal. 4. 4.　　　[7] Is. 48. 16.

CHAPTER 8

THE RAPTURE OF ST PAUL

22. Do you not suppose that Paul, who said that he was *caught up to the third heaven*, passed through these steps? But why *caught up*, and not simply brought up? In order that, if so great an apostle says he was *caught up* there whither he could not go by being taught or brought, I who am surely less than Paul shall not presume to be able to attain the third heaven by any strength or toil of my own, and so shall be neither confident of my strength nor diffident because of the toil. For he who is taught or brought is proved to be laboring himself by the very fact that he is following his instructor or conductor. He does something of himself to attain his physical or mental goal, so that he can say, *Yet not I, but the grace of God which was with me.* But he who is caught up, supported by someone else's strength, not his own, not knowing whither he is being borne, cannot be proud of himself either wholly or partly, since he does nothing [49] either by himself or with assistance. The apostle might have been brought or helped up to the first or second heaven; but to get to the third he had to be caught up. For we read that the Son came down to help us to rise to the first, and the Holy Ghost was sent to allure us to the second. But while the Father always cooperates with the Son and the Holy Ghost, we never read that he either came down from heaven or was sent over the earth. I do read, *The earth is full of the goodness of the Lord*, and, *Heaven and earth are full of thy glory*, and many similar passages. And I read of the Son, *But when the fulness of the time was come, God sent forth his Son.* And the Son says of himself, *The Spirit of the Lord hath sent me.* And again by the mouth of the same prophet he says, *And now the Lord God, and his Spirit, hath sent me.* And I read of the

Spiritus sanctus, quem mittet Pater in nomine meo:[8] et, *Cum assumptus fuero, mittam vobis eum*,[9] haud dubium quin [b] Spiritum sanctum. Patrem autem in sua persona, licet nusquam non sit, nusquam tamen invenio [c] nisi in coelis, ut in Evangelio, *Et* [d] *Pater meus qui in coelis est*: [10] et in oratione, *Pater noster qui es in coelis*.[11]

23. Unde nimirum colligo, quod quia Pater non descendit, Apostolus ut eum videret, ad tertium coelum ascendere quidem non potuit, quo tamen se raptum memoravit. Denique, *Nemo ascendit in coelum, nisi qui descendit de coelo*.[1] Et ne putes de primo dictum vel secundo, dicit tibi David: *A summo coelo egressio ejus*.[2] Ad quod iterum non subito raptus, non furtim sublatus, sed, *Videntibus*, inquit, *illis*, id est Apostolis, *elevatus est*.[3] Non sicut Elias, qui unum; non sicut Paulus, qui nullum (vix enim vel se ipsum testem aut arbitrum habere potuit, ipso perhibente, *Nescio, Deus scit*):[4] sed ut omnipotens, qui quando voluit descendit, quando voluit ascendit, pro suo arbitrio arbitros et spectatores, locum et tempus, diem et horam exspectans, *videntibus illis*, quos scilicet tanta visione dignatur; *elevatus est*. Raptus est Paulus, raptus est Elias, translatus est Enoch: Redemptor noster legitur *elevatus*, hoc est, ex se ipso levatus, non aliunde adjutus. Denique non currus vehiculo, non angeli adminiculo, sed propria virtute subnixum *suscepit eum nubes ab oculis eorum*.[5] Cur hoc? An fessum juvit? an pigrum impulit? an cadentem sustinuit? Absit. Sed suscepit eum ab oculis carnalibus discipulorum: qui etsi Christum noverant secundum carnem; sed ultra jam non noscerent. Quos ergo ad primum coelum per humilitatem Filius vocat, hos in secundo per charitatem Spiritus aggregat, ad tertium per contemplationem Pater exaltat. Primo humiliantur in veritate, et dicunt, *In veritate tua humiliasti me*.[6] Secundo congaudent

---

[b] *quin*, Mab.; *quia*, Ed. Cant. sine nota.
[c] *invenio*, Mab.; *invenis*, Ed. Cant. sine nota.
[d] *Et*, Mab. et omnia MSS praeter unum; deest in Ed. Cant.

[8] Joan. 14. 26.   [10] Matth. 16. 17.
[9] Joan. 16. 7.   [11] Matth. 6. 9.

[1] Joan. 3. 13.   [3] Act. 1. 9.   [5] Act. 1. 9.
[2] Ps. 18. 7.   [4] 2 Cor. 12. 2.   [6] Ps. 118. 75.

Holy Ghost, *But the Comforter, which is the Holy Ghost, whom the Father will send in my name.* Also, *If I depart, I will send him unto you,* meaning the Holy Ghost. But the Father in his own person, though there is no place where he is not, is found nowhere except in heaven, as in the Gospel, *My Father, which is in heaven,* and the prayer, *Our Father which art in heaven.*

23. From this I infer that, as the Father did not descend, the apostle was not able to ascend to the third heaven to see him, but said he was caught up. Moreover, *No man hath ascended up to heaven, but he that came down from heaven.* And lest you think it means from the first or second, David tells you, *His going forth is from the end of the heaven.* To this he was not suddenly caught up again, not secretly carried up, but *while they,* namely the apostles, *beheld, he was taken up.* Not like Elijah, with one witness; not like Paul, with none, for he could hardly have considered even himself a witness or observer when he said, *I cannot tell: God knoweth;* but like the Almighty, who descended when he willed and ascended when he willed, to himself alone beholden for beholders and spectators, time and place, day and hour; *while they,* those whom he honored with so great a spectacle, *beheld, he was taken up.* Paul was caught up, Elijah was caught up, Enoch was translated. Our Redeemer, we read, was taken up, that is, he took himself up, with no other's aid. Not mounted in a chariot, not supported by an angel, but relying on his own power, *a cloud received him out of their sight.* Why this? To assist him in his weariness? encourage him in his reluctance? keep him from falling? Hardly. But it received him out of the physical sight of his disciples, who knew Christ after the flesh, but not otherwise as yet. Therefore, those whom the Son calls to the first heaven through humility, the Spirit gathers in the second through love, and the Father exalts to the third through contemplation. In the first they are humbled in truth and say, *In thy truth thou hast humbled me.* In the second they rejoice in the truth and sing, *Behold, how good and how pleasant it is for brethren to dwell together in*

veritati, et psallunt,* *Ecce quam bonum, et quam jucundum habitare fratres in unum!* [7] De charitate quippe scriptum est, *Congaudet autem veritati.*[8] Tertio ad arcana veritatis rapiuntur, et aiunt, *Secretum meum mihi, secretum meum mihi.*[9]

* *psallunt*, Mab.; *psallant*, Ed. Cant. sine nota.
[7] Ps. 132. 1.   [8] 1 Cor. 13. 6.   [9] Is. 24. 16.

unity! for it is written of love that it *rejoiceth in the truth.* In the third they are caught up to the mysteries of truth and exclaim, *My secret to myself, my secret to myself!*

CAPUT 9

GEMITUS ET SUSPIRIA SANCTI BERNARDI, AD VERITATEM ANHELANTIS

24. Sed quid ego miser superflua magis loquacitate, quam spiritus vivacitate duos coelos superiores percurro, qui manibus pedibusque repens adhuc sub inferiore laboro? Ad quod tamen jam, ipso juvante, quo et vocante, mihi scalam erexi. Illic siquidem iter est, quo ostendat [a] mihi salutare Dei.[1] Jam Dominum desuper innixum suspicio, jam ad vocem veritatis exsulto. Vocavit me, et ego respondi illi: *Operi manuum tuarum porriges dexteram.*[2] Tu quidem, Domine, gressus meos dinumeras, sed ego lentus ascensor, fessus viator, diverticula quaero. Vae mihi, si tenebrae me comprehendant, aut si mea fuga fiat in hieme, vel in sabbato:[3] dum nunc ad lucem, cum tempus acceptabile et dies salutis sunt,[4] proficisci dissimulo. Quid moror? Ora pro me, fili, frater, socie, et particeps profectus mei, si quis est, in Domino. Ora Omnipotentem, quatenus sic pigrum roboret pedem, ut tamen *non veniat mihi pes superbiae.*[5] Etsi enim pes piger, ut ad veritatem ascendat, idoneus non est: tolerabilior tamen est [b] isto, qui in ea stare non potest, ut habes ibi, *Expulsi sunt, nec potuerunt stare.*[6]

25. Et hoc quidem de superbis. Sed quid de illorum capite? quid de illo, qui dicitur *rex super omnes filios superbiae?*[1] Et *ipse*, inquit, *in veritate non stetit:*[2] et alibi, *Videbam satanam cadentem de coelo.*[3] Quare hoc, nisi propter superbiam? Vae mihi, si et me viderit, qui *alta a longe cognoscit,*[4] superbientem; et illam in me terribilem intonet vocem: Tu quidem filius Excelsi eras, sed sicut homo morieris, et sicut unus de principi-

---

[a] *ostendat*, Mab.; *ostendam*, Ed. Cant. et unum MS.
[b] *tolerabilior tamen est*, Mab.; *tolerabiliter est tamen*, Ed. Cant. sine nota.

[1] Ps. 49. 23.	[3] Matth. 24. 20.	[5] Ps. 35. 12.
[2] Job 14. 15.	[4] 2 Cor. 6. 2.	[6] Ps. 35. 13.

[1] Job 41. 25.	[2] Joan. 8. 44.	[3] Luc. 10. 18.	[4] Ps. 137. 6.

CHAPTER 9

THE STEPS OF HUMILITY

24. But why am I, a poor wretch, running with idle chatter rather than quickness of spirit through the two upper heavens, when in fact I am laboriously crawling on all fours beneath the lowest? Yet I have already erected a ladder reaching up to this, with the aid of him who also calls me. For that is the path to where he shows me the salvation of God. I already look up to the Lord standing above it; I already rejoice at the voice of Truth. He has called me, and I have answered him, *To the work of thy hands thou shalt reach out thy right hand.* For now, O Lord, thou numberest my steps; but I, a slow climber, a weary wayfarer, keep looking for resting places. Woe to me if darkness overtake me, or if my flight be in the winter or on the sabbath day; if I neglect to start toward the light now in the accepted time and in the day of salvation. Why do I delay? Pray for me, my son, brother, comrade, and partner of my progress in the Lord, if I am making any. Pray to the Almighty to strengthen my sluggish foot, but so as to *let not the foot of pride come to me.* For although a sluggish foot is not capable of ascending to the truth, yet it is better than one which cannot stand in the truth, as it is said, *They are cast down, and shall not be able to rise.*

25. And this is said of the proud. But what of their head? what of him who is called *a king over all the children of pride*? *He abode not in the truth*, it is said; and elsewhere, *I beheld Satan fall from heaven.* Why this, if not because of pride? Woe to me if he who *knoweth the proud afar off* shall find me also exulting and shall thunder against me those terrible words: Thou wast a child of the most High; but thou shalt die like man, and fall like one of the princes. Who will not fear at the voice of this thunder? How much better for the sinew of

bus cades.⁵ Quis non ab hujus tonitrui voce formidet? O
quam salubrius ad tactum angeli nervus femoris Jacob emar-
cuit,⁶ quam angeli superbientis intumuit, evanuit, ruit. Utinam
et meum nervum angelus tangat ut marcescat, si forte ex hac
infirmitate incipiam proficere, qui ex mea firmitate non possum
nisi deficere. Lego profecto: *Quod infirmum est Dei, fortius
est hominibus.*⁷ Sic quoque Apostolus de suo nervo con-
questus, quem angelus non Domini, sed satanae colaphizabat,
responsum audivit: *Sufficit tibi gratia mea; nam virtus in infirmitate perficitur.* Quae virtus? Ipse Apostolus respondeat:
*Libenter gloriabor in infirmitatibus meis, ut inhabitet in me
virtus Christi.*⁸ Sed nondum forsitan intelligis, de qua specialiter dixerit, quia Christus omnes virtutes habuit. Sed cum
omnes habuerit, prae omnibus tamen unam, id est humilitatem,
nobis in se commendavit, cum ait: *Discite a me quia mitis sum
et humilis corde.*⁹

26. Libenter igitur et ego, Domine Jesu, gloriabor, si potero,
in mea infirmitate, in mei nervi contractione, ut tua virtus, id
est humilitas, perficiatur in me. Nam sufficit mihi gratia tua,
cum defecerit virtus mea. Pedem profecto gratiae fortiter
figens, et meum qui infirmus est, leniter trahens, securus
ascendam per scalam humilitatis: donec veritati adhaerens, ad
latitudinem transeam charitatis. Tunc psallam cum gratiarum
actione, et dicam: *Statuisti in loco spatioso pedes meos.*¹ Sic
arcta via cautius strictim inceditur, sic ardua scala tutius
pedetentim ascenditur; sic miro modo ad veritatem licet
pigrius tamen firmius claudicando acceditur. Sed *heu mihi,
quia incolatus meus prolongatus est!* ² *Quis dabit mihi pennas
sicut columbae,*³ quibus celerius volem ad veritatem, ut jam
requiescam in charitate? Quae quoniam desunt, *deduc me,
Domine, in via tua, et ingrediar in veritate tua,*⁴ et veritas
liberabit me.⁵ Vae mihi quod de illa descendi. Nisi enim prius
leviter, inaniter descendissem; in ascendendo tam diu, tam

---

⁵ Ps. 81. 6, 7.　　　⁷ 1 Cor. 1. 25.
⁶ Gen. 32. 25.　　　⁸ 2 Cor. 12. 9.　　　⁹ Matth. 11. 29.

---

¹ Ps. 30. 9.　　²Ps. 119. 5.　　³Ps. 54. 7.　　⁴Ps. 85. 11.　　⁵ Joan. 8. 32.

Jacob's thigh to wither at the touch of the angel, than to swell up, weaken, and collapse at the touch of the proud angel! Would that an angel might touch and wither my sinew too, if from this infirmity I should begin to progress, for in health I can only regress. I read truly, *The weakness of God is stronger than men.* Thus also the apostle, complaining that his own sinew had been buffeted by the angel not of the Lord but of Satan, received this answer, *My grace is sufficient for thee, for virtue is made perfect in weakness.* What virtue? Let the same apostle answer, *Most gladly therefore will I rather glory in my infirmities, that the virtue of Christ may rest upon me.* But perhaps you do not quite understand what virtue he was particularly referring to, since Christ had all virtues. While he did have all, yet one in particular he commends to us in himself, namely humility, saying, *Learn of me, for I am meek and lowly in heart.*

26. Most gladly, therefore, will I too, Lord Jesus, glory, if I may, in my infirmity, in the withering of my sinew, in order that thy virtue, namely humility, may be made perfect in me. For thy grace is sufficient for me, when my virtue has failed. Attaching my feeble feet firmly to grace, and slowly drawing them up, I will safely climb the ladder of humility, until, clinging to truth, I come to the fields of love. Then will I sing a song of thanksgiving and say, *Thou hast set my feet in a large room.* Thus straitly and cautiously we advance along the narrow way; thus securely, step by step, we climb the steep ladder; thus haltingly, slow but sure, we miraculously draw near to truth. But *woe is me, that my sojourning is prolonged! Oh that I had wings like a dove,* that I might fly away faster to truth, and be at rest in love! But since I have not, *teach me thy way, O Lord; I will walk in thy truth;* and the truth shall make me free. Alas that I ever descended from it! (50) Had I not first descended easily and foolishly, I would not have toiled so long and so hard in ascending. But why do I say I descended? I should say rather that I fell. Unless,

graviter non laborassem. Sed quid dico, Descendi? nam fortasse rectius Cecidi dixerim.ᵃ Nisi quia forte sicut nemo repente fit summus, sed gradatim quisque ascendit; sic nemo repente fit pessimus, sed paulatim descendit. Alioquin quomodo stabit illud: *Impius cunctis diebus vitae suae superbit?*⁶ Denique sunt viae, quae videntur hominibus bonae, et tamen ad malum deducunt.⁷

27. Est ergo via descensionis, sicut et ascensionis. Et via est ad bonum, et via est ad malum. Cave malam, elige bonam. Si per te non potes, ora cum propheta, et dic: *Viam iniquitatis amove a me.* Quomodo? *Et lege tua miserere mei;* illa scilicet lege, quam dedisti delinquentibus in via,¹ id est derelinquentibus veritatem, de quibus unus ego sum, qui vere a veritate cecidi. Sed numquid qui cadit, non adjiciet ut resurgat? ² Propter hoc *viam veritatis elegi,*³ qua humiliatus ascendam, unde superbiendo descendi. Ascendam, inquam, et psallam: *Bonum mihi, Domine, quod humiliasti me; bonum mihi lex oris tui super millia auri et argenti.*⁴ Duas tibi vias videtur David proposuisse, sed unam noveris esse; ipsam tamen a se diversam, et diversis nominibus appellatam, aut *iniquitatis* propter descendentes, aut *veritatis* propter ascendentes: quia et iidem gradus sunt ascendentium in solium, et descendentium; et eadem via accedentium ad civitatem, et recedentium; et unum ostium est ingredientium domum, et egredientium. Per unam denique scalam ascendentes Angeli, et descendentes Jacob apparuerunt.⁵ Quo spectant haec? Ut videlicet si ad veritatem redire cupis, non necesse sit viam quaerere novam quam non nosti, sed notam qua descendisti: quatenus reciprocis gressibus tua ipse vestigia sequens, per eosdem gradus humiliatus ascendas, per quos superbiendo descenderas: ita ut qui duodecimus superbiae fuit descendenti, primus humilitatis sit ascendenti; undecimus, inveniatur secundus; decimus, tertius;

ᵃ *Cecidi dixerim,* Mab.; *dixerim et "cecidi,"* Ed. Cant. et unum MS.
⁶ Job 15. 20.   ⁷ Prov. 14. 12.

¹ Ps. 24. 8.   ⁸ Ps. 118. 29, 30.
² Jer. 8. 4.   ⁴ Ps. 118. 71, 72.   ⁵ Gen. 28. 12.

perhaps, because, just as no one reaches the summit suddenly, but each one ascends step by step, so no one reaches the bottom suddenly but descends little by little. Otherwise how can it be that *the wicked man is proud all his days?* There are ways, in short, which seem good to men, but they lead to destruction.

27. There is then a way down and a way up, a way to the good and a way to evil. Shun the evil one, choose the good one. If you cannot do so of yourself, pray with the prophet and say, *Remove from me the way of lying.* How? *And grant me thy law graciously;* that law namely which thou hast given to the abandoned in the way, who have abandoned truth, and one of whom am I, surely fallen from truth. But shall not he who falls endeavor to rise again? This is why *I have chosen the way of truth*, by which I shall go up in humility thither whence I came down in pride. I shall go up, I say, singing, *It is good for me, O Lord, that I have been humbled. The law of thy mouth is better unto me than thousands of gold and silver.* David seems to have offered you two ways, but you know there is only one. Yet it is distinguished from itself and is called by different names, either *the way of lying* for those going down, or *the way of truth* for those going up. The same steps lead up to the throne and down; the same road leads to the city and from it; one door is the entrance of the house and the exit; Jacob saw the angels ascending and descending on the same ladder. What does all this mean? Simply that if you desire to return to truth, you do not have to seek a new way which you know not, but the known way by which you descended. Retracing your own path, you may ascend in humility by the same steps which you descended in pride, so that what was the twelfth step of pride going down is the first step of humility going up; the eleventh is found second; the tenth, third; the ninth, fourth; the eighth, fifth; the seventh, sixth; the sixth, seventh; the fifth, eighth; the fourth,

nonus, quartus; octavus, quintus; septimus, sextus; sextus, septimus; quintus, octavus; quartus, nonus; tertius, decimus; secundus, undecimus; primus, duodecimus. Quibus superbiae gradibus in te inventis, imo recognitis, jam non laboras in quaerendo viam humilitatis.

ninth; the third, tenth; the second, eleventh; and the first, twelfth. When these steps of pride are discovered or rather remembered in yourself, there is no difficulty in finding the way of humility.

CAPUT 10

DE PRIMO SUPERBIAE GRADU, QUI EST
CURIOSITAS

28. Primus itaque superbiae gradus est curiositas. Hanc autem talibus indiciis deprehendes. Si videris monachum, de quo prius bene confidebas, ubicumque stat, ambulat, sedet, oculis incipientem vagari, caput erectum, aures portare suspensas; e motibus exterioris ª hominis interiorem immutatum agnoscas. Vir quippe perversus *annuit oculo, terit pede, digito loquitur*; [1] et ex insolenti corporis motu, recens animae morbus deprehenditur: quam, dum a sui circumspectione torpescit, incuria sui curiosam in alios facit. Quia enim se ipsam ignorat, foras mittitur, ut haedos pascat.[2] Haedos quippe, qui peccatum significant, recte oculos auresque appellaverim: quoniam sicut mors per peccatum in orbem,[3] sic per has fenestras intrat ad mentem. In his ergo pascendis se occupat curiosus, dum scire non curat qualem se reliquerit intus. Et vere si te vigilanter, homo, attendas, mirum est si ad aliud unquam intendas. Audi, curiose, Salomonem; audi, stulte, Sapientem. *Omni custodia*, inquit, *custodi cor tuum*: ut omnes videlicet sensus tui vigilent ad id, unde *vita procedit*,[4] custodiendum. Quo enim a te, o curiose, recedis? cui te interim committis? Utquid audes oculos levare ad coelum,[5] qui peccasti in coelum? Terram intuere, ut cognoscas te ipsum. Ipsa te tibi repraesentabit, *quia terra es, et in terram ibis.*[6]

29. Duabus tamen causis inculpabiliter oculos levas, ut vel petas auxilium, vel impendas. Levavit oculos suos David in montes, ut peteret:[1] levavit et Dominus super turbas, ut

---

ª *exterioris*, Mab.; *exterioribus*, Ed. Cant. sine nota.
[1] Prov. 6. 13.   [3] Rom. 5. 12.   [5] Luc. 18. 13.
[2] Cant. 1. 7.   [4] Prov. 4. 23.   [6] Gen. 3. 19 (Vet. Lat.).

[1] Ps. 120. 1.

CHAPTER 10

THE FIRST STEP OF PRIDE, CURIOSITY [51]

28. The first step of pride, then, is curiosity, and you may recognize it by these marks. If you shall see a monk, whom you formerly trusted confidently, beginning to roam with his eyes, hold his head erect, prick up his ears, wherever he is standing, walking, sitting; you may know the changed inner man from the movements of the outer. For a wicked man *winketh with his eyes, speaketh with his feet, teacheth with his fingers*; and the strange movement of the body reveals a new disease in the soul, which has tired of introspection and which neglect of self makes curious toward others. For, as it knows not itself, it is sent forth to feed its kids. I shall rightly have called the eyes and ears kids, which signify sin; for just as death enters into the world by sin, so by these windows it enters into the mind. The curious man, therefore, occupies himself with feeding these, no longer curious to know how he has left himself within. And it would be strange indeed, O man, if while watchfully attending thyself thou shouldst likewise be extending thyself to aught else. Hearken to Solomon, thou curious fellow; hearken to the wise man, thou fool. *Keep thy heart*, he says, *with all diligence*; let all thy senses be alert for keeping that out of which *are the issues of life*. For whither wilt thou withdraw from thyself, thou curious fellow? To whom wilt thou commit thyself meanwhile? How dost thou dare lift thy eyes to heaven, when thou hast sinned against heaven? Look at the earth in order to know thyself. Only it will show thee an image of thyself, *for dust thou art, and unto dust shalt thou return*.

29. There are two reasons, however, for which you may lift up your eyes without reproach, namely, to seek help or to offer it. David lifted up his eyes unto the hills, to seek it; and the Lord lifted up his over the multitude, to offer it. The one

impenderet.² Alter miserabiliter, alter misericorditer, ambo inculpabiliter. Tu quoque si locum, tempus et causam considerans, tua vel fratris necessitate oculos levas; non solum non culpo, sed et plurimum laudo. Hoc enim excusat miseria, illud commendat misericordia. Sin alias, non Prophetae, non Domini, sed Dinae aut Evae, imo ipsius satanae imitatorem te dixerim. Dina namque dum ad pascendos haedos egreditur, ipsa patri, et sua sibi virginitas rapitur.³ O Dina, quid necesse est ut videas mulieres alienigenas? Qua necessitate? qua utilitate? An sola curiositate? Etsi tu otiose vides, sed non otiose videris. Tu curiose spectas, sed curiosius spectaris. Quis crederet tunc illam tuam curiosam otiositatem, vel otiosam curiositatem, fore post sic non otiosam, sed tibi, tuis, hostibusque tam perniciosam?

30. Tu quoque, o Eva, in paradiso posita es, ut cum viro tuo opereris et custodias illum: si injunctum perfeceris, quandoque transitura ad melius, ubi nec opus sit te in aliquo opere occupari, nec de custodia sollicitari. Omne lignum paradisi ad vescendum tibi conceditur, praeter illud, quod dicitur *scientiae boni et mali.*¹ Si enim caetera bona sunt, et sapiunt bonum, quid opus est edere de ligno, quod sapit etiam malum? *Non plus sapere, quam oportet sapere.*² Sapere enim malum, sapere non est, sed desipere. Serva ergo commissum, exspecta promissum; cave prohibitum, ne perdas concessum. Quid tuam mortem tam intente intueris? Quid illo tam crebro vagantia lumina jacis? Quid spectare libet, quod manducare non licet? Oculos, inquis, tendo, non manum. Non est interdictum ne videam, sed ne comedam. An non licet oculos quo volo levare, quos Deus in mea posuit potestate? Ad quod Apostolus: *Omnia mihi licent, sed non omnia expediunt.*³ Etsi culpa non est, culpae tamen indicium est. Nisi enim mens minus se curiose servaret, tua curiositas tempus vacuum non haberet. Etsi culpa non est, culpae tamen occasio est, et indicium com-

---

² Joan. 6. 5.   ³ Gen. 34. 1, 2.

¹ Gen. 2. 15–17.
² Rom. 12. 3.   ³ 1 Cor. 6. 12.

pitiably, the other pitifully, both blamelessly. If you also, considering the time, place, and cause, lift up your eyes because of your own or your brother's necessity, not only I do not condemn but I highly approve. For affliction excuses the one, while affection commends the other. But if for any other reason, then I will call you an imitator not of the prophet or the Lord but of Dinah or Eve or even Satan. For when Dinah goes out to feed her kids, her father loses his maid and she her maidenhood. O Dinah, why must thou go out to see the daughters of the land? What is the need? What is the use? Mere curiosity? Though thou seest them idly, thou art not idly seen. Thou lookest curiously, but art looked at more curiously. Who would then suppose that this curious idleness or idle curiosity would prove to be not idle but suicidal for thee, thy friends, and thy foes?

30. Thou too, O Eve, wast put into the Garden of Eden *to dress it and to keep it* with thy husband; destined, hadst thou fulfilled thy task, to pass on to a better, where there should be no need for thee to be occupied with any dressing or concerned with any keeping. Every tree of the garden is given thee to eat, save that which is called *of the knowledge of good and evil*. For if the others are good and of good sapor, why eat of the tree which has also the sapor of evil? *Not to be more sapient than it behoveth to be sapient*. For to be sapient of evil is not to be sapient but to be insipid. So keep the trust, trusting in the promise; forsake the forbidden, lest thou lose the allowed. Why regard so intently thy bane? Why cast wandering glances so frequently thither? Why does sight of it delight thee, when to bite is not allowed thee? It is my eyes, thou sayest, not my hand, which I reach out. Nor am I forbidden to see, but to eat. May I not lift up whither I will the eyes which God has placed in my power? To which the Apostle says: *All things are lawful unto me, but all things are not expedient*. Though it be no crime, yet it is the mark of a crime. For were not thy mind too careless of itself, thou wouldst have no free time for curiosity. Though it be no crime, yet it is the occasion of crime, the mark of one com-

missae, et causa est committendae. Te enim intenta ad aliud, latenter interim in cor tuum serpens illabitur, blande alloqui- tur. Blanditiis rationem, mendaciis timorem compescit, *Nequa- quam*, inquiens, *morieris*.⁴ Auget curam, dum incitat gulam: acuit curiositatem, dum suggerit cupiditatem. Offert tandem prohibitum, et aufert concessum: porrigit pomum, et surripit paradisum. Hauris virus peritura, et perituros paritura. Perit salus, non destitit partus. Nascimur, morimur: ideoque nasci- mur morituri, quia prius morimur nascituri. Propterea grave jugum super omnes filios tuos usque in hodiernum diem.

31. Sed et *tu*, *signaculum similitudinis*, non in paradiso, sed *in deliciis paradisi Dei* positus es.¹ Quid amplius quaerere debes? Plenus ergo sapientia, et perfectus decore, altiora te ne quaesieris, et fortiora te ne scrutatus fueris. Sta in te, ne cadas a te, si ambulas in magnis et in mirabilibus super te. Sed quid interim ex obliquo intendis ad aquilonem? Jam te video, jam te perspicio nescio quae supra te curiosius alta rimantem. *Ponam*, inquis, *sedem meam ad aquilonem*.² Caeteris astantibus coelicolis, dum tu sedere solus affectas, fratrum concordiam, totius coelestis patriae pacem, ipsius, quantum in te est, quietem Trinitatis infestas. Quo te tua, miser, curiositas ducit, ut prae- sumptione singulari non dubites civibus scandalum, injuriam facere Regi? *Millia millium ministrant ei, et decies centena millia assistunt ei*,³ ubi nemo sedere perhibetur, nisi solus is qui sedet super Cherubim,⁴ cui a caeteris ministratur: et tu nescio quae prae caeteris differentius prospiciendo, curiosius in- quirendo, irreverentius pervadendo, sedem tibi collocas in coelo, ut sis similis Altissimo? Quo fine? qua fiducia? Metire, insipiens, vires, pensa finem, excogita modum. Sciente hoc Altissimo praesumis,⁵ an nesciente? volente, an nolente? Sed quomodo malum quodcumque machinaris, aut velle, aut ignorare potest, cujus optima voluntas, cujus perfecta scientia

⁴ Gen. 3. 4.

¹ Ezec. 28. 12, 13.
² Is. 14. 13 (Vet. Lat.).   ⁴ Ps. 79. 2.
⁸ Dan. 7. 10.   ⁵ Judith 6. 15.

mitted and the cause of one to be committed. For while thou art intent on something else, the serpent meanwhile glides secretly into thy heart, speaking seductively. He blunts thy reason with blandishments and allays thy fear with lies, saying, *Ye shall not surely die*. Inciting thy greed, he aggravates thy need; exciting cupidity, he sharpens curiosity. He gives thee what thou wast forbidden to take and takes away all thou wast bidden to keep; he presents thee with fruit and prevents thee from paradise. Thou drinkest the venom, doomed to be mortal and mother of mortals. Thou hast lost deliverance but not delivery. We are born and die; and we are born mortal because we are in mortal sin before we are born.[52] And thus it is a grievous burden on all thy children even to the present day.

31. And thou, O *seal of resemblance*, wast put not in the garden but *in the pleasures of the paradise of God*. What further shouldst thou seek? Full of wisdom, therefore, and perfect in beauty, seek not what is above thee nor search out that which is too great for thee. Stay in thyself, lest thou fall from thyself, if thou wander among the great and marvelous things above thee. But why dost thou keep edging toward the north? Now I see thee, now I perceive thee scrutinizing too curiously all manner of lofty things above thee. *I will establish my seat in the north*, thou sayest. Thou, alone presuming to sit, while the other angels stand, art disturbing the concord of brethren, the peace of the whole celestial kingdom, the security of the Trinity itself, so far as in thee lies. Whither is thy curiosity leading thee, that thou dost not hesitate to attack the king and scandalize his subjects with such strange presumption, O unhappy one? *Thousand thousands minister unto him, and ten thousand times ten thousand stand before him*, and none sits, save only he *that sittest upon the cherubims*, that is ministered unto by the others; and thou, contemplating so arrogantly, investigating so curiously, approaching so irreverently those unknown things beyond what the others see, art establishing thy seat in heaven, that thou mayest be like the most High. To what end? Relying on what? Measure thy

est? Numquid autem et scire, et nolle non dubitas, sed non posse resistere putas? At vero nisi te conditum esse dubitaveris, dubitare te non crediderim de omnipotentia, sive de omnimoda scientia ac bonitate Conditoris, qui te de nihilo potuit, talem scivit, tantum condere voluit. Quomodo ergo Deum consentire aestimas, quod fieri nolit, ac refellere possit? An forte in te video compleri, imo a te initiari, quod post te, ac per te a tui similibus in terris frequentatum solet vulgariter dici: Privatus dominus temerarios nutrit? *An oculus tuus nequam est, quia ille bonus?* [6] De cujus bonitate dum fiduciam nefariam sumis, factus es et contra scientiam impudens, et contra potentiam audax.

32. Hoc est enim, o impie, hoc est quod cogitas; haec est iniquitas, quam meditaris in cubili tuo,[1] et dicis: Putas Creator opus suum destruat? Scio quidem quia non latet Deum qualiscumque cogitatio mea: Deus enim est. Nec placet ei talis cogitatio mea, quia bonus est. Sed nec si velit, ego effugiam manus ejus, quia potens est. Numquid tamen mihi timendum est? Si enim cum bonus sit, non potest illi placere meum malum, quanto minus suum? Meum quippe dixerim contra ejus voluntatem aliquid velle: suum autem, si vindicet sese. Tam ergo quodcumque scelus non valet velle ulcisci, quam nec vult, nec valet sua bonitate privari. Fallis te, miser, fallis te, non Deum. Te, inquam, fallis, et mentitur iniquitas sibi,[2] non Deo. Dolose quidem agis, sed in conspectu ejus. Te ergo fallis, non Deum. Et quia de magno ejus bono in te, tu magnum in eum excogitas malum, merito iniquitas tua invenitur ad odium.[3] Quae namque major iniquitas, quam ut inde Creator a te contemnatur, unde plus amari merebatur? Quae major iniquitas, quam cum de potentia Dei non dubites, quin [a] te scilicet destruere possit qui condere potuit; confisus tamen de multa ejus dulcedine, qua speras eum nolle vindicare cum possit; mala pro bonis, odium retribuas pro dilectione? [4]

[6] Matth. 20. 15.

[a] *quin*, Mab.; *qui*, Ed. Cant. sine nota.
[1] Ps. 35. 5.
[2] Ps. 26. 12.
[3] Ps. 35. 3.
[4] Ps. 108. 5.

strength, O fool; weigh the end; consider the means. Art thou thus presuming with the knowledge of the most High, or without? With his approval, or without? But how can he either approve or not know any evil thou mayest hatch, he whose will is always good, whose knowledge is perfect? Or perhaps, not doubting that he knows and disapproves, thou believest that he is unable to resist? But unless indeed thou doubtest thy creation, I do not believe thou hast any doubt of the omnipotence or of the infinite knowledge and goodness of the Creator who had the power, the skill, and the will to create thee from nothing. How then dost thou suppose that God will allow that which he disapproves and is able to prevent? Perhaps I see fulfilled in thee, in fact originated by thee, a common maxim often used after thee and with thy aid by thy disciples on earth: A familiar master breeds contemptuous servants.[53] *Is thine eye evil because he is good?* Impious confidence in his goodness makes thee oppose his omniscience with impudence and his omnipotence with recklessness.

32. For this, O accursed one, this is what thou ponderest; this is the mischief which thou devisest upon thy bed, saying: Do you think the Creator will destroy his own work? I know indeed that my every thought is evident to him, for he is God. Nor can this thought of mine be acceptable to him, for he is good. Nor shall I escape his hand, if he so wills, for he has power. And yet need I to be afraid? For if my evil act cannot be pleasing to him, since he is good, how much less can his own! It would be mine to oppose his will; but his, if he should avenge himself. Therefore he is unable to wish to be revenged for any crime, insofar as he is unwilling and unable to be deprived of his own goodness. Thou deceivest thyself, unhappy one; thou deceivest thyself, not God. Thou deceivest, I say, thyself, and thine iniquity lies to itself, not to God. Thou art doing deceitfully, but in his sight. Therefore thou deceivest thyself, not God. And, because from his great goodness to thee thou art devising a great evil to him, thy iniquity is truly found to be hateful. For what greater iniquity, than that the

33. Haec, inquam, iniquitas, non ira momentanea, sed odio digna est sempiterno, qua tuo dulcissimo et altissimo Domino, licet invito, desideras tamen ac speras aequari, quatenus semper videat quod doleat, dum te socium habeat cum nolit, nec dejiciat cum possit; quin potius eligat ipse dolere, quam te patiatur perire. Possit quidem dejicere si velit, sed prae dulcedine, ut aestimas, velle non possit. Certe si talis est qualem putas, tanto nequius agis, si non amas. Et si ille aliquid fieri patitur contra se potius, quam ipse aliquid faciat contra te; quanta malitia est, ut vel tu non parcas illi, qui sibi non parcit, parcendo tibi? Absit tamen ab ejus perfectione, ut quia dulcis est, justus non sit, quasi simul dulcis et justus esse non possit: cum melior sit justa dulcedo, quam remissa; imo virtus non sit dulcedo sine justitia. Quia igitur gratuitae Dei bonitati, qua gratis factus es, ingratus existis, justitiam vero quam expertus non es, non metuis; ideoque audacter committis culpam, de qua tibi falso promittis impunitatem: jam ecce justum senties, quem bonum nosti, cadens in foveam, quam paras auctori: ut dum scilicet talem in eum poenam machinaris, qua tamen valeat carere si velit, sed ut putas non valeat velle; et ideo nec carere ea utique bonitate, qua neminem expertus es illum punisse: talem justus Deus justissime in te retorqueat poenam, qui nec valet, nec debet pati suam impune bonitatem offendi: sic utique temperans in vindicta sententiam, ut, si velis resipiscere, non neget veniam; secundum tamen duritiam tuam et cor impoenitens,[1] non possis velle, et ideo nec poena carere.

[1] Rom. 2. 5.

Creator should be despised by thee for that very reason for which he deserves to be loved the more? What greater iniquity, than that, when thou hast no doubt of God's power, that he who could create can destroy thee, yet trusting in his loving-kindness, because of which thou hopest that he will refuse to take the vengeance he can, thou returnest *evil for good, and hatred for love*.

33. This iniquity, I say, deserves not passing wrath but everlasting hate,[54] when thou yearnest and hopest to be made equal to thy most loving and lofty Lord, even against his will, so that he would forever have before his eyes a cause for grief, having thee for a peer although unwilling, and not casting thee down although able, but choosing rather to be grieved himself than to suffer thee to perish. He could indeed cast thee down if he so willed, but because of his loving-kindness, thou thinkest, he cannot so will. Surely if he is such as thou believest, thou art acting all the more vilely in not loving him. And if he suffers anything to be done against himself rather than do anything against thee, how great is thy wickedness in not sparing him who does not spare himself in sparing thee! But far be it from his perfection that, because he is kind, he should not be just; as if he could not be both kind and just together, since a just is better than an indulgent kindness; indeed, kindness without justice is not a virtue at all. Because thou art ungrateful for God's gracious goodness, by grace of which thou wast made, thou dost not fear the justice thou hast not learned to know, and so thou sinnest boldly, falsely promising thyself impunity. But now behold, thou fallest into the pit destined for its own maker, and learnest that he whom thou knewest to be good is also just. For the injury which thou contrivest for him, which he could avoid if he so willed, yet in thy belief could not so will without losing that very goodness by which, as thou knewest, he had never punished anyone; that injury the just God most justly turns back upon thee, for he neither can nor should suffer his goodness to be blasphemed with impunity. He so softens the sentence of punishment that, shouldst thou wish to recover

34. Sed jam audi calumniam: *Coelum*, inquit, *mihi sedes est, terra autem scabellum pedum meorum*.[1] Non dixit, Oriens, aut Occidens, aut Una aliqua coeli plaga: sed, Totum coelum mihi sedes est. Non potes ergo in parte sedere coeli, cum ille totum elegerit sibi. In terra non potes, quia scabellum pedum ejus est. Terra etenim locus solidus est, ubi sedet Ecclesia, fundata supra firmam petram. Quid facies? E coelo pulsus, in terris remanere non potes. Elige ergo tibi in aere [2] locum, non ad sedendum, sed ad volandum: ut qui tentasti concutere statum aeternitatis, poenam sentias propriae fluctuationis. Te ergo fluctuante inter coelum et terram, sedet Dominus *super solium excelsum et elevatum*,[3] et plena est omnis terra majestate ejus, ut nusquam nisi in aere invenias locum.

35. Seraphim namque aliis quidem alis suae contemplationis de throno ad scabellum, de scabello ad thronum volantia, aliis caput Domini pedesque velantia,[a][1] ad hoc ibi posita puto, ut sicut peccanti homini paradisi per Cherubin prohibetur ingressus, ita et per Seraphin tuae curiositati modus imponatur: quatenus nec coeli jam magis impudenter, quam prudenter arcana rimeris, nec Ecclesiae mysteria cognoscas in terris; sed solis contentus sis cordibus superborum, qui nec in terra esse dignantur sicut caeteri hominum, nec sicut Angeli volant ad coelum. Licet vero et caput in coelo, et pedes in terra a te abscondantur; quiddam tamen tibi medium videndum ad invidendum duntaxat permittitur: dum suspensus in aere, descendentes quidem per te, et ascendentes Angelos intueris; sed quid vel audiant in coelis, vel nuntient terris,[b] penitus nescis.

36. O Lucifer, qui mane oriebaris, imo non jam lucifer, sed noctifer, aut etiam mortifer, rectus cursus tuus erat ab oriente ad meridiem, et tu praepostero ordine tendis ad aquilonem? Quanto magis ad alta festinas, tanto celerius ad occasum declinas. Velim tamen curiosius, o curiose, intentionem tuae curiositatis inquirere. *Ponam*, inquis, *sedem meam ad aquilo-*

---

[1] Is. 66. 1.   [2] Eph. 2. 2.   [3] Is. 6. 1.

[a] *velantia*, Mab.; *volantia*, Ed. Cant. sine nota.
[b] *terris*, Mab.; *in terris*, Ed. Cant. sine nota.   [1] Is. 6. 2.

thyself, he will not refuse forgiveness; but after thy hardness and impenitent heart thou canst not so wish, and so thou canst not escape from thy punishment either.

34. But now see how thou art restricted. *The heaven*, he says, *is my throne, and the earth is my footstool.* He does not say, the East, or the West, or any one quarter of heaven; but, all heaven is my throne. Therefore thou canst not sit in any region of heaven, since he has taken it all for himself. Nor on earth either, because it is his footstool. For the earth is a solid body, where the Church is set, founded upon a firm rock. What shalt thou do? Expelled from heaven, thou canst not remain on earth. Take therefore a place in the air, not to sit on but to fly in, so that thou who didst attempt to shake the eternal mayest feel thy own volatility as requital. While thou, therefore, art vacillating between heaven and earth, the Lord is sitting *upon a throne, high and lifted up*, and the whole earth is full of his glory, so that thou canst find a place only in the air.

35. For the seraphim, flying from the throne to the footstool and from the footstool to the throne on wings of contemplation and covering the face and the feet of the Lord with their other wings, were so placed, I think, in order that, just as the entrance to paradise is forbidden to sinful man by cherubim, so a bound may be set to thy curiosity by seraphim. Thus thou canst neither search out the secrets of heaven, more maliciously than judiciously, nor learn the mysteries of the Church on earth; but canst dwell only in the hearts of the proud, who neither deign to live on earth like other men, nor fly to heaven like angels. Both head in heaven and feet on earth are hidden from thee. As to what is between, thou mayest behold but not be told; suspended in the air thou seest the angels descending and ascending by thee, but what they hear in the heavens or announce to the lands thou knowest not at all.

36. O Lucifer, thou who wast wont to rise at dawn, now no longer a herald of light, but of night and of death, thy proper orbit was from the east to the south. And dost thou

nem.[1] Nec aquilonem hunc corporalem, nec sedem hanc (cum sis spiritus) intelligo materialem. Puto autem per *aquilonem*, reprobandos homines fuisse designatos; per *sedem*, potestatem in illos. Quos utique in praescientia Dei, quanto ei vicinior, tanto caeteris perspicacior praevidens, nullo quidem sapientiae radio coruscantes, nullo spiritus amore ferventes, velut vacuum repereris locum, affectasti super illos dominium, quos quadam tuae astutiae claritate perfunderes, tuae malitiae aestibus inflammares: ut quomodo Altissimus sua sapientia ac bonitate omnibus filiis obedientiae[2] praeerat, ita et tu super omnes filios superbiae rex[3] constitutus, tua eos astuta malitia, ac maliosa astutia regeres, per quod Altissimo similis esses. Sed miror cum in praescientia Dei tuum praevideris [a] principatum, cur non in eadem praevidisti et praecipitium? Nam si praevidisti, quae insania fuit, ut cum tanta miseria cuperes principari, ut malles misere praeesse, quam feliciter subesse? Aut non expediebat participem esse plagarum illarum luminosarum, quam principem tenebrarum harum? Sed credibilius est, quod non praevidisti: aut propter illam causam, quam superius dixi, quia [b] Dei bonitatem attendens, dixisti in corde tuo, *Non requiret*,[4] propter quod, o impie, Deum irritasti; aut quia viso principatu, in oculo statim superbiae trabes excrevit, qua interposita casum videre non potuit.

37. Sic Joseph cum suam praevidisset exaltationem,[1] non tamen praescivit sui venditionem, quamvis propior esset venditio, quam exaltatio. Non quod tantum patriarcham in superbiam crediderim incidisse: sed ut ejus exemplo pateat, quod hi qui futura praevident per spiritum prophetiae, etsi non omnia, non ideo tamen [a] putandi sunt nulla vidisse. Quod si quis contendat in eo quod sua somnia adhuc adolescentulus narrabat,

---

[a] *praevideris*, Mab.; *provideris*, Ed. Cant. sine nota.
[b] *quia*, Mab.; *quin*, Ed. Cant. sine nota.
[1] Is. 14. 13 (Vet. Lat.).   [3] Job 41. 25.
[2] 1 Pet. 1. 14.   [4] Ps. 10 sec. Heb. 13.

---

[a] *tamen*, Mab.; deest in Ed. Cant. sine nota.
[1] Gen. 37. 6–9.

turn toward the north in an unnatural course? The more thou hastenest in rising, the quicker thou fallest in setting. Yet I should like to search out more curiously the purpose of thy curiosity, thou curious one. *I will establish my seat in the north*, thou sayest. I do not believe this north to be physical or this seat material, for thou art a spirit. But I interpret *the north* to mean sinful men, and *seat*, power over them. Such men thou couldst indeed foresee in God's prescience, so much more clearly than others as thou wast nearer to him. None of them was radiant with flashes of wisdom, none of them burned with spiritual love. As if finding an empty place, thou didst assume dominion over those whom thou couldst imbue with the brilliance of thy cunning and inflame with the warmth of thy malice, so that, just as the most High, by his wisdom and goodness, was lord of all the children of obedience, so might thou be made a king over all the children of pride, ruling them by thy cunning malice and malicious cunning, and in that way be like the most High. But I wonder why, when thou didst prophesy thy principality through God's prescience, thou didst not likewise prophesy thy precipitate fall. For if thou didst foresee it, what madness was it that thou shouldst wish to rule in such great wretchedness, preferring preeminence in misery to subjection in felicity? Were it not better to be a citizen of those luminous lands than lord of the land of darkness? But it is more likely that thou didst not foresee it; either for that reason which I mentioned above, because, considering God's goodness, thou hast said in thy heart, *Thou wilt not require it*, wherefore, O wicked one, thou hast contemned God; or else because, thy sovereignty foreseen, immediately the beam of pride grew out in thy eye, which, thus blinded, could not see thy fall.

37. Thus Joseph foresaw his exaltation but not his enslavement, though the enslavement was nearer than the exaltation. Not that I would suspect so great a patriarch of having fallen into pride; but let it appear from his case that those who foresee the future through the spirit of prophecy, even if they do not see all, should not be thought to have seen

quorum tunc mysterium ignorabat, vanitatem posse notari;
ego tamen mysterio magis sive simplicitati pueri deputandum
arbitror, quam vanitati. Quae tamen, si qua fuit, per ea quae
passus legitur, potuit expiari. Nonnullis enim aliqua aliquando
de se per revelationem jucunda monstrantur, quae etsi humanus
animus absque ulla vanitate scire non potest, non minus ideo
eveniet quod monstratum est; sic tamen ut illa vanitas im-
punita non sit, qua de magnitudine aut revelationis [2] aut pro-
missionis in se vel leviter exsultavit. Sicut enim medicus, non
solum unguento, sed et igne utitur et ferro, quo omne quod
in vulnere sanando superfluum excreverit, secet et urat, ne
~~sanitatem,~~ quae ex unguento procedit, impediat: sic medicus
animarum Deus hujusmodi animae procurat tentationes, im-
mittit tribulationes, quibus afflicta et humiliata, gaudium vertat
in luctum, revelationem putet illusionem. Unde fit ut et
vanitate careat, et veritas revelationis non pereat. Sic Pauli
extollentia per stimulos carnis reprimitur,[3] et ipse revelationibus crebris attolitur. Sic Zachariae infidelitas linguae obliga-
tione mulctatur,[4] et angeli veritas suo in tempore manifestanda
non mutatur. Sic, sic *per gloriam et ignobilitatem* [5] sancti
proficiunt, dum inter singularia dona quae recipiunt, communi
hominum vanitate pulsari se sentiunt: ut dum per gratiam
supra se aliquid cernunt, non obliviscantur quod sunt.

38. Sed quid de revelationibus ad curiositatem? De quibus
ut haec per excessum intermiscerem, inde sumpta occasio est,
cum ostendere vellem, reprobum angelum ante casum suum
sic potuisse praevidere illam, quam post accepit, in reprobos
homines dominationem, ut tamen suam non praesciret damna-
tionem. De quo etiam nonnullis quaestiunculis motis magis,
quam solutis, totius disputatiunculae haec summa sit: quod
per curiositatem a veritate ceciderit, quia prius spectavit curiose, quod affectavit illicite, speravit praesumptuose. Jure

nothing. Some may claim that vanity can be observed in the fact that, as a mere boy, he was telling his dreams, the hidden meaning of which he did not then understand; but I should say that it is to be attributed to their strangeness or to his boyish innocence rather than to any feeling of vanity. But if there was any, it was atoned for by what he is said to have suffered. For sometimes good tidings about himself are revealed to a man, which, though human nature cannot hear them without some feeling of vanity, none the less come true; yet in such a way that the vanity in which he has exulted even a little through the abundance of the revelation or promise does not go unpunished. For as a physician uses not only an ointment but also fire and knife to cut out and burn all superfluous matter which has grown up in the wound he is healing, lest it hinder the healing effect of the ointment; so God the physician of souls afflicts with temptations, inflicts tribulations on such a soul, which is so cast down and humbled by them that its joy turns to grief and it thinks the revelation a mockery. In this way the vanity is lost and the truth of the revelation is saved. Thus Paul's exaltation proceeds with frequent revelations, while his exultation is checked by a thorn in the flesh. Thus Zacharias is tongue-tied for his lack of faith, while the angel's unchangeable words come true in their own time. Thus, thus it is that saints progress *by honor and dishonor* when, because of their peculiar gifts, they feel themselves disturbed by vulgar vanity. And so, although they see through grace a something higher than themselves, they still remember what they are.

38. But what has revelation to do with curiosity? The opportunity arose to interpolate this discussion of it by way of digression when I wanted to show how the bad angel before his fall might have foreseen that domination over bad men which he later obtained, without however foreknowing his damnation. A few little questions about this have been raised rather than solved; and this is the whole matter in a nutshell: through curiosity he fell from truth, because he first curiously observed what he then unlawfully coveted and

igitur in gradibus superbiae primum curiositas vindicat sibi, quae etiam inventa est initium omnis esse peccati.[1] Sed nisi haec citius cohibeatur, in levitatem animi, quae secundus gradus est, cito delabitur.

[1] Ecclus. 10. 15.

boldly aspired to. Curiosity therefore rightly claims first place among the steps of pride, for it is shown to be the beginning of all sin. But it will quickly fall, unless more quickly checked, into frivolity, which is the second step.

CAPUT 11

DE SECUNDO GRADU SUPERBIAE, QUI EST LEVITAS ANIMI

39. Monachus enim, qui sui negligens, alios curiose circumspicit, dum quosdam suspicit superiores, quosdam despicit inferiores: et in aliis quidem videt quod invidet, in aliis quod irridet. Inde fit ut pro mobilitate oculorum levigatus animus, nulla utique sui cura aggravatus, modo per superbiam ad alta se erigat, modo per invidiam in ima demergat: nunc per invidiam nequiter tabescit, nunc pro excellentia pueriliter hilarescit. In altero nequam, in altero vanus, in utroque superbus existit: quia et quod superari se dolet, et quod superare se gaudet, amor propriae excellentiae facit. Has autem animi vicissitudines nunc pauca et mordacia, nunc multa et inania; nunc risu, nunc luctu plena, semper vero irrationabilia indicant verba. Compara, si vis, hos duos primos superbiae gradus summis duobus humilitatis: et vide si non in ultimo curiositas, in penultimo levitas cohibetur. Id ipsum in caeteris reperies, si alterutrum comparentur. Sed jam ad tertium docendo, non descendendo veniamus.

CHAPTER 11

THE SECOND STEP OF PRIDE, FRIVOLITY [55]

39. For the monk who neglects himself to become curious about other men, respects some as superior, rejects others as inferior; sees in some cause for envy, in others cause for ridicule. Thus it comes about that the soul, made frivolous by its wandering eyes and not sobered by any self-examination, first is exalted to the pinnacle of pride, then is plunged into the depths of envy. Now it is consumed with sinful envy; now it rejoices childishly in its own excellence. In one case it is found sinful, in the other silly, in both proud; for love of its own excellence makes it both grieve to be surpassed and rejoice to surpass others. These vicissitudes of the soul are marked by speech first brief and biting, then lengthy and empty; now full of merriment, now of sadness; but always uncalled for. Compare, if you will, these first two steps of pride with the last two of humility, and see if curiosity is not repressed on the last, frivolity on the next to the last. You will find the same thing in the others, if they are compared respectively. But now let us come to the third — in our argument, not in our action.

CAPUT 12

DE TERTIO GRADU SUPERBIAE, QUI EST INEPTA LAETITIA

40. Proprium est superborum, laeta semper appetere, et tristia devitare, juxta illud: *Cor stultorum ubi laetitia.*[1] Unde et monachus, qui duos jam superbiae gradus descendit, dum per curiositatem ad animi levitatem devenit, cum gaudium quod semper appetit, frequenti videt interpolari tristitia, quam de bonis alterius contrahit; impatiens suae humiliationis, fugit ad consilium falsae consolationis. Ex illa denique parte, qua sua sibi vilitas, et aliena excellentia monstratur, restringit curiositatem, ut totum se transferat in contrariam partem: quatenus in quo ipse videtur praecellere, curiosius notet; in quo alter praecellit, semper dissimulet: ut dum devitat quod triste putatur, laetitia continuetur. Sicque fit ut quem sibi vicissim vindicabant gaudium et tristitia, sola possidere incipiat inepta laetitia. In hac autem tertium tibi gradum constituo: accipe quibus eam[a] signis vel in te deprehendas,[b] vel in altero. Illum qui ejusmodi est, aut raro, aut nunquam gementem audies, lacrymantem videbis. Putes, si attendas, aut sui oblitum, aut ablutum a culpis. In signis scurrilitas, in fronte hilaritas, vanitas apparet in incessu. Pronus ad jocum, *facilis ac promptus in risu.*[2] Cunctis quippe quae in se contemptibilia, et ideo tristia noverat, a memoria rasis; bonisque, si qua sentit in se, adunatis vel simulatis ante oculos mentis, dum nil cogitat nisi quod libet, nec attendit si licet; jam risum tenere, jam ineptam laetitiam dissimulare non valet. Ut enim vesica collecto turgida vento, punctoque forata exiguo, si stringitur, crepitat dum detumescit; ac ventus egrediens non passim effusus, sed strictim emissus crebros quosdam sonitus reddit: sic monachus, ubi

---

[a] *eam*, Mab.; *eum*, Ed. Cant. sine nota.
[b] *deprehendas*, Mab.; *apprehendas*, Ed. Cant. sine nota.
[1] Eccl. 7. 5.
[2] Benedictus, *Regula*, cap. 7.

CHAPTER 12

THE THIRD STEP OF PRIDE, FOOLISH MIRTH [56]

40. It is the custom of the proud always to seek what is cheerful and avoid what is gloomy, as it is written, *The heart of fools is in the house of mirth*. Thus the monk who has already descended two steps of pride, falling through curiosity to frivolity, finds the pleasure he is always seeking frequently interrupted by the sorrow he derives from another man's good. Not being able to bear his own humiliation, he takes refuge in false consolation. Henceforth he restrains his curiosity from the direction which reveals his own weakness and another's excellence, to give himself over entirely to the opposite direction. He takes careful notice of that in which he himself seems to be preeminent, but always overlooks that in which another is preeminent, so that everything unpleasant may be avoided and his mirth may be uninterrupted. And thus it comes about that he whom joy and sadness were contending for now begins to be possessed solely by foolish mirth. This, however, I consider the third step; learn by what signs you may detect it either in yourself or in another. He who is in this way seldom or never will be heard sighing or seen weeping. You would think, to watch him, that he either had no conscience or else had no sins to be conscious of. Facetiousness appears in his gestures, merriment in his face, vanity in his stride. He likes to make jokes; he is *easily and quickly moved to laughter*. Everything contemptible, and therefore unpleasant, which he knows in himself is erased from memory. He gathers together the good things, if he finds any in himself, or else creates them in the mind's eye. Thinking only of what pleases him, without regard to whether it be proper, he can no longer restrain his laughter or conceal his foolish mirth. For just as a windbag with a small vent, if compressed when it is distended with air, will whistle as it deflates, and

vanis scurrilibusque cor suum cogitationibus impleverit, propter disciplinam silentii non inveniens ventus vanitatis qua
plenius egrediatur, inter angustias faucium per cachinnos ex-
cutitur. Saepe vultum pudibundus abscondit, claudit labia,
dentes stringit; ridet tamen nolens, cachinnat invitus. Cumque
os pugnis obstruxerit suis, per nares adhuc sternutare auditur.

the escaping air, not leaking out but shot out, keeps making a noise, so the monk who has filled his heart with silly and ludicrous thoughts, finding no outlet for the blasphemous blast because of the rule of silence,[57] lets it escape from his throat in snorts. He keeps covering his face from shame, he compresses his lips, he grinds his teeth; he laughs without wanting to, he guffaws involuntarily. And when he blocks his mouth with his fists, you can hear him chortle through his nose.

CAPUT 13

DE QUARTO GRADU SUPERBIAE, QUI EST JACTANTIA

41. At postquam vanitas crescere, et vesica grossescere coeperit, necesse est ut ampliori foramine, laxato sinu, ventositas eructetur,* alioquin rumpetur. Sic monachus inepta redundante laetitia, dum risu, vel signis eam aperire non sufficit, in Heliu verba prorumpit: *En venter meus, quasi mustum absque spiraculo, quod lagunculas novas dirumpit.*[1] Aut loquetur ergo, aut rumpetur. *Plenus est enim sermonibus, et coarctat eum spiritus uteri sui.*[2] Esurit et sitit auditores, quibus suas jactitet vanitates, quibus omne quod sentit, effundat: quibus, qualis, et quantus sit, innotescat. Inventa autem occasione loquendi, si de litteris sermo exoritur, vetera proferuntur et nova; volant sententiae, verba resonant ampullosa. Praevenit interrogantem, non quaerenti respondet.[b] Ipse quaerit, ipse solvit, et verba collocutoris imperfecta praecidit. Cum autem pulsato signo necesse est interrumpi colloquium, horam longam, breve queritur intervallum; quaerit licentiam, ut ad fabulas revertatur post horam, non ut quempiam aedificet, sed ut scientiam jactet. Aedificare potest, sed non aedificare intendit. Non curat te docere, vel a te doceri ipse quod nescit; sed ut scire sciatur quod scit. Quod si de religione agitur, statim visiones et somnia proferuntur. Deinde laudat jejunia, commendat vigilias, super omnia orationes exaltat; de patientia, de humilitate, et de singulis virtutibus plenissime, sed vanissime disputat: ut tu scilicet, si audieris, dicas, quod *ex abundantia cordis os loquitur*, et quia *bonus homo de bono thesauro suo profert bona.*[3] Si ad ludicra sermo convertitur,[c] in his quanto

* *eructetur*, Ed. Cant.; *eructuetur*, Mab.
[b] *respondet*, Mab.; *respondit*, Ed. Cant. sine nota.
[c] *convertitur*, Mab.; *convertatur*, Ed. Cant. sine nota.
[1] Job 32. 19.
[2] Job 32. 18.
[3] Matth. 12. 34, 35.

CHAPTER 13

THE FOURTH STEP OF PRIDE, BOASTFULNESS [58]

41. But when increasing vanity begins to make the wind-bag swell, then the wind must be belched out through a larger opening, a wider passage, else it will burst. Likewise the monk swollen with foolish mirth, when laughter and gestures do not suffice to let it out, bursts forth in the words of Elihu, *Behold, my belly is as wine which hath no vent; it is ready to burst like new bottles.* He must either talk or burst. *For he is full of matter, the spirit within him constraineth him.* He hungers and thirsts after hearers, to whom he may vaunt his vanities, to whom he may pour forth all his feelings, to whom his character and greatness may become known. An occasion for talking having been found, if mention of literature arises, ancients and moderns are brought forth. Opinions fly around, weighty words resound. He interrupts a questioner, he answers one who does not ask. He himself puts the questions, he himself solves them, he cuts short his fellow speaker's unfinished words. But when the signal makes it necessary to break up the discussion, he complains that the long hour is a short time, and seeks permission to return to his narration after the hour, not to edify anyone but to display his learning. He is able to edify, but he does not try to. He does not care to teach you, or to learn from you what he does not know, but to know that you know that he knows. If the discussion is about religion, he immediately brings up visions and dreams. Then he praises fasts, commends vigils, exalts prayers above all. He gives the fullest but emptiest discussion of patience, of humility, of each and every virtue, so that if you should hear him you would say that *out of the abundance of the heart the mouth speaketh*, and that *a good man out of the good treasure of the heart bringeth forth good things.* If the conversation turns to lighter matters, he is found no less

assuetior, tanto loquacior invenitur. Dicas, si audias,[a] rivum
vanitatis, fluvium esse scurrilitatis os ejus, ita ut severos quoque
et graves animos in levitatem concitet risus. Et ut totum in
brevi colligam, in multiloquio nota jactantiam. In hoc habes
quartum gradum et descriptum, et nominatum. Fuge rem, et
tene nomen. Hac eadem cautela jam accede ad quintum, quem
nomino singularitatem.

[a] *audias*, Mab.; *audies*, Ed. Cant. sine nota.

loquacious than familiar with them. You would say if you heard him that his mouth was a stream of frivolity, a river of scurrility, such that it excites even stern and grave souls to light laughter. And to sum it up briefly, in the multitude of words you may recognize boastfulness. In this you have the fourth step both described and named. Avoid the thing and keep the name. Now, with this same warning, proceed to the fifth, which I call singularity.

CAPUT 14

DE QUINTO GRADU SUPERBIAE, QUI DICITUR SINGULARITAS

42. Turpe est ei, qui se supra caeteros jactat, si non plus caeteris aliquid agat, per quod ultra caeteros appareat. Proinde non sufficit ei *quod communis monasterii regula, vel majorum cohortantur exempla.*[1] Nec tamen melior esse studet, sed videri. Non melius vivere, sed videri vincere gestit, quatenus dicere possit: *Non sum sicut caeteri hominum.*[2] Plus sibi blanditur de uno jejunio, quod caeteris prandentibus facit, quam si cum caeteris septem dies jejunaverit. Commodior sibi videtur una oratiuncula peculiaris, quam tota psalmodia unius noctis. Inter prandendum crebro solet oculos jactare per mensas, ut si quem minus comedere viderit, victum se doleat, et incipiat idipsum sibi crudeliter subtrahere, quod necessarium victui indulgendum praeviderat, plus gloriae metuens detrimentum, quam famis cruciatum. Si quem macriorem, si quem pallidiorem prospexerit, vilem se aestimat, nunquam requiescit. Et quoniam vultum ipse suum videre non potest, qualem se scilicet intuentibus offert; manus quas potest et brachia spectans, palpat costas, humeros attrectat et lumbos: ut secundum quod corporis sui membra, vel minus, vel satis exilia probat, pallorem ac colorem oris discernat. Ad omnia denique sua strenuus, ad communia piger. Vigilat in lecto, dormit in choro: cumque aliis psallentibus ad vigilias tota nocte dormitet, post vigilias aliis in claustro quiescentibus solus in oratorio remanet: exscreat, et tussit, gemitibus ac suspiriis aures foris sedentium de angulo implet. Cum autem ex his quae singulariter, sed inaniter agit, apud simpliciores ejus opinio excreverit, qui profecto opera probant quae cernunt, sed unde prodeant non discernunt; dum miserum beatificant, in errorem inducunt.

[1] Benedictus, *Regula*, cap. 7.
[2] Luc. 18. 11.

CHAPTER 14

THE FIFTH STEP OF PRIDE, SINGULARITY [59]

42. It is disgraceful for him who vaunts himself above other men if he does not do something more than other men by which he may appear superior to other men. Consequently he is not satisfied with *what the common rule of the monastery or the example of his seniors enforces.* He strives, however, not to be but to appear superior. He does not long to lead a better life, but to seem to surpass, so that he may say, *I am not as other men are.* He gets more pleasure from one fast which he keeps while the others are eating than if he had fasted a week with the others. He considers one little prayer of his own more praiseworthy than the whole psalmody of a night. At dinner he keeps constantly looking around the tables, and if he sees anyone eating less than himself, he grieves that he is beaten and begins mercilessly to deprive himself of even that food which he had planned to allow as indispensable, fearing the damage to his reputation more than the pangs of hunger. If he discovers anyone more haggard, anyone more cadaverous, he despises himself, he gets no rest. And since he cannot see his own face as others see it, he looks at his hands and arms which he can see, he pokes his ribs, he feels his shoulders and loins, so that he may guess the pallor or color of his face according as he finds the limbs of his body satisfactorily emaciated or not. Zealous for himself, indifferent to the community, he keeps vigil in bed, he sleeps in the choir. Although he sleeps the night out while the others are saying psalms at matins, when the others are resting in the cloister after matins [60] he alone remains in the oratory. He spits and coughs; from his corner he fills the ears of those outside [61] with groans and sighs. But although these things which he does with singularity but without sincerity raise his reputation among the more innocent, who praise the works they see without discerning whence they proceed, the poor wretch is grievously deceived when they call him blessed.

CAPUT 15

DE SEXTO GRADU SUPERBIAE, ID EST ARROGANTIA

43. Credit quod audit, laudat quod agit, et quod intendat non attendit. Obliviscitur intentionem, dum amplectitur opinionem. Quique de omni alia re plus sibi credit, quam aliis; de se solo plus aliis credit, quam sibi: ut jam non verbo tenus, aut sola operum ostentatione suam praeferat religionem, sed intimo cordis credat affectu se omnibus sanctiorem: et quidquid de se laudatum agnoverit, non ignorantiae aut benevolentiae laudatoris, sed suis meritis arroganter adscribit. Unde post singularitatem, sextum sibi gradum jure arrogantia vindicavit. Post hanc praesumptio invenitur, in qua septimus gradus constituitur.

CHAPTER 15

THE SIXTH STEP OF PRIDE, CONCEIT [62]

43. He believes all they say, he approves his own way, his motives do not matter. He forgets his own motives, and embraces their opinion of him. And he who believes himself rather than others in all other matters, concerning himself alone believes others rather than himself, so that now no longer merely in words or works does he exalt his own piety, but in the depths of his heart he believes that he is more holy than all other men. And whatever he hears praised about himself he conceitedly ascribes, not to the ignorance or benevolence of the speaker, but to his own merits. After singularity, therefore, conceit rightly claims sixth place. And after this we find audacity, which constitutes the seventh step.

CAPUT 16

DE SEPTIMO GRADU SUPERBIAE, QUI EST
PRAESUMPTIO

44. Qui enim alios se praecellere putat, quomodo plus de
se, quam de aliis non praesumat? Primus in conventibus resi-
det, in consiliis primus respondet: non vocatus accedit, non
jussus se intromittit: reordinat ordinata, reficit facta. Quidquid ipse non fecerit aut ordinaverit, nec recte factum, nec
pulchre aestimat ordinatum. Judicat judicantes, praejudicat
judicaturis. Si, cum tempus advenerit, non promoveatur ad
Prioratum; suum abbatem aut invidum judicat, aut deceptum.
Quod si mediocris ei aliqua obedientia injuncta fuerit, indig-
natur, aspernatur, arbitrans se non esse minoribus occupan-
dum, qui se ad majora sentit * idoneum. Sed qui sic promp-
tulus ad omnia magis temere, quam libere se consuevit ingerere,
impossibile est eum aliquando non errare. Ad praelatum autem
pertinet errantem arguere. Sed quomodo culpam suam con-
fitebitur, qui nec esse putat, nec putari culpabilis patitur?
Propterea cum ei culpa imputatur, crescit, non amputatur.
Si ergo cum argutus fuerit, declinare cor ejus videris in verba
malitiae,[1] in octavum gradum, qui dicitur defensio peccatorum,
noveris corruisse.

* *sentit*, Mab.; *sensit*, Ed. Cant. sine nota.
[1] Ps. 140. 4.

CHAPTER 16

THE SEVENTH STEP OF PRIDE, AUDACITY [63]

44. Must not he who thinks himself superior to others be more forward than others? In assemblies he is seated first, in councils he speaks first. He comes unsummoned, he intrudes unbidden. He reregulates the regulations, he does over what is already done; whatever he has not done or regulated, he considers neither correctly done nor fairly regulated. He judges the judges, and prejudges their judgments. If when the time comes he is not promoted to the priorate, he judges his abbot to be either jealous or deceived. If some petty obedience is assigned to him, he indignantly disdains it, thinking that he ought not to be occupied with lesser things when he knows himself capable of greater ones. But he who has the habit of offering himself for everything with such willingness, though more audaciously than graciously, cannot but err sometimes. It is the duty of the superior to reprove one who errs. But how shall he confess his guilt who neither thinks himself culpable nor tolerates his being thought so? For that reason, the fault for which he is taken to task is not removed but grows greater. If, therefore, when he is being reproved, you see his heart incline to evil words, you may know that he has fallen to the eighth step, which is called excusing sins.

CAPUT 17

DE OCTAVO GRADU SUPERBIAE, QUI EST DEFENSIO PECCATORUM

45. Multis vero modis fiunt *excusationes in peccatis.*[1] Aut enim dicit qui se excusat, Non feci; aut, Feci quidem, sed bene feci; aut, Si male, non multum male; aut, Si multum male,[a] non mala intentione. Si autem et de illa, sicut Adam vel Eva, convincitur, aliena suasione excusare se nititur. Sed qui procaciter etiam aperta defendit, quando *occultas et malas cogitationes, cordi suo advenientes, humiliter revelaret abbati?* [2]

[a] *aut, Si multum male*, Mab.; desunt in Ed. Cant. sine nota.
[1] Ps. 140. 4.
[2] Benedictus, *Regula*, cap. 7.

CHAPTER 17

THE EIGHTH STEP OF PRIDE, EXCUSING SINS ⁽⁶⁴⁾

45. There are many ways of making *excuses in sins*. For he who excuses himself may say, I did not do it; or, I did it indeed, but it was right; or, if wrong, it was not very wrong; or, if very wrong, it was not with bad intent. If nevertheless he is convicted of it, like Adam or Eve, he attempts to excuse himself on the ground that he was beguiled by someone else. But if he shamelessly defends even his open offences, how is he to *manifest to his abbot humbly the secret and evil thoughts of his heart?*

CAPUT 18

DE NONO GRADU SUPERBIAE, QUI EST
SIMULATA CONFESSIO

46. Licet vero genera haec excusationis eatenus mala [a] judicentur, quatenus ore prophetico *verba malitiae* [1] appellentur; multo tamen periculosior est fallax ac superba confessio, quam pervicax et obstinata defensio. Nonnulli enim cum de apertioribus arguuntur, scientes si se defenderent, quod sibi non crederetur; subtilius inveniunt argumentum defensionis, verba respondentes dolosae confessionis. *Est* quippe, ut scriptum est, *qui nequiter humiliat se, et interiora ejus plena sunt dolo.* [2] Vultus demittitur, prosternitur corpus: aliquas sibi lacrymas extorquent, si possunt; vocem suspiriis, verba gemitibus interrumpunt. Nec [b] solum qui ejusmodi est, objecta non excusat, sed ipse quoque culpam exaggerat: ut dum impossibile aliquid, aut incredibile culpae suae ore ipsius additum audis, etiam illud, quod ratum putabas, discredere possis; et ex eo quod falsum esse non dubitas dum confitetur, in dubium veniat quod quasi certum tenebatur. Dumque affirmant quod credi nolunt, confitendo culpam defendunt, et aperiendo tegunt; quando et confessio laudabiliter sonat in ore, et adhuc iniquitas occultatur in corde: quatenus magis ex humilitate, quam ex veritate confiteri putet qui audit, aptans eis illud Scripturae, *Justus in principio sermonis accusator est sui.* [3] Malunt enim apud homines veritate periclitari, quam humilitate, cum apud Deum periclitentur utrinque. Aut si adeo culpa manifesta sit, quod nulla penitus tegi versutia possit; nihilominus tamen vocem, non cor poenitentis assumunt, qua notam, non culpam deleant, dum ignorantiam manifestae transgressionis, decore recompensant publicae confessionis.

[a] *mala*, Mab.; *male*, Ed. Cant. sine nota.
[b] *nec*, Mab. et omnia MSS praeter unum; *non*, Ed. Cant.
[1] Ps. 140. 4.
[2] Ecclus. 19. 23.   [3] Prov. 18. 17 (Vet. Lat.).

CHAPTER 18

THE NINTH STEP OF PRIDE, HYPOCRITICAL CONFESSION [65]

46. Although these kinds of excuses are considered so evil that they are called by the prophet *evil words*, nevertheless a false and proud confession is much more perilous than a willful and stubborn defense. For there are some who, when they are reproved for their more obvious sins, knowing that they will not be believed if they excuse themselves, contrive a more subtle method of defense by responding with a deceitful confession. *There is* indeed, as it is written, *one that humbleth himself wickedly, and his interior is full of deceit.* The face drops, the body is prostrate, they squeeze out some tears if they can. They interrupt their voice with sighs, their words with groans. This sort of man not only does not deny the charges against him but exaggerates his guilt himself, so that, hearing from his own lips something impossible and incredible added to his guilt, you may disbelieve even that which you thought was established; that which you cannot doubt to be false when it is confessed brings into question that which was considered certain. Asserting what they do not wish to have believed, they condone their guilt by confessing it, they conceal it by revealing it. The confession sounds laudable on the lips, and the iniquity is so well hidden in the heart that the hearer thinks they are confessing from humility rather than from veracity, applying to them that verse, *The just man begins his speech by accusing himself.* For with men they prefer to risk their name for veracity rather than humility, although with God they risk both. But if their guilt is so manifest that no ingenuity can conceal it, they assume none the less the voice, not the heart, of a penitent, and thus wipe out the stigma, not the guilt, making up for the infamy of a manifest transgression by the honor of a public confession.

47. Gloriosa res humilitas, qua ipsa quoque superbia palliare se appetit, ne vilescat! Sed haec cito tergiversatio a praelato deprehenditur, si ad hanc superbam humilitatem non leviter flectitur, quo magis dissimulet culpam, vel differat poenam. *Vasa figuli probat fornax*,[1] et tribulatio vere poenitentes discernit. Qui enim veraciter poenitet, laborem poenitentiae non abhorret: sed quidquid sibi pro culpa quam odit injungitur, tacita conscientia patienter amplectitur. In ipsa quoque obedientia duris ac contrariis rebus obortis, quibuslibet irrogatis injuriis sustinens non lassescit,[2] ut in quarto gradu stare se indicet humilitatis. Cujus vero simulata confessio est, una vel levi contumelia, aut exigua poena interrogatus,[3] jam humilitatem simulare, jam simulationem dissimulare non potest. Murmurat, frendet, irascitur; nec in quarto stare humilitatis, sed in nonum superbiae gradum corruisse probatur, qui secundum quod descriptus est, recte simulata confessio appellari potest. Quanta putas tunc confusio * sit in corde superbi, cum fraus decipitur, pax amittitur, laus minuitur, nec culpa diluitur? Tandem notatur ab omnibus, judicatur ab omnibus: eoque vehementius omnes indignantur, quo falsum conspiciunt quidquid de eo prius opinabantur. Tunc opus est praelato, ut eo minus illi parcendum putet, quo magis omnes offenderet, si uni parceret.

ᵃ *confusio*, Mab. et veteres Edd.; *confessio*, Ed. Cant. sine nota.
[1] Ecclus. 27. 6.
[2] Benedictus, *Regula*, cap. 7.
[3] Sap. 2. 19.

47. A glorious thing is the humility which pride itself tries to put on as a mantle, lest it become disgusting. But this subterfuge is soon detected by the superior, if he does not treat this proud humility with such gentleness as to dissemble the guilt or defer the punishment even further. *The furnace trieth the potter's vessels*, and affliction reveals the truly penitent. For he who truly repents does not abhor the pain of penitence but patiently and with a quiet mind bears all that is enjoined him for the guilt which he detests. In the exercise of his obedience he does not weary in suffering all that is inflicted on him, things contrary to nature and even at times unjust, so that he shows himself to be standing on the fourth step of humility. But he whose confession is hypocritical, when tried with one slight reproach or petty punishment, can no longer be hypocritically humble, no longer hide his hypocrisy. He grumbles, grinds his teeth, grows angry, and proves himself not to be standing on the fourth step of humility but to have fallen to the ninth step of pride, which, thus described, may well be called hypocritical confession. How great must be the confusion in the heart of the proud, when fraud is found out, pardon is lost, reputation shattered, and guilt not washed away! At last he is branded by all, condemned by all, abhorred by all the more vehemently as they realize that their former opinion of him was false. And now the superior is bound to consider that he cannot pardon him, for the reason that pardoning one will be an offence to them all.

CAPUT 19

DE DECIMO GRADU SUPERBIAE, QUI EST REBELLIO

48. Hic nisi eum miseratio superna respiciat, ut (quod valde talibus difficile est) universorum judiciis tacitus acquiescat; frontosus mox et impudens factus, tanto deterius, quanto desperatius in decimum gradum per rebellionem corruit: quique prius latenter arrogans fratres contempserat, jam patenter inobediens etiam magistrum contemnit.

49. Sciendum namque, quod omnes gradus, quos in duodecim partitus sum, in tres tantummodo colligi possunt: ut in sex superioribus contemptus fratrum, in quatuor sequentibus contemptus magistri, in duobus, qui restant, consummetur contemptus Dei. Notandum quoque, quod hi duo ultimi superbiae gradus, qui et humilitatis ascendendo primi inveniuntur; sicut extra congregationem ascendendi sunt, ita in congregatione descendi non possunt. Quod autem ante ascendi debeant, ex hoc aperte intelligi datur, quod de tertio gradu in Regula legitur: *Tertius*, inquit, *gradus est, ut quis pro Dei amore omni obedientia se subdat majori.*[1] Si ergo in tertio gradu subjectio collocatur, quae procul dubio fit,[a] quando primum novitius conventui sociatur; consequens est, quod duo jam anteriores transcensi intelligantur. Denique ubi fratrum concordiam, et [b] magistri sententiam monachus spernit, quid ultra in monasterio, nisi scandalum facit?

[a] *fit*, Mab.; *sit*, Ed. Cant. sine nota.
[b] *et*, Mab.; *ac*, Ed. Cant. et unum MS.
[1] Benedictus, *Regula*, cap. 7.

CHAPTER 19

THE TENTH STEP OF PRIDE, DEFIANCE [66]

48. Unless the divine compassion looks down upon him so that (what is very difficult in such cases) he yields in silence to the general condemnation, he soon becomes shameless and brazen, and the more so the more desperately he is plunging down to the tenth step by defiance. He who before contemned the brethren in secret conceit now contemns even the master in open disobedience.

49. For notice that all the steps which I have divided into twelve might be arranged in three only, so that on the upper six contempt of the brethren, on the next four contempt of the master, on the remaining two contempt of God is consummated. Note likewise that these last two steps of pride, which are also found to be the first of humility in ascending, just as they must be ascended outside the monastery, likewise cannot be descended within the monastery. That they should be ascended before entrance may be clearly seen from what is said in the Rule about the third step. *The third step*, it says, *is reached when a man, for the love of God, submits himself with all obedience to a superior*. If therefore submission, which undoubtedly occurs when the novice first joins the convent, occurs at the third step, it follows that the two prior ones are understood as having already been passed over. And indeed, when a monk spurns the society of the brethren and the judgment of the master, what more can he do in a monastery except create a scandal?

CAPUT 20

DE UNDECIMO GRADU SUPERBIAE, QUI EST LIBERTAS PECCANDI

50. Post decimum itaque gradum, qui rebellio dictus est, expulsus vel egressus de monasterio statim excipitur ab undecimo. Et tunc ingreditur vias, quae videntur hominibus bonae, quarum finis (nisi forte Deus eas illi sepserit) demerget eum in profundum inferni,[1] id est in contemptum Dei. *Impius* siquidem *cum venerit in profundum malorum, contemnit.*[2] Potest autem undecimus gradus appellari libertas peccandi, per quam monachus, cum jam nec magistrum videt quem timeat, nec fratres quos revereatur; tanto securius, quanto liberius sua desideria implere delectatur, a quibus in monasterio tam pudore, quam timore prohibebatur. Sed etsi jam vel fratres, vel abbatem non timet, nondum tamen Dei penitus formidine caret. Hanc ratio, tenuiter adhuc submurmurans, voluntati proponit, nec sine aliqua dubitatione quaeque primum illicita perficit; sed, sicut is qui vadum tentat, pedetentim, non cursim vitiorum gurgitem intrat.

[1] Prov. 16. 25 (Vet. Lat.); Benedictus, *Regula*, cap. 7.
[2] Prov. 18. 3 (Vet. Lat.).

CHAPTER 20

THE ELEVENTH STEP OF PRIDE, FREEDOM TO SIN [67]

50. After the tenth step, therefore, which is called defiance, he is expelled or withdraws from the monastery, and forthwith finds himself on the eleventh. And now he enters upon the ways which seem good to men but which (unless God shall hedge them in for him) will plunge him at last into the depths of hell, that is, into contempt of God. For *when the wicked cometh, then cometh also contempt.* The eleventh step may be called freedom to sin, whereby the monk, no longer seeing either a master to fear or brethren to respect, is allured into satisfying his own desires, with the confidence of freedom, whereas shame as well as fear withheld him from them in the monastery. But although now he has neither brethren nor abbot to be afraid of, he has not yet lost all fear of God. The rational faculty, still faintly whispering, opposes the will with this fear, and he commits the first offences with considerable hesitation; but, like a man trying to ford a stream, he is drawn into the whirlpool of vice, not all at once but little by little.

CAPUT 21

DE DUODECIMO GRADU SUPERBIAE, QUI EST CONSUETUDO PECCANDI

51. At postquam terribili Dei judicio prima flagitia impunitas * sequitur, experta voluptas libenter repetitur, repetita blanditur. Concupiscentia reviviscente sopitur ratio, ligat consuetudo. Trahitur miser in profundum malorum, traditur captivus tyrannidi vitiorum, ut carnalium ita voragine desideriorum absorptus, suae rationis divinique timoris oblitus, *dicat insipiens in corde suo: Non est Deus.*[1] Jam indifferenter libitis pro licitis utitur, jam ab illicitis cogitandis, patrandis, investigandis animus, manus, vel pedes non prohibentur: sed quidquid in cor, in buccam, ad manum venerit; machinatur, garrit, et operatur, malevolus, vaniloquus, facinorosus. Quemadmodum denique ascensis his omnibus gradibus, corde jam alacri et absque labore pro bona consuetudine justus currit ad vitam: sic descensis impius eisdem, pro malo usu non ratione se gubernans, non timoris freno retentans, intrepidus festinat ad mortem. Medii sunt qui fatigantur, angustiantur: qui nunc metu cruciantur gehennae, nunc pristina retardati consuetudine, descendendo vel ascendendo laborant. Supremus tantum et infimus currunt absque impedimento, et absque labore. Ad mortem hic, ad vitam ille festinat; alter alacrior, alter proclivior. Illum alacrem charitas, hunc proclivem cupiditas facit. In altero amor, in altero stupor laborem non sentit. In illo denique *perfecta charitas*, in isto consummata iniquitas *foras mittit timorem.*[2] Illi veritas, huic caecitas dat securitatem. Potest ergo duodecimus gradus appellari consuetudo peccandi, qua Dei metus amittitur, contemptus incurritur.

---

* *impunitas*, Mab.; *impunitus*, Ed. Cant. sine nota.
[1] Ps. 13. 1.
[2] 1 Joan. 4. 18.

CHAPTER 21

THE TWELFTH STEP OF PRIDE, HABITUAL SINNING [68]

51. But when by the terrible judgment of God impunity follows the first lapses, the tasted pleasure is repeated freely, and found sweet. As lust awakens, reason is lulled to sleep, and the habit becomes binding. The wretch is drawn into the depths of sin, the captive is given over to the tyranny of vice, so that, swallowed up by a whirlpool of carnal desires and forgetting both his own reason and the fear of God, *the fool saith in his heart, There is no God*. He now allows himself to do whatever he pleases, he no longer keeps his mind, hands, or feet from improper thoughts, deeds, or explorations; but whatever comes to his heart, lips, or hand he ponders maliciously, prattles boastfully, or performs viciously. In the same way that the good man who has gone up all these steps finally flies toward life with eager heart and without exertion because of his good habits, so the wicked man who has gone down the same hastens toward death without trepidation because of his evil ways, not restraining himself by reason, not refraining from aught through fear. It is those midway who grow weary and are distressed, now tormented by the fear of hell, now held back by old habits as they strive to go up or down. Only the highest and the lowest fly without hindrance or exertion. The former eager for life, the latter prone to death, they hasten along. Love makes the one eager, lust makes the other prone; sympathy feels no exertion in the one, apathy in the other. In the former *perfect love*, in the latter consummate wickedness, *casteth out fear*. Truth makes one secure, blindness the other. The twelfth step, therefore, may be called the habitual sinning by which the fear of God is lost and contempt of God incurred.

CAPUT 22

AN ET QUOMODO ORANDUM PRO DESPERATIS, ET MORTUIS SECUNDUM ANIMAM

52. *Pro tali* jam, inquit Joannes apostolus, *non dico ut quis oret.*[1] Sed numquid dicis, o Apostole, ut quis desperet? Imo gemat qui illum amat. Non praesumat orare, nec desistat plorare. Quid est quod dico? An forte ullum remanet spei refugium, ubi oratio non invenit locum? Audi credentem, sperantem, nec tamen orantem. *Domine*, inquit, *si fuisses hic, frater meus non fuisset mortuus.* Magna fides, qua credidit sua praesentia Dominum mortem prohibere potuisse si adfuisset. Modo autem quid? Absit ut quem credidit vivum potuisse servare, mortuum dubitet posse resuscitare. *Sed et nunc*, inquit, *scio quia quaecumque poposceris a Deo, dabit tibi Deus.*[2] Deinde quaerenti ubi posuissent eum, respondet: *Veni, et vide.*[3] Quamobrem? O Martha, magna nobis fidei tuae insignia tribuis: sed quomodo cum tanta fide diffidis? *Veni*, inquis, *et vide.* Cur, si non desperas, non sequeris, et dicis, Et resuscita? si autem desperas, cur Magistrum sine causa fatigas? An forte fides aliquando recipit, quod oratio non praesumit? Denique appropinquantem cadaveri prohibes, et dicis: *Domine, jam fetet; quatriduanus enim est.*[4] Desperando dicis hoc, an dissimulando? Sic quippe ipse Dominus post resurrectionem *finxit se longius ire,*[5] cum mallet cum discipulis remanere. O sanctae mulieres Christi familiares, si fratrem vestrum amatis, cur ejus misericordiam non flagitatis, de cujus potentia dubitare, pietate diffidere non potestis? Respondent: Sic melius tanquam non orantes oramus, sic efficacius quasi diffidenter confidimus. Exhibemus fidem, perhibemus affectum: scit ipse, cui non est opus ut aliquid dicatur, quid desideremus. Scimus

[1] 1 Joan. 5. 16.
[2] Joan. 11. 21, 22.
[3] Joan. 11. 34.
[4] Joan. 11. 39.
[5] Luc. 24. 28.

CHAPTER 22

CONCLUSION

52. *For such a one*, says the Apostle John, *I do not say that he shall pray*. But dost thou say, O Apostle, that he shall despair? Rather let him groan who loves such a one. Let him not presume to implore, nor ever cease to deplore. What do I say? Can there be any haven for hope where prayer finds no place? Hear one who believes, who hopes, but does not pray. *Lord*, she says, *if thou hadst been here, my brother had not died*. Great faith, by which she believed that the Lord could have prevented death by his presence had he been there. But what then? She could hardly believe anyone able to save the living and doubt that he could raise the dead. *But I know*, she says, *that even now, whatsoever thou wilt ask of God, God will give it thee*. Then when he asks where they have laid him, she replies, *Come and see*. Why? O Martha, thou art giving us sure tokens of thy faith, but how with such great trust canst thou mistrust? *Come and see*, thou sayest. If thou dost not despair, why dost thou not go on and say, And raise him? But if thou dost despair, why dost thou importune the Master without cause? Is it perhaps that faith sometimes receives what prayer does not presume? Then as he approaches the corpse thou dost stop him, saying, *Lord, by this time he stinketh: for he hath been dead four days*. Sayest thou this in despair or in dissimulation? In the latter way indeed the Lord himself, after the resurrection, *made as though he would have gone further*, when he intended rather to stay with the disciples. O holy women, intimate friends of Christ, if ye love your brother, why do ye not implore the mercy of him whose power ye cannot doubt, whose love ye cannot mistrust? They reply: We pray better in this way, as if not praying; we trust more efficaciously in this way, as if mistrustful. We expose our faith; we disclose our devotion; he knows what we

quidem quod omnia potest: sed hoc tam grande miraculum, tam novum, tam inauditum, etsi ejus subest potentiae, multum tamen excedit universa merita humilitatis nostrae. Sufficit nobis potentiae locum, pietati dedisse occasionem; malentes patienter exspectare quid velit, quam impudenter quaerere quod forsitan nolit. Denique quod nostris meritis deest, verecundia fortasse supplebit. Petri quoque post gravem lapsum lacrymam quidem video, sed precem non audio: nec tamen de indulgentia dubito.

53. Disce et in Matre Domini magnam in mirabilibus fidem habere, in magna fide verecundiam retinere. Disce verecundia decorare fidem, reprimere praesumptionem. *Vinum*, inquit, *non habent*.[1] Quam breviter, quam reverenter suggessit, unde pie sollicita fuit! Et ut discas in hujusmodi magis pie gemere, quam petere praesumptuose; pietatis aestum pudoris temperans umbra, conceptam precis fiduciam verecunde suppressit. Non frontose accessit, non palam locuta est, ut audacter coram omnibus diceret: Obsecro, fili, defecit vinum, contristantur convivae, confunditur sponsus; ostende quid possis. Sed licet haec aut multo plura pectus aestuans, fervens loqueretur affectus; privatim [a] tamen potentem pia Filium mater adiit, non potentiam tentans, sed voluntatem explorans. *Vinum*, inquit, *non habent*. Quid modestius? quid fidelius? Non defuit pietati fides, voci gravitas, efficacia voto. Si ergo illa, cum mater sit, matrem se oblita non audet petere miraculum vini; ego vile mancipium, cui permagnum est Filii simul ac Matris esse vernaculum, qua fronte praesumo pro vita petere quatriduani?

54. Duo etiam in Evangelio caeci visum, alter accepisse, alter recepisse leguntur: alter quem amiserat, alter quem nunquam habuerat; unus scilicet excaecatus, alter vero caecus natus. Sed qui excaecatus, miserabilibus mirisque clamoribus miram misericordiam meruit: qui vero caecus natus, tanto misericordius, quanto mirabilius nullis suis precibus praeventum sui illuminatoris beneficium nihilo minus sensit. Illi

[a] *privatim*, Mab.; *privatum*, Ed. Cant. sine nota.
[1] Joan. 2. 3.

want without our needing to tell him anything. We know indeed that he is omnipotent, but this miracle so great, so novel, so unheard of, while within his power, nevertheless far exceeds the whole merit of our humility. It suffices us to have given his power an occasion, his love an opportunity, preferring to await patiently what he wills than to seek impudently what perhaps he does not will. And it may be that our modesty will make up for what our merit lacks. Likewise after Peter's grievous sin I see tears indeed but hear no prayers, nor do I doubt its remission.

53. Learn also from the Lord's mother how to have much faith in miracles but to preserve modesty in such faith. Learn to adorn faith with modesty, to repress audacity. *They have no wine*, she says. With what few, what reverent words she suggested what she was anxious about. And that you might learn to utter a grievous groan rather than a presumptuous prayer in such a case, she tempered the warmth of love with the shade of shame and modestly suppressed the trust she had in prayer. She did not step up boldly and speak openly, saying before all, Please, son, the wine has run short, the guests are inconvenienced, the bridegroom is embarrassed, show what you can do. Though a warm heart, a glowing sympathy might have said this or much more, yet the loving mother came privately to her omnipotent son, not to test his omnipotence but to discover his will. *They have no wine*, she says. What could be more modest, more trustful? Her love did not lack faith, nor her words dignity, nor her prayer efficacy. If then she, although his mother, forgets she is his mother and does not venture to ask for the miracle of wine, how shamelessly would I, a vile slave whose greatest honor is to be the chattel of the son as well as of the mother, presume to ask for the life of one who is four days dead!

54. Two blind men are said in the gospel, one to have received, the other to have recovered, sight; one having lost it, the other never having had it; that is, one having been blinded and the other born blind. The one who had been blinded merited the miraculous mercy through his pitiful

denique dictum est, *Fides tua te salvum fecit*: huic autem non.[1]
Duos quoque recens mortuos, tertium jam quatriduanum, lego
resuscitatos: solam tamen in domo adhuc positam, precibus
patris; duos autem ex insperata magnitudine pietatis.[2]

55. Simili etiam forma si contigerit (quod Deus avertat)
aliquem de nostris fratribus, non in corpore, sed in anima
mori; quamdiu adhuc inter nos erit, pulsabo et ego meis qualiscumque peccator, pulsabo et fratrum precibus Salvatorem.
Si revixerit, lucrati erimus fratrem:[1] si vero non mereamur
exaudiri, ubi jam vel tolerare vivos, vel tolerari a vivis non
poterit, sed incipiet efferri, semper quidem fideliter gemo, sed
jam non ita fiducialiter oro. Non aperte audeo dicere, Veni,
Domine, suscita mortuum nostrum: corde tamen suspenso
tremulus intro clamare non cesso, Si forte, si forte, si forte
*desiderium pauperum exaudiet Dominus, praeparationem cordis
eorum audiet auris ejus;*[2] et illud, *Numquid mortuis facies
mirabilia, aut medici suscitabunt, et confitebuntur tibi?* et de
quatriduano: *Numquid narrabit aliquis in sepulcro misericordiam tuam, et veritatem tuam in perditione?*[3] Potest interim
Salvator, si vult, improvise et insperate occurrere nobis, la-
crymisque portantium motus, non precibus, mortui vitam
reddere vivis, aut certe jam sepultum revocare a mortuis.
Mortuum autem dixerim illum, qui sua peccata defendens, in
octavum jam corruit gradum. *A mortuo* enim, *tanquam qui
non est, perit confessio.*[4] Post decimum vero, qui tertius est
ab octavo, jam effertur in libertatem peccandi, quando expel-
litur a consortio monasterii. At postquam quartum transierit,
jam recte quatriduanus dicitur, dum in quintum decidens per
consuetudinem sepelitur.

---

[1] Luc. 18. 35–43; Joan. 9.
[2] Marc. 5. 35–42; Luc. 7. 11–15; Joan. 11.

---

[1] Matth. 18. 15.

[2] Ps. 87. 11, 12.

[2] Ps. 10 sec. Heb. 17.

[4] Ecclus. 17. 26.

and unnatural cries, but the one born blind, though not praying for it, none the less received an even more merciful, because more miraculous, boon from his enlightener. To the former it was said, *Thy faith hath saved thee*; but not to the latter. I read also that two newly dead and a third dead four days were restored; but only one, the girl lying in the house, by the prayers of her father, the other two by an unexpected plenitude of pity.

55. In like manner, if it should happen (which God forbid) that any of our brethren should die, not physically but spiritually, so long as he is still among us I will knock at the Savior's door, both with my own prayers, whatever a sinner can avail, and with those of the brethren. If he is restored, we have gained our brother. But if we are not worthy to be heard, when he can no longer either endure the living or be endured by them, but must be carried out, I will continue faithfully to groan but will no longer pray with equal confidence. I shall not dare to say openly, Come, Lord, raise up our dead. None the less, with heart choked up and trembling body, I will not cease to cry inwardly. If perchance, if perchance, if perchance *the Lord will hear the desire of the humble, he will prepare their heart, he will cause his ear to hear.* And again, *Wilt thou show wonders to the dead? shall the dead arise and praise thee?* And concerning the four days dead, *Shall thy loving-kindness be declared in the grave? or thy faithfulness in destruction?* The Savior can, if he will, come to us suddenly and unexpectedly, and, moved by the tears, not the prayers, of the bearers, restore to the living the life of the dead, or even recall from the dead one already buried. But I should call him dead who has already fallen to the eighth step by excusing his sins. For *confession perisheth from the dead, as from one who is not.* After the third step of death (the tenth) he is carried out into freedom to sin, when he is expelled from the fellowship of the monastery. And after he has passed the fourth he is rightly called dead four days, and when he falls to the fifth through habitual sin, he is buried.

56. Absit autem a nobis, ut etiam pro talibus, etsi palam
non praesumimus, vel in cordibus nostris orare cessemus: cum
Paulus eos quoque lugeret, quos sine poenitentia mortuos
sciret.[1] Etsi enim a communibus orationibus ipsi se excludunt,
sed ab affectibus * omnino non possunt. Viderint tamen in
quanto periculo sint, pro quibus Ecclesia palam orare non
audeat, quae fidenter etiam pro Judaeis, pro haereticis, pro
Gentilibus orat. Cum enim in Parasceve nominatim oretur
pro quibuslibet malis, nulla tamen mentio fit de excom-
municatis.

57. Dicis forsitan, frater Godefride, me aliud quam tu
quaesisti, quam ipse promisi, tandem exhibuisse, cum pro
gradibus humilitatis, superbiae gradus videar descripsisse. Ad
quod ego: Non potui docere nisi quod didici. Non putavi
congruum me describere ascensiones, qui plus descendere,
quam ascendere novi. Proponat tibi beatus Benedictus gradus
humilitatis, quos ipse prius in corde suo disposuit: [1] ego quid
proponam non habeo, nisi ordinem meae descensionis. In quo
tamen, si diligenter inspicitur, via forsitan ascensionis reperitur.
Si enim tibi Romam tendenti homo inde veniens obviaret,
quaesitus viam, quid melius quam illam, qua venit, ostenderet?
Dum castella, villas et urbes, fluvios ac montes, per quos transierit, nominat, suum denuntians iter, tuum tibi praenuntiat:
ita ut eadem loca recognoscas eundo, quae ille pertransiit
veniendo. In hac similiter nostra descensione gradus ascen-
sorios fortasse reperies, quos ascendendo melius tu in tuo
corde, quam in nostro codice leges.

* *affectibus*, Mab. et Ed. Cant. et plura MSS; *effectibus*, vetustiora MSS
et Mills in Anglica translatione.
[1] 2 Cor. 12. 21.

---

[1] Ps. 83. 6.

56. Far be it from us to cease praying in our hearts even for such, though we dare not openly, when Paul bewailed even those whom he knew to have died impenitent. For though they exclude themselves from our common prayers, they cannot do so from our hearts. Nevertheless let them see in what great peril they are for whom the Church does not dare to pray openly, although it prays fearlessly even for Jews, for heretics, for heathen. For on Good Friday we pray specifically for all kinds of wicked men, but no mention is made of the excommunicate.

57. You may say, Brother Godfrey, that I have set forth something other than what you requested and I promised, as I seem to have described the steps of pride instead of the steps of humility. I reply, I could only teach what I had learned. I who know more about going down than going up did not think it would be proper for me to describe the way up. Let Saint Benedict tell you about the steps of humility, which he first set up in his own heart; I have nothing to tell you about except the order of my own descent. Yet if this is carefully examined, the way up may be found in it. For if when going to Rome you should meet a man coming from there and ask him the way, what way could he tell better than that which he had come? In naming the castles, towns and cities, rivers and mountains, along which he has passed, he describes his own road and prescribes yours, so that you may recognize the same places in going which he has passed along in coming. Similarly in this descent of mine you will find, perhaps, the steps leading up, and ascending will read them in your own heart better than in my book.

NOTES

NOTES

The *Mellifluous Doctor* Saint Bernard, Abbot of Clairvaux, Doctor of the Church, was born at Fontaines, near Dijon in Burgundy, in 1090, became a Cistercian monk in 1112, founded the monastery of Clairvaux in 1115, and died there in 1153.

1. (Title)

The correct title of this essay is "The Steps of Humility," *De Gradibus Humilitatis* (or, as in the MSS followed by the Cambridge edition, *Super Humilitatis Gradibus*), and not "The Steps of Humility and Pride," *De Gradibus Humilitatis et Superbiae*, as in the editions. The author entitled it *De Gradibus Humilitatis*, and in the Retractation (a sort of "preface to the second edition") he protested against the corruption of the title already prevalent, apparently, in his own day. There is only one set of steps, as he explicitly states. They are the steps of Jacob's ladder, which is allegorically interpreted by Benedict as our life in the world, and are called by him the "steps of humility or discipline." Bernard says that they might better be called steps of pride for one who is descending them. But to change the title or to divide the work into two parts, called "Steps of Humility" and "Steps of Pride" respectively, as the editors do, is to obscure the author's meaning and destroy the perfect unity of the essay.

The Latin chapter titles are taken from Mabillon's edition; the English chapter titles are by the translator.

2. (Mabillon's Preface, 1) *Bernard's first production*.

There is no good reason for calling this Bernard's first work. The words *primum opus illius* occur in the biography, but *primum* is to be construed as an adverb, being followed in the next sentence by *inde*, "next." "If anyone desires to know how careful a judge and examiner of himself he was from the beginning, let him regard first his work on the *Steps of Humility*. Next, if the religious devotion of a pious mind is sought, let him proceed to the homilies in *Praise of the Virgin Mother*, and that book which he published on *Loving God*" — and so on, listing the various virtues shown by his various works, not in chronological order (*Vita prima* 3, 8, 29, *Opera*, Vol. II, 2211). The "little book entitled *De Humilitate*," *libellum qui inscribitur de Humilitate*, mentioned in Letter 18 (*Opera* 163), cannot be this essay, which is not entitled *De Humilitate*, but *De Gradibus Humilitatis*, a title the correctness of which Bernard insists on in the Retractation. The letter, far from proving that the *Steps of Humility* was his first work, proves that it was not, but was later than the lost *De Humilitate*, the sermons on *Missus Est*, and the *Apology*. It was probably written after *Loving God*, in which the possibility of mystical experience, taken for granted in the *Steps of Humility*, is denied; and before the sermons on Canticles, in which the mystical Bridegroom is identified with the second person of the Trinity, instead of the first, as in the essay.

The lost *De Humilitate* is probably the *De Humilitate* found in column

1070 of Volume II of Mabillon's edition of Bernard's works (*Pat. Lat.* 184, 793). It was published with two other essays under the title *De Statu Virtutum*. Mabillon says it is not by Bernard, but suggests no reason why not. It is obviously by a Benedictine abbot, is typically Bernardine in doctrine and style, bears the title of the book mentioned in Bernard's letter, and is attributed in the only known MS to "Abbot Bernard."

3. (Mabillon's Preface, 1) *Until he retracts.*

Mabillon both misquotes Manricus and misrepresents Bernard. Manricus does not say, *donec rem a se excogitatam retractaret*, but *donec a se excogitatum ipse notaret, quasi minoris ex eo fidei futurum*, "until he had pointed out that this had been thought out by himself, as if it would be for that reason of less credence" (*Annales Cistercienses* 1121, 2, 3). Bernard was always careful to distinguish among understanding, faith, and opinion. In the Retractation he pointed out that the theory concerning seraphim was his opinion, and therefore fallible and subject to correction by a better opinion, fearing that the word *puto*, instead of the more explicit *opinor*, might not have made this sufficiently clear. But he did not retract the opinion, or deny himself the right to express opinions. His language here is entirely consistent with the two passages which Mabillon, following Manricus, refers to as "modifying the earlier statement" (Sermon 4 on *Missus Est*, 12, XB 74; *Baptism* 5, 18, *Opera* 1421; the former is earlier, not only than the Retractation, but than the *De Gradibus Humilitatis* itself).

The same theory concerning seraphim occurs in a sermon with the explicit warning, "I am saying however what I feel; I am not indeed speaking positively, but by a sort of conjecture and opinion." (Sermon 5 for 1st Sunday of November, 7, XB 441.)

4. (Mabillon's Preface, 2) *Only four works.*

It is not clear why Mabillon says four, for the letter mentions only three, namely: (1) the "little book entitled *De Humilitate*," which Mabillon identifies with the *Steps of Humility*; (2) a series of four sermons entitled *In Praise of the Virgin Mother*, on the Gospel for the Annunciation, *Missus est angelus Gabriel* (Luc. 1. 26), written when Bernard was confined by sickness (XB 32); and (3) the so-called *Apology*, addressed to William of St Thierry, a discussion of monastic customs largely devoted to a criticism of the allegedly unmonastic customs of the Cluniacs (*Opera* 1221).

5. (Mabillon's Preface, 2) *Letter 320.*

Now known as Letter 317 (*Opera* 604). In this brief but interesting historical document, written in 1138, Bernard, with unrestrained jubilation, announces to his prior the termination of the papal schism and his own imminent triumphal return from Rome to Clairvaux.

6. (Author's Preface) *Brother Godfrey.*

Godfrey de la Roche, Bernard's cousin, was one of those who accompanied him to Citeaux in 1112, and one of the original monks of Clairvaux in 1115. He was appointed first abbot of Fontenay, the second daughter of Clairvaux, in 1119, but returned some years later to Clairvaux, where he was prior until 1139, when he was elected bishop of Langres, the diocese where Clairvaux was located, after Bernard himself had been elected but had refused to accept. He eventually retired to Clairvaux again in 1162 and died there in 1165. The *Steps of Humility* was probably written while he was prior of Clairvaux (cf. Mabillon's Preface). Wurm (*Gottfried*, 6), Vacandard (*Vie*, I, 158), Luddy (*Life*, 83), Mills (translation, vii), and Williams (*St Bernard of Clairvaux*, 28) say that it was written while he was abbot of Fontenay, and was therefore composed primarily for the monks there, rather than for Bernard's own monks at Clairvaux. Certainly nothing in the essay itself suggests this, and Godfrey is not referred to as an abbot. Their opinion seems to be inferred from two untenable premises — that the *Steps of Humility* is the book referred to in the letter written in 1127, and that Godfrey returned to Clairvaux some time later than this — after 1130 according to Williams, about 1135 according to Mills. But it would seem that he had already returned by 1126, for his signature *Godefridus prior de Clarevalle* appears as witness to a deed also witnessed by Bishop Joceran, who died April 16, 1126 (E. Petit, *Histoire des Ducs de Bourgogne de la Race Capétienne*, II, 220, no. 259; cf. Manricus, *Annales Cistercienses*, 1127, 4, 6; Vacandard, *Vie*, I, 399, note 1). For Godfrey's life, see H. J. Wurm, *Gottfried Bischof von Langres* (Wurzburg, 1886).

7. (Author's Preface) *A dilemma between this fear and love.*

Most of Bernard's essays are prefaced by a similar apology for writing them. *Consideration:* "My speech, glad yet reluctant, both wills and wills not to come forth; for majesty and love contend in bidding it contrariwise. The latter urges, the former forbids. But your condescension, in not commanding but requesting although you would more fittingly command, has solved the difficulty. For when majesty yields so condescendingly, why should modesty not yield?" (*Opera* 1005.) *Office of Bishops:* "The favor of him who asks is flattering, but the demand of that which is asked is terrifying. For who am I to write to bishops? But on the other hand who am I to disobey bishops? I am forced on one hand to grant, on the other to deny, what I am asked. To write to such eminence is above me; to disobey it is beyond me. Danger on both sides; but the greater seems to threaten on the side of disobedience." (*Opera* 1101.) *Precept and Dispensation:* "With what reason shall I keep silent longer? Yet with what effrontery shall I speak? By frequent letters and messages you force me either to reveal my ignorance or to refuse the duty of love. I prefer to be found lacking in that which puffs up than in that which edifies." (*Opera* 1174.) *Apology:* "If up until now I have agreed either reluctantly or not at all to write what you have asked me, it was not because I refused to do what I was asked, but because I did not presume to do what I was incapable of. But now a new and urgent reason has put to flight my former modesty, and I am forced to give vent to my grief either competently or incompetently, the very necessity giving me confidence." (*Opera* 1222.) *In Praise of the New Warfare:* "I have put it off for some time; not because the request seemed a thing to be despised, but lest an easy and immediate assent should be found blameworthy in case I who have no skill should presume to do what a better could accomplish better, and a very necessary thing should perhaps be rendered less perfect through me." (*Opera* 1253.) *Loving God:* "But because both the learned and the unlearned have the custom of making excuses of this sort, and it is not easily known which excuse proceeds really from ignorance and which from modesty, if obedience to the prescribed task does not make it clear; accept of my poverty what I have, lest by keeping silent I should be reputed a philosopher." (*Opera* 1329.) These expressions do not seem to be insincere. Just as Bernard wanted to keep monastic seclusion, and took a special vow never to leave Clairvaux except on urgent business of the Church or the Order, but was compelled to travel extensively; so he wanted to keep monastic silence, giving expression to his thoughts only in the sermons which it was his duty as abbot to preach to his own monks, but was frequently urged to speak elsewhere or to write a book. He consented to write only when he felt that the particular case involved an obligation of charity which must take precedence over the obligation of monastic silence and humility. That is why we have so few books, and no systematic discussion of mysticism, by one who wrote with such facility, and could have discussed mysticism with such authority.

8. (1) *I am the truth, promising life.*

Truth, the end to which humility is a means, is itself a means to a higher end, eternal life. Cf. Sermon 2 for Ascension, 6: "Thou art the way, the truth, and the life — the way in example, the truth in promise, the life in reward" (XB 370). The sequel will show that the truth to which humility is an end is truth in yourself, which is like all knowledge an end in itself, but not the highest good. It leads eventually, however, to the highest good, eternal life or beatitude, which includes knowledge of God, or Truth in itself. Bernard proceeds to give an alternative, equally true, interpretation of the verse in which the "life" is taken as the grace of strength to persevere in humility.

9. (2) *The Zion of speculation.*

"Speculative consideration is that which collects itself in itself and, so far as divinely assisted, withdraws itself from human affairs in order to contemplate God" (*Consideration* 5, 2, 4, *Opera* 1074). This mystical recollection is the hilltop to which the steps of humility lead, and from which, after the laborious climb, a clear view of truth is finally attained.

10. (3) *The double circumcision.*

That is, physical and spiritual. Just as historically Truth, that is, Christ, appeared after the fulfillment of these twelve fundamental precepts of the Law of Moses, so mystically Truth appears after the ascension of these twelve steps of the Rule of Benedict.

11. (3) *It makes the yoke of Truth easy, and its burden light.*

Matth. 11. 30. Benedict says: "When all these steps of humility have been mounted the monk will presently attain to that love of God which is perfect and casteth out fear. By means of this love everything which before he had observed not without fear, he shall now begin to do by habit, without any trouble and, as it were, naturally. He acts now not through fear of hell, but for the love of Christ, out of a good habit and a delight in virtue." (*Rule*, chap. 7.) Cf. Sermon 85 on Canticles, 8: "Where there is love there is not labor but savor" (*Opera* 3190).

12. (5) *Who will bid me even to that half-way but sweet banquet of love?*

Bernard himself is still partaking of the first banquet. He repeats this assertion, using a different metaphor, at the beginning of Chapter 9. Unless he is guilty of excessive humility, this indicates that, to say nothing of the second banquet, he is not yet partaking of the third — that is, at the time of writing the *Steps of Humility* he has not yet experienced mystical contemplation. He already, however, has a clear understanding of the path which leads to it. (But cf. Mabillon's note to Misc. Sermon 46, in which he argues that Bernard's self-deprecations are not always to be taken as applying literally to himself.)

13. (5) *Turn to truth, learn to love, and partake of the fruits of wisdom.*
The three rewards of humility are (1) truth — as was explained in the first chapter; (2) love — as is explained in this chapter; and (3) those "fruits of wisdom" which are served in the first banquet, namely the bread of sorrow and the wine of remorse.

14. (5) *Christ is the end of the law.*
Rom. 10. 4. Historically Truth incarnate as Christ was the end of the Mosaic Law. Mystically knowledge of truth in yourself, as will be explained in the next chapter, is the end of the Benedictine ladder of humility. Historically Christ introduced the era of grace. Mystically knowledge of truth in yourself makes you receptive of the grace of love.

15. (5) *Love.*
Even if the slip of the pen which wrote *gratiam* instead of *charitatem* was made by the author himself, it cannot be what he meant. The last two sentences are a syllogism: Truth gives love to those to whom it is revealed; it is revealed to the humble; ergo it gives love to the humble. Furthermore, the whole point of the chapter, of which these sentences are a summary, is that humility leads to love. To write *grace* instead of *love* not only invalidates the syllogism but deprives the chapter of all sense. The psychological explanation of the slip of the pen is obvious, since *Humilibus autem dat gratiam* (Jac. 4. 6; 1 Pet. 5. 5) is a favorite text with Bernard. (Mills, although he did not emend this passage in his critical text, found it impossible to render it literally in his English translation. But instead of changing *grace* to *love*, he changed *love* to *grace* in the preceding sentence — which makes an equally valid syllogism but not equally good sense.)

16. (6) *Sick sympathize with sick, and hungry with hungry.*
These are simple examples of the fundamental principle of Bernard's epistemology, that like knows like. He proceeds to make a more profound application of this principle.

17. (6) *Just as pure truth is seen only with a pure heart, so a brother's misery is truly felt with a miserable heart.*
These two propositions, examples of the principle that like knows like, are an epitome of Bernard's epistemology. Pure truth, or Truth in itself, which is God, is directly known, that is contemplated, not merely known about, only when the spiritual vision has been purified by humility and love. A brother's misery, that is a neighbor as he actually is in the state of sin, is directly known, that is loved and literally sympathized with, only when the knower has become himself subjectively miserable by the awareness of his own objectively miserable state.

18. (6) *Who willed his passion in order to learn compassion.*

The fundamental law that like knows like applies even to God. Man knows about God, to a certain extent, by reason and faith. God knows about man, perfectly, by his infinite wisdom. But man can know God directly, that is by contemplation, only by being deified, as Bernard calls it in *Loving God*, that is by purifying himself through humility and love so as to restore the *likeness* of God in which he was originally created. God can know fallen man directly, that is by sympathy, only by being humanified, that is incarnated, thus acquiring, if not sin itself, all the miseries which are the consequences of sin. Likewise he can love man only by being incarnated, love and knowledge being two aspects of sympathy, which is harmony of will.

19. (12) *Not because he could not consummate it in the one, but because he could not fulfill our needs without the other.*

Although God had the *power* to redeem man by his omnipotence without resorting to incarnation or any other device beyond his mere fiat, nevertheless he would not have had the *will* to do so except for his love for man which resulted from the sympathy for, that is direct knowledge of, man which he acquired, and could only have acquired, as a man. Therefore the redemption would have been impossible without the incarnation — not because justice required the sacrifice of a God-man, but because of the law that only like can know or love like.

Cf. above (sec. 9): "Him who could cure them, being God; wanted to cure them, being their neighbor; and understood them, having suffered the same things."

20. (12) *How could we imagine that superhuman compassion?*

God's eternal and impassive love for man is so unlike anything in our experience that it could not evoke a corresponding love for him in us. The incarnation is necessary, therefore, not only in order that God should learn to love us by sympathy, but in order that we should learn to love him. Reason teaches us to know about God, and it teaches us to love him as our benefactor ("loving God for your own sake"), but it does not teach us to know him directly or to love him by sympathy. But we are able to know Jesus as a fellow-man and love him as a fellow-sufferer, and in knowing and loving him we know and love God incarnate in him — which would be impossible without the incarnation. This necessity does not apply to mystics, who proceed by a process of purification to direct knowledge and love of the eternal Word. But few men are mystics. Ordinary Christians know and love God only in his human form, and even in heaven their greatest beatitude, before the resurrection, is the presence of the human Christ (cf. Sermon 4 for All Saints', 2, XB 630).

Cf. above (sec. 9): "When should we dare to approach him, remaining in his impassivity?"

21. (12) *If that pity free from pain had not come first.*

If God's love for man presupposes his incarnation, the incarnation itself presupposes a preexisting eternal love. Likewise, if man's love for his neighbor presupposes his humility, the humility itself presupposes a preexisting good will, that is a sort of love, which leads him to enter the monastic life where humility can be learned. God's eternal love for man is impassive. The man's preexisting good will is a rational, passionless sort of love, being the partial subjection of the will to the enlightened reason (the first step of humility). But both man and God have to pass through the discipline of humility before attaining the passionate love of sympathy.

22. (13) *I do not say make yourself what you are not, but observe what you are.*

Cf. Augustine: "The Son of God came as a man, and was *made* humble: it is commanded to you to *be* humble, it is not commanded to you to be *made* from man a brute: God was *made* man; do you, man, know that you *are* a man: your whole humility is to know yourself." (*In Joan.* 25, 16, *Pat. Lat.* 35, 1604.)

23. (14) *Some saint.*

Augustine, *De Genesi ad Litteram*, 11, 14, 18 (*Pat. Lat.* 34, 436).

24. (15) *Erect a way of ascent in his heart.*

Cf. Benedict: "If we would scale the summit of humility, and swiftly gain the heavenly height which is reached by our lowliness in this present life, we must set up a ladder of climbing deeds." (*Rule*, chap. 7.)

25. (18) *From justice to mercy.*

The progress follows the order of the Beatitudes, as given in the Vulgate: *beati pauperes spiritu, mites, qui lugent, qui esuriunt et sitiunt justitiam, misericordes, mundo corde, pacifici.*

Bernard did not apply the seventh beatitude to the mystical path in his doctrine, but he exemplified it in his own life, descending from his pure-hearted vision of God to become a peacemaker in the world.

26. (19) *These three things.*

This chapter is somewhat confusing because the three obstacles overcome by the three virtues are not always given in the correct order, the order of the Beatitudes. The three obstacles by which the spiritual vision is obscured are (1) a perverse will toward sinning, (2) the weakness of the flesh, and (3) ignorance. (1) A perverse will toward sinning is overcome by *sorrow and remorse* (the first of the three banquets), which destroy the delight taken in sinning. Such sorrow and remorse begin after "that thorough self-examination which makes a man contemptible in his own sight" (above, sec. 2). (2) The weakness of the flesh is overcome by a *desire for justice* so strong that it moves us to act in spite of the body's natural inertia. Such desire begins when the purely rational humility, by which we recognize ourselves to be what we truly are, is succeeded by a voluntary humility, by which we will to act and to be treated justly, that is, in accordance with our real littleness (cf. Sermon 42 on Canticles, 6, *Opera* 2927). (3) Ignorance is overcome by *active charity*, which leads us to know *about* other men, as we never do so long as we are concerned only with ourselves. Such charity begins when you "observe what you are, that you are wretched indeed, and so learn to be merciful, a thing you cannot know in any other way" (above, sec. 13). All three obstacles, therefore, are overcome by humility.

27. (19) *Ignorance and weakness and willfulness.*

That is: willfulness and weakness and ignorance, respectively.

28. (19) *Be excusable.*

That is, at the Last Judgment, which is referred to in the sequel — unless, as seems more likely, *erunt* is an error for *erant*.

29. (19) *Truth needy, naked, and weak.*

That is, in their neighbors. The threefold purification resulting from humility, by which we know ourselves, leads to love, by which we know our neighbors.

30. (19) *Weakness or ignorance or willfulness.*

That is: willfulness or weakness or ignorance, respectively.

31. (19) *To such a heart Truth promises to appear in his splendor.*

But not immediately, for there is a further stage of purification, as is clear from other passages in the essay; and it seems obvious that the soul which is weeping, hungering for justice, and devoted to works of mercy is still in the state where truth is found *harsh*. The spiritual vision — *oculus* (or *acies*) *cordis* (or *mentis*) — consists of understanding and love, and its organs are the reason and the will. The process by which they are purified involves three steps. (1) Humility shows us truth in ourselves. (2) As a result of this humility and awareness of truth in ourselves, we proceed to the threefold process of purification described in this chapter. (3) As a result of this process, we come to love our neighbors; and this is the state (the second of the three banquets) where truth is found *loving*. It is this love which finally purifies the spiritual vision for contemplation, as is said above (sec. 6): "After the spiritual vision has been purified by this brotherly love, they enjoy the contemplation of truth in its own nature"; and then truth is found *pure*. The first step involves the reason alone, for we can be forced by reason to know ourselves even against our will. The second step is the subjection of the will to the reason. The third step is the freeing of the will from the reason's domination (Sermon 9 on Canticles, 2, *Opera* 2704), although its cooperation is still required. The second step is the end of the purification of the reason, but it is the beginning of the purification of the will — as is emphasized in the following chapter.

The sentence, *To such a heart Truth promises to appear in his splendor*, may also be understood in a different sense, perhaps justified by the preceding context, although less relevant to the argument of the chapter. Weeping, hungering for justice, and works of mercy, even if they do not lead to love, are themselves merits sufficient for salvation. To such a heart, therefore, Truth promises to appear in his splendor — not in mystical contemplation but at the Last Judgment.

32. (19) *Three steps or states of truth.*

That is, of direct knowledge. Bernard's doctrine may be considered either identical with or contrary to the Socratic doctrine that moral virtue is the result of knowledge, depending on which steps are being compared. His doctrine is that virtue and knowledge result from each other in progressive steps. As a result of the moral discipline of the twelve steps of humility, you attain knowledge of yourself by reason. As a result of knowledge of yourself, you undertake the moral discipline of active charity. As a result of active charity, you attain knowledge of your neighbors by love. As a result of knowledge of your neighbors, you are purified for the moral discipline of contemplation. As a result of contemplation, you attain knowledge of God by ecstasy.

33. (19) *Reason, by which we examine ourselves, leads us to the first.*

Reason alone gives adequate knowledge of the self. But it must be remembered that Bernard uses *reason* in contrast to the other faculties of the soul, *will* and *memory*, and especially in contrast to *love*, which is a function of the will. He does not use *reason* in contrast to *revelation* or *faith*. Understanding, faith, and opinion are all functions of the reason. Bernard means that reason alone, that is, without the will, leads to the first step of truth. He does not mean that reason alone, that is, without being enlightened by faith, leads to it.

34. (19) *Love, by which we sympathize with others, entices us to the second.*

This is Bernard's solution of the modern philosophical problem, How can the solipsist be refuted? Bernard would say that he cannot be refuted rationally. The only true knowledge is direct knowledge, and reason, even when enlightened by faith, gives direct knowledge only of the self. The self, to be sure, is very complicated; modern philosophy has shown that it includes, for example, the forms of intuition and categories of understanding which determine the form of the phenomenal world, and these belong to the domain of "pure reason." But it does not include other selves. Other selves cannot be known directly by reason. But they can be known directly by love, which is a function of the will, a faculty distinct from the reason, because love, being an agreement of two substantially distinct wills, apprehends the other will in apprehending its own.

Descartes, undertaking to construct a philosophy by reason alone, easily established that he was and what he was, but had to resort to arguments of doubtful cogency in order to go further. A lover would have no such difficulty. If the first axiom of reason is *Cogito ergo sum*, the first axiom of love is *Amo te ergo es*.

35. (19) *Purity, by which we are lifted to invisible heights, snatches us up to the third.*

Bernard's most famous disciple describes the same threefold path to God in language more beautiful even than his. It is Bernard who leads Dante to God, and this seems to indicate that he derived his doctrinal inspiration chiefly from Bernard, just as he derived other kinds of inspiration from Virgil and Beatrice. He has three guides on the anagogic path. His first guide is Virgil, who symbolizes enlightened reason. As Vacandard says: "Virgile apparaît au moyen-âge comme l'oracle du paganisme. Ce n'est pas seulement un poète, un maître en l'art des vers, que Dante et ses contemporains saluent en lui, c'est encore et surtout un sage, à qui n'échappe aucun des secrets de la philosophie morale. C'est un disciple de Platon; c'est un héritier des traditions antiques. C'est de plus, un prophète." * His second guide is Beatrice, who symbolizes love. As Love says in the *New Life* (sec. 24): "He who should inquire delicately touching this matter, could not but call Beatrice by mine own name, which is to say, Love; beholding her so like unto me." The popular interpretation of Beatrice as theology, apparently due to an attempt to make Dante Thomas's disciple instead of

* Vacandard, *Le Rôle de Saint Bernard dans la Divine Comédie* (Rouen, 1883), p. 9.

Bernard's, although the former plays a relatively minor role in the *Comedy*, seems manifestly absurd, for Beatrice was not a theologian, but the girl whom Dante loved. His third guide is Bernard, who symbolizes contemplation. He says: "Fly with thine eyes through this garden; for seeing it will prepare thy look to mount further through the divine radiance" (*Par.* 31) — thus indicating the two kinds of contemplation he distinguished in Sermon 62 on Canticles (*Opera* 3037). On the upward path, Virgil conducts Dante through purgatory, where he recognizes his own sins, pride first of all; Beatrice conducts him through paradise, where he enjoys the communion of saints; Bernard conducts him, purified by his passage through purgatory and paradise, to the vision of absolute Truth.

36. (21) *First, when the Son of God, who is the Word and wisdom of the Father.*

That is, the Son incarnate as revealer of the Christian faith. Faith in his revelation comes *first*, at the beginning of the path which leads to knowledge.

Bernard's doctrine on faith and understanding may be expressed by saying that we *can* understand perfectly without faith but *don't*. Reason has the potency of understanding, but it is through faith that this potency is brought into act.

Understanding is infallible; a false judgment cannot be understood. Man, having the faculty of reason, is able to understand. Even unregenerate man, although unable to avoid sinning, is able to avoid erring — not without grace, but without saving grace. The infidel can understand himself and God just as well as the believer, although he cannot have the believer's further knowledge of God's essence by faith which transcends understanding. If most infidels (as well as nominal believers) do not understand themselves or God, it is for two reasons. First, they do not devote the attention of their infallible understanding to themselves or God, but through curiosity devote it to the unimportant things of the world, understanding them truly but not profitably. Secondly, even if considering themselves or God, through pride they do not try to understand, but content themselves with mere opinion, which is fallible. Therefore, although understanding never fails, reason, when corrupted by curiosity and pride, does fail, that is, fails to understand. Since the rational man is willfully curious or proud, he is to blame for his failure to understand.

The reason can be enlightened by any means God wills, and so even the infidel is capable of enlightenment. But the means by which God does will to enlighten the reason of people in general is faith, that is, the Christian revelation. This faith is not belief in the facts which are to be understood, for they are intelligible rather than credible, but the threefold belief in God * which precedes all belief in facts. It is belief in the precepts, miracles, and promises of the incarnate Word. Moved by the promises and assured by the miracles, the true believer observes the precepts. This is the first step of humility. "The first step of humility," says Benedict, "is reached when a man, with the fear of God always before his eyes, does not allow himself to

* Qua credimus in Deum, qua credimus Deum, qua credimus Deo. (Misc. Sermon 45, 5, XB 913.)

forget, but is ever mindful of all God's precepts, remembering that such as contemn God fall into hell for their sins and that life eternal awaits such as fear him." The fundamental precept is to imitate the example of Christ's humility. As the believer progresses in humility, he overcomes curiosity and pride and so purifies the reason for understanding himself and God. He can then say with the prophet (above, sec. 15): "After I learned the truth by believing in Christ,* that is, imitating his humility, it was itself exalted in me by my confession; but I was greatly humbled."

Understanding, therefore, is dependent on faith psychologically but not logically. Once attained, it relies only on reason, and its arguments are sufficiently cogent to compel any man to accept them, provided he will attend to them rationally. The tenets of the Christian faith, on the other hand, are dependent on faith in Christ both psychologically and logically. They rely only on authority, and the infidel cannot be compelled to accept them by any rational argument. Even the believer cannot understand them. The intelligible and the credible form two domains of knowledge, equal in certainty but differing in clarity.†

37. (21) *Weighed down by the flesh, captive to sin, blinded by ignorance, and given over to external things.*

(1) Weighed down by the flesh. Cf. *Precept and Dispensation* 20, 59: "*The corruptible body is a load upon the soul* (Sap. 9. 15). Not the body simply, but the corruptible body; the corruption, not the nature, of the body being onerous. Wherefore those who groan within themselves wait for the redemption of their body (Rom. 8. 23), not for its loss." (*Opera* 1212.)

(2) Captive to sin. Cf. *Grace and Free Choice* 7, 21: "Man received at his creation the lesser degree of both freedoms together with full freedom of choice, and when he sinned he fell from both. He fell from ability not to sin into inability not to sin, freedom of counsel being completely lost. And likewise from ability not to be confounded into inability not to be confounded, freedom of enjoyment being completely lost." (*Opera* 1380.)

(3) Blinded by ignorance. Cf. Misc. Sermon 45, 2: "The fall of the reason is threefold. For its function was to distinguish between good and evil, true and false, expedient and inexpedient; but in making these distinctions it is now blinded by such great darkness that it often leads the judgment to the contrary, taking evil for good, false for true, harmful for expedient, and conversely. Surely it would never err in these matters if it were never deprived of the light by which it was created." (XB 912.)

(4) Given over to external things. Curiosity about external things, the

---

* In Christum credendo (the *fides praeceptorum*).

† For Bernard's doctrine on faith and understanding see: Letter 18, 2 (*Opera* 161); *Consideration* 5, 3, 5–6 (*Opera* 1074); *ibid.* 5, 14, 30 (*Opera* 1093); *Loving God* 2, 6 (*Opera* 1333); *Abelard's Errors* 1, 1 (*Opera* 1442); Sermon 3 for Ascension, 1–2 (XB 370); Misc. Sermon 10, 1 (XB 777); Misc. Sermon 45, 2–5 (XB 912); Sermon 31 on Canticles, 3 (*Opera* 2864); Sermon 76 on Canticles, 6 (*Opera* 3140); Sermon 85 on Canticles, 2 (*Opera* 3186).

first step of pride, is the first step which leads to sin, either original or actual; see chapter 10 below.

38. (21) *Gently purged, ardently energized, and made merciful.*

This is the triple purification described in the preceding chapter: gently purged, willfulness being overcome by weeping; ardently energized, weakness being overcome by hungering for justice; made merciful, ignorance being overcome by devotion to works of mercy.

39. (21) *By this second conjunction of the Spirit of God and the human will, love is created.*

The will, having been "anointed" by the Holy Ghost, that is, purified in the threefold manner described, is then "extended," that is, the benevolence which it naturally feels for itself is extended to its neighbors. It is thus extended "even to its enemies" in the extreme case of those who obey the evangelical command to love your enemies; but elsewhere Bernard explains this impossible command as referring to active charity only (Sermon 50 on Canticles, 3, *Opera* 2968). As soon as the good will is thus extended to its neighbors, love, that is, a harmony of two wills, comes into existence.

40. (21) *A finally perfected soul.*

That is, restored to the likeness of God. Cf. *Grace and Free Choice* 10, 35: "We need also the aid of him whose example has provoked us to such things, so that by it we may be conformed through wisdom and *changed into the same image from glory to glory, even as by the Spirit of the Lord* (2 Cor. 3. 18)." (*Opera* 1388.) God, that is, God the Son incarnate, has *provoked* us to right action by his example, that is, has called the reason 'to understand what is right. But it is necessary for the same God, that is, God the *Spirit of the Lord*, to *aid* us, that is, to move the will to desire what is right. With this example and this aid we are *changed into the same image*, that is, into the likeness of God. Cf. Misc. Sermon 45, 4: "The Son of God, therefore, sent by the Father, came and gave faith; after the Son, was sent the Holy Ghost, who gave and taught love. And so by these two, that is faith and love, was aroused hope of returning to the Father. And this is the trinity, namely faith, hope, love, with which as with a trident that changeless and blessed Trinity has brought back the changeable, fallen, and wretched trinity from the slime of the abyss to its lost beatitude." (XB 913.) In this sermon the association of the divine persons with the theological virtues and with the faculties of the soul, suggested by the valid association of the Son with faith and reason and of the Holy Ghost with love and will, is completed by a forced association of the Father with hope and memory. Similarly, in the *Steps of Humility*, the association of the divine persons with the steps of the anagogic path, suggested by the valid association of the Son with humility and of the Holy Ghost with love, is completed by the untenable association of the Father with contemplation.

41. (21) *The Father unites this soul to himself as a glorious bride.*

This is the only glaring inconsistency in Bernard's works. The identification of the Bridegroom, that is, the object of mystical contemplation, with the Father is incompatible with the doctrine of the sermons on Canticles, in which he is always identified with the Word. If we accept the latter, which is Bernard's definitive doctrine, as being true, we must reject the other as erroneous. It seems to be based, not on any intuition or argument or authority, but merely on a fanciful attempt to carry out the association, suggested by the relation of the Son to humility and of the Holy Ghost to love, to its obvious but untenable conclusion. Certainly no cogent argument can be derived from the three not very relevant scriptural citations given in the preceding section. The correct relation is to associate humility, love, and contemplation with the incarnate Word, the Holy Ghost, and the eternal Word respectively. Christ teaches us humility by his example, and gives us, through his own doctrine in the gospels and through that of his body the Church, the faith by which our reason is enlightened. The Holy Ghost, entering our hearts, infuses love. The divine Word, not incarnate, is contemplated in mystical ecstasy. But the Father transcends all human comprehension, at least before the resurrection.*

This point, which is of fundamental importance for the epistemology of Christian mysticism, may receive some light from modern philosophy. Hume demonstrated that science is impossible because scientific knowledge is knowledge of the laws governing the external object, and the subject, limited to its own experience, has no means of discovering the laws of that which is outside its experience. Kant refuted Hume by showing that, although Hume's argument was sound, he was wrong in concluding that it invalidated scientific knowledge, because he did not understand what science is. It is necessary to go beyond the Cartesian analysis of the all into subject and object. It is necessary to subdivide the object into reality and appearance. With regard to the reality, or thing in itself, Hume's argument is sound, and no knowledge is possible. But with regard to the appearance, or phenomenon, knowledge is possible, because its laws are determined by the subject, as Kant undertook to demonstrate. Science is possible because it is concerned, with the objective world to be sure, but with its appearance, not its reality. But in demonstrating the possibility of science Kant at the same time demonstrated the impossibility of mysticism. Mysticism, however variously it may be described, is essentially, by definition, knowledge of reality, as contrasted with the knowledge of mere appearance, which, the mystics maintain, is all that is given in ordinary or scientific knowledge. But reality, the thing in itself, is just what Kant showed to be unknowable. If the mystics have forms of intuition and categories of understanding different from those of other people, then no doubt the world appears to them differently than it appears to the others, but this peculiar world of the mystics is only a different appearance, a different phenomenal world, and could at best claim only equal validity with the ordinary phenomenal world. Mysticism, therefore, defined as knowledge of reality, seems to be impossible, just as science, defined as knowledge of the external object, seemed to be impossible before Kant's explanation of it. Ouspensky demonstrated the possibility of mysticism in a manner similar to that in which Kant demonstrated the possibility of science. He undertook to demonstrate that the world as it appears to the mystics, differing from the world as it appears to others

* Cf. Sermon 4 for All Saints', 3 (XB 631); Misc. Sermon 41, 12 (XB 902); Sermon 31 on Canticles, 2 (*Opera* 2863).

because the mystics apprehend it emotionally instead of conceptually, is itself that very reality of which the world of ordinary experience is an appearance. It is the four-dimensional hypersolid * of which the phenomenal world is a three-dimensional cross-section. We may say, therefore, that, just as in order to understand the possibility of science we must subdivide the object into reality and appearance, so in order to understand the possibility of mysticism we must subdivide reality into what we may call ultimate reality and proximate reality. Science is knowledge of the object, but of its appearance, not its reality. Mysticism is knowledge of its reality, but of its proximate reality, not its ultimate reality. The ultimate reality, which is the thing in itself, is absolutely unknowable, as Kant rightly maintained. But the proximate reality is knowable to those who have purified their souls to the extent of getting rid of the forms of intuition and categories of understanding which make scientific knowledge possible by obscuring reality. The proximate reality itself, no less than the phenomenal world, is only an appearance of the unknowable ultimate reality. But relative to the phenomenal world it is reality, and upon the truth of this fact is based the mystics' claim to a superior knowledge – superior not merely in quantity or quality, that is, extent or subtlety, but superior as truth is superior to illusion, as reality is superior to appearance.

Ultimate reality, proximate reality, and appearance are absolutely one, because they are identical, being the same thing considered from different points of view. Yet they are absolutely three, because they are more different from each other than any other things whatever, all other divisions or distinctions being merely subdivisions within one of these, which are the most basic categories possible. Ultimate reality is ultimate, itself derived from nothing, all else derived from it. Proximate reality is derived from ultimate because it is an appearance of it. Appearance is derived from proximate reality because it is an appearance of it, yet not in quite the same way as proximate reality is derived from ultimate. Appearance is also an appearance of, and so derived from, ultimate reality. Their relations, therefore, are those of the Christian Trinity.

The thing in itself, as described by Kant, is incorporeal and eternal because transcending space and time, unknowable and ineffable because transcending all categories of understanding, the cause of all things which are, yet not in the same sense in which one phenomenon is called cause of another. This is exactly how the theologians describe God – that is, God as transcendent, or God the Father. They also describe God as immanent, that is, the Spirit of God in this temporal phenomenal world. This is the divine in things, in Bernard's language the "being of all things," that is, that which is truly real in things, the *given*, as distinguished from that which is illusory or apparent, the *a priori*. The Holy Ghost dwells in us and in all creatures, and even in ordinary experience we apprehend immanent God whenever we apprehend the truly divine, and so truly real, in ourselves or in other things.

* Cf. Eph. 3. 17: That ye, being rooted and grounded in love, may be able to comprehend with all saints what is the breadth, and length, and depth, and height.

But the theologians also describe the divine Word or Wisdom. Unlike the Holy Ghost, which moves in this temporal phenomenal world, it is eternally immoveable, and so transcends this world and cannot be known by the knowledge of this world. Unlike the Father, it does not transcend the knowledge of those pure souls who apprehend the objective world not in space and time but *sub specie aeternitatis*. It is the proximate reality which man is capable of knowing but because of his corruption does not know ordinarily. The Word, not the Father or the Holy Ghost, although all three are one same Truth, is the object of mystical contemplation, and because it is apprehended by love, not by concepts, it is rightly called the Bridegroom of the soul.

42. (21) *If thou know not thyself, go feed thy kids.*

The whole verse reads: *If thou know not thyself, O fairest among women, go forth, and follow after the steps of the flocks, and feed thy kids beside the tents of the shepherds.* Cant. 1. 7 (Douai trans.) Bernard interprets it as follows: "Man made in honor, when he understands not this honor, deserves by such ignorance to be likened to the sheep, as sharers in his present corruption and mortality. So it comes to pass that by not knowing himself the creature marked off by the gift of reason begins to be herded with the flocks of irrational beings, when, ignorant of his own glory which is within, he is led away by his own curiosity to be conformed outwardly to sensible things; and he becomes one of the rest, because he understands not that he has received something beyond the rest. And so we must greatly beware of this ignorance, by which we may think of ourselves less than ourselves; but not less, nay even more, of that by which we attribute more to ourselves." (*Loving God* 2, 4, *Opera* 1332.) Humility, knowing yourself, means to know that you are in a state of sin. To be in a state of sin means to be potentially blessed but actually miserable. Neither the angels, who are actually blessed, nor the animals, who are not even potentially blessed, are in a state of sin. To acquire humility through learning by faith that you are in a state of sin, means to lower yourself in your own estimation only if you formerly thought you were an angel. If you were a materialist and so thought you were an animal, to learn that you are in a state of sin means to raise yourself in your own estimation. The doctrine of sin is that we are capable of being better than we are. It is the only ground of hope and optimism.

43. (21) *The hearts of its neighbors.*

This sentence shows the three steps of the purifying process: (1) the school of humility, where the soul learns to know itself; (2) the leadership of the Holy Ghost, by which it overcomes willfulness, weakness, and ignorance; (3) the introduction into the hearts of its neighbors by love. Only after it has been introduced into the hearts of its neighbors by love, as well as adorned with good habits and holy virtues, is it capable of contemplation.

44. (21) *The chamber of the King.*

Cf. Sermon 23 on Canticles, 9: "The chamber of the King is to be sought in the mystery of mystical contemplation (*in theoricae contemplationis arcano*)." (*Opera* 2799.)

45. (21) *About half an hour.*

This phrase, taken from Scripture, may not be intended to indicate literally the approximate duration of a mystical ecstasy. It is, however, the only suggestion concerning this subject in Bernard's works. Cf. Pascal: "From about half past ten in the evening till about half an hour after midnight, Fire." (*Mémorial, Oeuvres*, IV, p. 4.) Cf. William James: "Mystical states cannot be sustained for long. Except in rare instances, half an hour, or at most an hour or two, seems to be the limit beyond which they fade into the light of common day." (*Varieties of Religious Experience*, p. 381.)

46. (21) *Searches out the secrets of truth.*

Cf. William James: "Although so similar to states of feeling, mystical states seem to those who experience them to be also states of knowledge. They are states of insight into depths of truth unplumbed by the discursive intellect. They are illuminations, revelations, full of significance and importance, all inarticulate though they remain; and as a rule they carry with them a curious sense of authority for after-time." (*Ibid.*, p. 380.)

47. (21) *That it may feed on the memory of them when it returns to itself.*

Cf. William James: "Mystical states, strictly so called, are never merely interruptive. Some memory of their content always remains, and a profound sense of their importance. They modify the inner life of the subject between the times of their recurrence." (*Ibid.*, p. 381.)

48. (21) *Hears unspeakable words.*

Cf. William James: "The handiest of the marks by which I classify a state of mind as mystical is negative. The subject of it immediately says that it defies expression, that no adequate report of its contents can be given in words." (*Ibid.*, p. 380.)

In these two sentences Bernard describes all four of James's "marks" of mystical experience: ineffability, noetic quality, transiency, passivity.

49. (22) *He does nothing.*

Cf. William James: "Although the oncoming of mystical states may be facilitated by preliminary voluntary operations, as by fixing the attention, or going through certain bodily performances, or in other ways which manuals of mysticism prescribe; yet when the characteristic sort of consciousness once has set in, the mystic feels as if his own will were in abeyance, and indeed sometimes as if he were grasped and held by a superior power." (*Ibid.*, p. 381.)

50. (26) *Alas that I ever descended from it!*

This refers not to original sin but to the descent of the steps of pride, as is clear from the sequel. There is something illogical in Bernard's statement that no one reaches either the top or the bottom except by passing all the steps. Where then does one begin? Benedict seems to assume that the monk starts from a state of utter depravity and proceeds upward, slowly or rapidly, by the steps of humility. Bernard, in saying that the upward path can be recognized as the same path which has been descended, indicates that a monk is more apt to be perfectly humble at the beginning of his monastic career, and that lack of humility should be attributed to a fall. With regard to himself, he may be looking back to his days as a humble monk at Citeaux as the period before his own fall.

Bernard considers a monk's actual spiritual state to be less important than the direction of his progress. It is better to be on the fourth step of humility than on the fourth step of pride, although the monk on the latter is much more humble than the one on the former.

51. (28) *The First Step of Pride, Curiosity*.

"The twelfth step of humility is reached when a monk not only has humility in his heart, but even shows it also exteriorly to all who behold him. Thus, whether he be in the oratory at the 'Work of God,' in the monastery, or in the garden, on a journey, or in the fields, or wheresoever he be, sitting, standing, or walking, always let him, with head bent and eyes fixed on the ground, bethink himself of his sins and imagine that he is arraigned before the dread judgment of God." (Benedict, *Rule*, chap. 7. The quotations from the *Rule* are from Gasquet's translation.)

52. (30) *Because we are in mortal sin before we are born*.

Literally: Because first we die before we are born. That is, the soul dies before the body is born. The soul dies when it is separated from its "soul," which is God; just as the body dies when it is separated from its soul, which is an image of God. The death of the soul is effected by sin; that of the body, by the penalty of sin. We are spiritually dead when we are physically born. The soul is restored to life when it is reunited with its "soul," God, that is, Truth; just as the body is restored to life when it is reunited with its soul at the resurrection. The resurrection of the soul is effected by Christ's first coming; that of the body, by his second coming. (Misc. Sermon 116, XB 1012.)

53. (31) *A familiar master breeds contemptuous servants. Privatus dominus temerarios nutrit*.

This is a form of the common proverb, *Familiarity* (that is, condescension) *breeds contempt*. The meaning is made clear by the following section, which shows that Satan's contempt of God is particularly reprehensible because it was due to God's excessive kindness, the very thing which should have aroused love instead of contempt.

This proverb occurs in the Vulgate: *Qui delicate a pueritia nutrit servum suum, postea sentiet eum contumacem*. (Prov. 29. 21.) Also in the *Scala Paradisi* or *Scala Claustralium* of Guigo the Carthusian: *Vulgare proverbium est, quod nimia familiaritas parit contemptum*. (8, 9, *Bernardi Opera*, Vol. II, 654.) Bernard himself says elsewhere, and with a similar reference to ingratitude toward God: *Hoc nempe est, quod vulgari proverbio dicitur: Familiaris dominus fatuum nutrit servum*. (Misc. Sermon 27, 5, XB 842.)

A 12th century example of the use of *privatus* in the sense of *familiaris* is found in the rhymed book of etiquette called *Facetus*, couplet 15:

> Noli privatus nimis aut affabilis esse;
> qui nimis est privatus, eum vitare necesse.[*]

The second verse shows that *privatus* is a synonym, not an antonym, of *affabilis*, as it is hardly necessary to avoid one who is too shy.

54. (33) *Not passing wrath but everlasting hate*.

According to Bernard, the devil's sin, which was attempting to usurp

---

[*] Carl Schroeder, *Der deutsche Facetus* (*Palaestra*, Band 86, Berlin, 1911), p. 15. Cf. *ibid.*, p. 300.

God's power, is deserving of hatred, and so punished severely; whereas man's original sin, which was seeking knowledge elsewhere than from God, is deserving merely of wrath, and so punished very lightly (*mitissimae poenae*) in the case of those, for example unbaptized infants, who neither have been redeemed nor have committed actual sins deserving of hatred. (Sermon 69 on Canticles, 3–4, *Opera* 3090.)

55. (39) *The Second Step of Pride, Frivolity.*

"The eleventh step of humility is reached when a monk, in speaking, do so quietly and without laughter, humbly, gravely and in a few words [*pauca verba et rationabilia*; cf. Bernard's *semper vero irrationabilia*] and not with a loud voice."

56. (40) *The Third Step of Pride, Foolish Mirth.*

"The tenth step of humility is attained to when one is not easily and quickly moved to laughter." Cf. *Grace and Free Choice* 5, 14: Nulla autem verior miseria, quam falsa laetitia (*Opera* 1375).

57. (40) *The rule of silence.*

"Whatever, therefore, has to be asked of the prior, let it be done with all humility and with reverent submission. But as to coarse, idle words, or such as move to laughter, we utterly condemn and ban them in all places. We do not allow any disciple to give mouth to them." (Benedict, *Rule*, chap. 6.)

58. (41) *The Fourth Step of Pride, Boastfulness.*

"The ninth step of humility is reached when a monk restrains his tongue from talking, and, practicing silence, speaks not till a question be asked him, since Scripture says, *In the multitude of words there wanteth not sin* (Prov. 10. 19)."

59. (42) *The Fifth Step of Pride, Singularity.*

"The eighth step of humility is reached when a monk does nothing but what the common rule of the monastery, or the example of his seniors, enforces." Cf.: "What is done without leave of the spiritual Father will be reckoned presumption and vain-glory, and merit no reward." (*Rule*, chap. 49.)

Cf. Misc. Sermon 24, 1: "The devil persuades some to keep singular fasts, by which the others are scandalized, not because he loves fasting but because he delights in scandal." (XB 827.) Cf. Sermon 19 on Canticles, 7 (*Opera* 2769); Sermon 33 on Canticles, 1 (*Opera* 2882); Sermon 46 on Canticles, 6 (*Opera* 2948); Sermon 64 on Canticles, 5 (*Opera* 3050).

The editor of the Cambridge edition remarks: "Bernard's precept was wiser than his practice, for he nearly brought his life and work to a premature close by illnesses largely caused by his excessive austerities." His precept was that we owe the body health and nothing else; asceticism should be carried to the point, but only to the point, beyond which the health of the body would be endangered (Misc. Sermon 16, 2, XB 795) — but always, of course, in conformity with obedience to the Rule and to the abbot.

60. (42) *When the others are resting in the cloister after matins.*

"The brethren shall get up at the eighth hour of the night by reasonable calculation, so that having rested till a little after midnight they may rise refreshed. Let the time that remains after matins be used, for those brethren who need it, for the study of the Psalter or lessons." (*Rule*, chap. 8.)

61. (42) *He fills the ears of those outside.*

"If any brother wish to pray privately let him go into the oratory, without ostentation, and say his prayers, not with a loud voice, but with tears and an earnest heart." (*Rule*, chap. 52.)

62. (43) *The Sixth Step of Pride, Conceit.*

"The seventh step of humility is reached when a man not only confesses with his tongue that he is most lowly and inferior to others, but in the depths of his heart believes so."

63. (44) *The Seventh Step of Pride, Audacity.*

"The sixth step of humility is reached when a monk is content with all that is mean and vile; and in regard to everything enjoined him accounts himself a poor and worthless workman."

64. (45) *The Eighth Step of Pride, Excusing Sins.*

"The fifth step of humility is reached when a monk manifests to his abbot, by humble confession, all the evil thoughts of his heart and his secret faults."

65. (46) *The Ninth Step of Pride, Hypocritical Confession.*

"The fourth step of humility is reached when any one in the exercise of his obedience patiently and with a quiet mind bears all that is inflicted on him, things contrary to nature, and even at times unjust, and in suffering all these he neither wearies nor gives over the work."

66. (48) *The Tenth Step of Pride, Defiance.*

"The third step of humility is reached when a man, for the love of God, submits himself with all obedience to a superior."

67. (50) *The Eleventh Step of Pride, Freedom to Sin.*

"The second step of humility is reached when any one not loving self-will takes no heed to satisfy his own desires, but copies in his life what our Lord said, *I came not to do mine own will but that of him who sent me* (Joan. 6. 38)."

68. (51) *The Twelfth Step of Pride, Habitual Sinning.*

"The first step of humility is reached when a man, with the fear of God always before his eyes, does not allow himself to forget, but is ever mindful of all God's commandments."

APPENDICES

APPENDIX A

THE METAPHYSICAL PRESUPPOSITIONS OF CISTERCIAN MYSTICISM ACCORDING TO ISAAC OF STELLA

Bernard's theory of knowledge is based on the fundamental metaphysical presupposition that, in the full sense of being, God alone is. This principle, implicit in all his works and explicitly stated in his essay on *Consideration*,[1] is not developed in detail by Bernard, because his writings are concerned not with the theory of universals which precedes his theology logically but with the ethical consequences which precede it in urgency. The principle is, however, developed by his contemporary Isaac, the English abbot of the Cistercian monastery of Stella near Poitiers. Isaac was an admirer of Bernard[2] but cannot be considered his disciple. In many points his doctrine accords with Bernard's and was probably influenced by it,[3]

---

[1] 5, 6, 13 (*Opera* 1081).   [2] *Pat. Lat.* 194, 1869 c.

[3] E.g.: Qui ad pure incorporeum cernendum aciem mentis erigit, non solum omne corpus vel corporis similitudinem, sed etiam cogitationum universam volubilitatem transcendat, necesse est. (1701 c.)

Subdatur itaque sicut operatio voluntati, sic voluntas vel affectio rationi; ratio autem sapientiae et verbo Dei. (1703 d.)

Charitas ergo via, veritas vita, charitas similitudo, veritas imago, charitas meritum, veritas praemium; charitate itur, veritate statur. (1744 b.)

Quid enim proximius animo suo ipsius corpore, quod non solum diligere debet, sed odire non valet? (1774 a.)

Visitor diluculo, et subito, probor; assumor, et statim deseror; erigor, et statim dejicior, sicut qui per montana graditur, et planum iter non invenit. (1786 d.)

Virtus vero tota in veritate charitatis et in charitate veritatis consistit, tantum ex veritate illuminans ad cognoscendum, quantum ex charitate inflammans ad diligendum. Sicut enim sine charitate scientia inflat, sic sine scientia charitas oberrat. (1836 c.)

Liberum enim arbitrium quid aliud est quam libera cum ratione voluntas? Ex ratione arbitrium, ex voluntate liberum. (1847 a.)

Datur [gratia] libero arbitrio, quia solum salvatur; sed ideo datur, quia sine gratia non salvatur. (1847 d.)

Ea demum amicitia vera est, cum amico propter amicum idem velle, et idem nolle. (1852 b.)

Deus omnia quae habet, haec est. (1876 b.)

but in many others it is quite different from anything found in Bernard's works.[4] His metaphysics is found in his sermons for Sexagesima.[5]

All things which exist, exist either through themselves or

[4] E.g.: Dixisti enim, o insipiens, in corde tuo, extra cor tuum ipse: *Non est Deus* (Ps. 13. 1), quod tamen nec dicere potuisses, si is quem negas, non esset, sine quo nihil esse posset. Si ergo es ipse qui dixisti: procul dubio et is de quo dixisti. Quidquid enim est, aut principium est, aut de principio esse, necesse est. Quare si de principio es, necessario est principium, unde es: aut si principium ipse es, tunc quod esse negas, es. (1759 b.)

Si nunquam Deus fuit, hoc semper verum fuit. Quod si hoc semper fuit verum, ab aeterno aliquid fuit verum. Unde et ab aeterno veritas fuit, quia hoc verum fuit. (1759 d.)

Videtis, fratres, quantas patimur angustias, quanta languemus verborum inopia, cupientes de indicibili aliquid proprie dicere, docere de incomprehensibili. Totum equidem, ut non solum credatis aliis, sed ut intelligatis ipsi haud posse intelligi quid sit Deus, aut comprehendi. Sed neque hoc, dilectissimi, nostra infirmitate, aut hebetudine vel obtusitate, sed sua ipsius virtute et subtilitate. Unde sancta illa, et sublimia, et pennata seraphim alis quae volatum significant contemplationis, visa sunt velare faciem ejus et pedes, quatenus non velet eis principium et finem sua ignorantia, sed Dei incomprehensibilis supersapientia. (1762 d.)

Sunt itaque mentis rationalis tria exercitia; propter praesentia, praeterita, et futura, ex tribus ejus naturalibus potentiis, ratione, memoria, ingenio. Ingenium exquirit incognita, ratio judicat inventa, memoria recondit dijudicata, et offert adhuc dijudicanda. (1767 a.)

Antequam sensibilis iste mundus fieret, nihil omnino minus erat, quam nunc est, imo infinite amplius, quam in hac sensibilitate existat. Totum enim, quod in exemplo patet, prodiisse de exemplari necesse est: sed totum quod est in exemplari, in exemplum venisse, nondum verum est. Ibi enim non solum quae facta sunt, sed quaecunque fieri possunt, pulchrius et verius existunt, ubi non mutabilia et vana, sed veritas et vita sunt. (1769 a.)

Haud enim praedestinavit Deus talem non posse perire, qui cum sit liberi arbitrii, in alterutrum flecti potest: nec aliter ac vivit, posse vivere; sed simpliciter sic vivere, et non perire. Valde namque diversa sunt, non perire, et non posse perire. Alterum ergo praedestinavit, alterum minime, qui tamen utrumque donavit. (1803 a.)

Sensu igitur corpora percipit, imaginatione corporum similitudines, ratione vero corporum dimensiones, et similia; insuper primum videlicet incorporeum ad subsistendum tamen indigum corpore, ac per hoc loco et tempore. Intellectu quidem fertur super omne quod corpus est, vel corporis, vel ullo modo corporeum; percipitque spiritum creatum, qui ad subsistendum non eget corpore, ac per hoc nec loco, licet sine tempore esse minime possit, cum naturae mutabilis sit. Intelligentia denique utcunque, et quantum naturae fas est, cernit ipsum solum summe et pure incorporeum: quod nec corpore ut sit, nec loco ut alicubi, nec tempore ut aliquando, eget. (1880 c.)

[5] For Isaac's psychology, see his essay on *The Soul*. For his theory of free choice, see sermons 34 and 46.

not through themselves. If not through themselves, they exist
through another to which they adhere in order to exist, and
are called adherents or accidents. If through themselves, they
are called substances. For example, Man exists through himself, and any particular man exists through himself, but his
wisdom or folly, tallness or shortness, whiteness or blackness
exist not through themselves but through him. It is the property of accidents, which include the nine other categories, to
adhere to substances, and it is the property of substances to be
susceptible of contrary accidents and therefore mutable. All
substances exist through themselves, but they may exist in
either of two ways. They may, like Man, exist only abstractly
in nature and the reason and the understanding; or they may,
like any particular man, exist both in nature and in act, both
in reason and in reality, both in understanding and in status.
The latter are numerically one both in reason and in reality,
and are substances in the strict sense; they are called first substances. The former are suspended in the understanding and
conceived confusedly by the mind as common to many par-
ticulars; they are called second substances. First substances
exist in themselves, but second substances exist only in the
first substances which exist in reality. Any particular man
exists in himself, but Man exists only in the various men, and
if there were no men, Man would exist nowhere and so would
not be at all. Second substances exist of themselves, but first
substances exist only of the second substances which preexist
in reason. Man exists of himself, requiring for his existence
nothing but the differentiated genus mortal rational animal,
but a particular man exists only of Man, and if there were no
such thing as Man there could be no particular men exemplify-
ing it. All things, therefore, are imperfect — accidents do not
exist through themselves, second substances do not exist in
themselves, first substances do not exist of themselves. All
things are dependent on something else for their being and
therefore, considered alone by themselves, are not. Accidents
are the forms [6] by which generic second substances are differ-

---

[6] In 1755 c, for *complectitur, nulla omnino erit secunda*, read *complectitur,
nulla omnino erit forma.*

entiated into specific second substances and by which specific second substances are exemplified in first substances. Accidents are nothing apart from the second substances of which they are determinations. Second substances are nothing apart from the first substances in which they are posited. First substances are nothing apart from the accidents by which they are differentiated. All separate things are nothing, and therefore all combinations are nothing, for a combination of two nothings can produce only nothing. All creatures composed of matter and form are nothing, because matter is mere substance, which is nothing, and form is mere accident, which is nothing. *If a man think himself to be something, when he is nothing, he deceiveth himself.*[7] If God can say *I am who am,*[8] all others must confess, I am who am not. As the Prophet says,[9] *All nations before him are as nothing; and they are counted to him less than nothing, and vanity.*[10]

That which is most worthy and than which nothing can be better, must exist through itself, of itself, and in itself. It must be immutable,[11] for it is obvious that the immutable is better than the mutable, and this is confirmed by the authority of the apostle: *with whom is no variableness, neither shadow of turning.*[12] Being immutable, it is simple and one.[13] One, it transcends all second substances, for unity is the principle of all things. Simple, it transcends all first substances, which are compounded of matter and form. Immutable, it transcends all substance whatever, corporeal or incorporeal, for mutability is the property of substance.[14] It is not any of all things;

[7] Gal. 6. 3.
[8] Ex. 3. 14.
[9] Is. 40. 17.
[10] Sermon 19.
[11] In 1757 d, for *conmutabilis* read *immutabilis*.
[12] Jac. 1. 17.
[13] *Quod est unum, simplex et stabile est* (1757 d); the argument seems to require transposing *unum* and *stabile*. But for Isaac the fundamental divine attributes (unity, simplicity, immutability) are equivalent (cf. 1764 d); he is not constructing a rigorous deductive system like Anselm of Canterbury, but refreshing his monks with spiritual food.
[14] Sermon 20.

still less is it nothing at all; neither is it, like Plato's matter, intermediate between something and nothing. One before all things, simple after all things, immutable above all things — it is the creator, sustainer, and ruler of the universe.[15] This super-substance alone truly is, since all else has been shown to be nothing. Being better than any substance, it alone deserves to be worshiped, even if it does not exist, since it can at least be thought.

Its existence, however, is demonstrable. The atheist, if he concedes his own existence, must admit that his own first cause is either himself or something else — in the latter case he acknowledges God's existence; in the former he is himself God. If anything exists, the one simple immutable cause of all diversity and composition and motion must exist. The eternal existence of truth itself, which the atheist must concede if he claims his own doctrine to be eternally true, proves the existence of the immutable — unless something mutable and consequently temporal has existed from eternity, which is absurd. These proofs are based not on verbal inference but on the nature of God.[16] If anything exists, the first cause of all things must exist. Even if no thing exists (as was in fact the case before the creation), still he exists who can bring into existence everything which either is or can be.[17]

Having found that God is and what he is not, we must inquire what he is. This is not absolutely impossible. God is ineffable — intrinsically so, not merely through the weakness of our understanding. But something can be affirmed truly, although not accurately, even of the ineffable. Divine theology, which describes God literally, can affirm nothing of him, but denies all attributes to him. Symbolic theology, which

[15] Isaac's doctrine frequently recalls that of John Scotus Erigena, especially this phrase: Principium, unde omnia ducuntur ad esse; finis continens omnia, ne recidant ad non esse; aeternitas movens et regens omnia per esse (1758 d).

[16] I.e., not on the epistemological definition of God as that than which nothing greater can be thought (as in Anselm), but on the metaphysical definition of God's essence as that than which nothing better can be.

[17] Sermon 21.

describes God metaphorically, calls him a lion, a bird, etc. Between the two is rational theology, which describes God neither literally nor metaphorically but by understatement. God is truly wise and just — but not in the same way that a man is wise or just; and to call him wise or just is to fall short of the truth.

God's simplicity means that he is whatever he has. Since he is that than which nothing better can be, he is obviously wise and just, i.e. has wisdom and justice, and consequently is wisdom and justice. This is absurd, because he is not anything, yet it is true in the sense of understatement. Just as he is called supersubstance, so he can be called superwisdom and superjustice, and similarly of other attributes. This means that he is the source of wisdom and of justice and of all things — not as one thing is the source of another of the same nature (as the spring is the source of the river), but as the efficient cause, like an artisan, whose nature is different from that of the artefact he makes. But this too is an understatement, because the artisan only makes artefacts which are of the same nature as his raw material, whereas God creates things from nothing, annihilates things into nothing, changes one sort of thing into another, increases without adding, and decreases without taking away. He is no thing, but the efficient cause of all things; truly existing in himself, yet giving to other things a different sort of existence. As unity, he is not any number, but is the efficient cause of all numbers; e.g., two is merely twice unity (not two unities, for there is only one), and so in two nothing but unity truly exists. As simplicity, he is the efficient cause of all compounds. As immutability, he is the efficient cause of all motion. He is the essence of all things — not that mutable essence by reason of which they are truly nothing, but the immutable essence by which all things are truth and life together once and forever, the source and efficient cause of essence, wisdom, justice, and all things — having them and being them not as they are in things but whence they are in things. Through the good and beautiful things which are made the understanding tries to discern that best and most beautiful by which they are made.[18]

In God we must distinguish what he is from what he has — not in denotation, for they are identical, but with regard to his being and his having respectively. What he is has what he has. The latter, therefore, is of the former, while the former is not of anything. Hence the latter is called the offspring, or (as we usually say) the Son, of the former; while the former is, to continue the metaphor, called the Father of the latter. Rational theology distinguishes, therefore, between God as wisdom and God as wisdom of wisdom, between God as justice and God as justice of justice, etc. The relation between Father and Son is ineffable. Just as there is no noun to describe what God is, so there is no verb to describe what God does — for one reason because none of the tenses of our grammar refers to eternal action. Resorting to understatement and choosing the most nearly suitable verb from human psychology, we say that God speaks — but with the reservations that it is not speaking and is not in the present tense. The human soul has three faculties: memory, reason, and inventiveness — directed to the past, present, and future respectively.[19] Inventiveness searches out unknown things. Reason judges things found by inventiveness or regurgitated by memory, speaking them either audibly in the mouth of the body or by meditation in the mouth of the heart. Memory stores away things judged by reason and regurgitates them to be judged again. In God there is nothing corresponding to memory or inventiveness, for he has nothing past or future. Everything which he has, he has simultaneously present, or rather super-simultaneously superpresent in eternity. Everything which he has, therefore, he is eternally speaking, and so what he has is called his Word.[20] In it all things exist actually, that is by

[18] Sermon 22.

[19] The soul, intermediate between God and body, has God-like simplicity with respect to its natural faculties and body-like complexity with respect to its accidental virtues. It is its faculties but is not its virtues. (1876 b.)

[20] Sermon 23.

eternally present prescience, but also potentially, for it is the source, that is the exemplar, of all things which are or can be. All things exist in the immutable exemplar, where they are truth and life, more truly than in the substantial example, where they are mutable and unreal. The creation, by which sensible things are made, does not, therefore, bring anything into being, for all created things existed even more truly before their creation, together with the infinity of things never yet created.

It remains to inquire why there should have been a creation at all, why that which is infinite wills to supplement itself by that which is nothing, and especially why Plato says God rejoiced with great joy [21] and Genesis says he saw everything to be very good, after creating the world, when he could find greater clarity of vision, greater goodness, and greater occasion for rejoicing within himself. The solution is to be found in this very interior rejoicing itself. If what God is rejoices in, and loves, what God has, this joy or love must be identical with God, because of his simplicity, and yet it is neither Father nor Son, because it proceeds from both, and so it is a third element, which we call the Holy Ghost. God is light (to make an understatement). A light gives light by shining, and these three things — to be a light, to shine, and to give light — are identical, yet distinguishable. The light which is given comes from the light which shines and from its shining; the shining comes from the light which shines; the light which shines has no source but itself. But it is the nature of light to be visible. The light which shines is visible through its shining because it gives light. Light is precious just because it is visible — that is, giveable, receivable, and enjoyable. Its whole use lies in its gift, that is, the light which is given.[22] This is true whatever understatement we employ. Whether we call the Holy Ghost light, goodness, joy, or love; its nature is to be giveable, receivable, and enjoyable, and to share itself with others. God therefore wills to be enjoyed — not through any

[21] Timaeus 37 c.
[22] Sermon 24.

necessity or desire, but through the very nature of his intrinsic goodness and joy, which is to extend itself to others, that they may share in that goodness and joy.[23] Compelled by his own goodness and joy, a compulsion which is the highest freedom, he created the rational soul capable of enjoying him. He made it rational in order to search him out in itself and in all things, concupiscible in order to love and desire him, irascible in order to reject all things opposing this contemplation and delight; and he created the corporeal world for its service. The highest good of the rational soul is to do that for which it is made, namely, to enjoy God by contemplation, to see the light which shines by the light which it gives.[24] And as that to which a light which shines gives light is not another light but darkness, which is nothing; so that by which true being is shared is not another being but non-being, which is nothing apart from the being it shares.

[23] Cf. Bernard, Sermon 18 on Canticles, 4 (*Opera* 2763).
[24] Sermon 25.

APPENDIX B

BERNARD'S CRITICISM OF PETER ABELARD'S THEOLOGY

Bernard's criticism of Peter Abelard's doctrine [1] concerned rather subtle points of theology. He objected to Abelard's saying that the Holy Ghost, although of the same substance as the Father, is not of the substance of the Father; that God, although able to do whatever he wills, could not have done other than he has willed; that the dominion which the devil justly had, with God's permission, over man derived its validity from that permission; that, although Christ is a person of the Trinity, the person of Christ is not a person of the Trinity; that grace, being ineffectual unless it is accepted, is ineffectual before it is accepted; that the accidents of bread and wine, which remain with the substance of body and blood, do not become accidents of the body and blood; that ignorance is reprehensible rather than sinful; that the Church's power of binding and loosing is absolute only within the present Church; and that temptation is sin only when yielded to. The emotional bitterness aroused by these subtleties seems hard to understand, especially since Abelard's only purpose was to defend the doctrine of the Church. The bitter feeling can only be explained by some fundamental misunderstanding which made it impossible for the two antagonists to see each other's point of view.

One such misunderstanding was the difference in their fundamental categories of epistemology. Abelard thought in terms of the traditional distinction of faith and understanding, while Bernard made a threefold distinction of faith, understanding, and opinion. He divided the field of invisible things, which are not subject to empirical knowledge, among these

[1] Cf. especially Abelard, *Introduction to Theology* (*Pat. Lat.* 178, 979); and Bernard, *Abelard's Errors* (*Opera* 1433).

three ways of knowing, and asserted that each is supreme in its own domain.[2] For example, the domain of faith includes the Trinity,[3] the redemption,[4] and baptism;[5] that of understanding includes God,[6] freedom,[7] and immortality;[8] and that of opinion includes angels,[9] the immaculate conception,[10] and the validity of illicit sacraments.[11]

Abelard followed the patristic tradition, derived from Augustine and Anselm, of faith seeking understanding. In the first book of his *Introduction to Theology* he expounded the faith as given by authority; in the second and third he explained it rationally. He acknowledged the difficulty of understanding the unintelligible,[12] but asserted that it is the task of theology to do so, for only thus can the true faith be defended against infidels, heretics, and philosophers. Faith seeking understanding means that the same doctrines are first to be believed and then, so far as possible, understood, and consequently that faith and understanding have the same domain, which is the whole of theology.

Bernard proceeded from faith to understanding only in the sense that without some antecedent faith one would not become interested in theology at all. He taught that belief in Christ's precepts, miracles, and promises leads a man to consider himself and God, and leads him to the humility by which his reason is purged of pride and curiosity and therefore free to understand God.[13] But within theology he proceeded from understanding to faith, following understanding as far as pos-

---

[2] *Consideration* 5, 3, 5–6 (*Opera* 1074).
[3] *Ibid.* 5, 8, 18 (*Opera* 1085). Cf. Sermon 76 on Canticles, 6 (*Opera* 3140).
[4] *Loving God* 3, 7 (*Opera* 1334).
[5] Sermon 5 on Canticles, 1 (*Opera* 2683).
[6] Sermon 31 on Canticles, 3 (*Opera* 2864).
[7] *Grace and Free Choice* 2, 3–4 (*Opera* 1367).
[8] Sermon 81 on Canticles, 5 (*Opera* 3166).
[9] *Consideration* 5, 4, 7 (*Opera* 1076). Cf. *Steps of Humility*, Retractation; *Baptism* 5, 18 (*Opera* 1421).
[10] Letter 174, 1 (*Opera* 389). Cf. *ibid.* 9 (*Opera* 393).
[11] Letter 69, 2–3 (*Opera* 220); Letter 403, 1 (*Opera* 719).
[12] Cf. 1046 d, 1059 c.
[13] Misc. Sermon 45, 4 (XB 913). Cf. *Steps of Humility* 4, 15.

sible, and resorting to faith only when understanding failed. He did not consider the task of theology to be to understand the unintelligible, which is impossible, but to understand the intelligible, relegating the unintelligible to the domain of faith, the doctrines of which are credible only because they are unintelligible.[14] He criticized Abelard for not distinguishing these two domains.

Being prepared to give a reason for everything, even those things which are above reason, he presumes both against reason and against faith. For what is more contrary to reason than to try to transcend reason by reason? And what is more contrary to faith, than to refuse to believe whatever he cannot attain by reason?[15]

Even worse, from Bernard's point of view, than Abelard's failure to distinguish the domain of faith from that of understanding, was his failure to make the even more fundamental distinction between the domain of certitude (which includes the domains of faith and understanding) and that of opinion. Bernard had perfect confidence in his own infallibility both in expounding the faith and in arguing rationally. Abelard, more humble, had no such confidence, but admitted his human fallibility and acknowledged himself ready to retract immediately wherever he might be shown to have erred against either faith or reason[16] — a possibility which never occurred to Bernard. Bernard's confidence in his own infallibility resulted from his limiting it to the domains of faith and understanding, two infallible ways of knowing. To Bernard Abe-

---

[14] *Consideration* 5, 3, 6 (*Opera* 1075).

[15] *Abelard's Errors* 1, 1: Dum paratus est de omnibus reddere rationem, etiam quae sunt supra rationem, et contra rationem praesumit, et contra fidem. Quid enim magis contra rationem, quam ratione rationem conari transcendere? Et quid magis contra fidem, quam credere nolle, quidquid non possit ratione attingere? (*Opera* 1442.) Cf. Thomas Aquinas, *Summa Theol*. I, 46, 2, response: "So that the world had a beginning is credible, but not demonstrable or knowable. And it is useful to consider this, lest anyone, presuming to demonstrate what is of faith, should bring forward reasons that are not cogent, so as to give occasion to unbelievers to laugh, and to think that such are the grounds on which we believe things that are of faith."

[16] 980 a.

lard's humility was mere confusion of thought, and his desire
to be corrected in matters of faith or reason was mere hypocrisy — as if any educated Catholic could misstate the faith or
any rational creature reason irrationally, unless prejudiced by
emotion! [17]   Abelard confused faith with opinion when he
defined faith as a supposition concerning invisible things.[18]
Bernard's most fundamental criticism of Abelard, namely that
in defining faith he confused certitude with supposition,[19]
was meaningless in Abelard's categories. In the final retractation in which he endeavored to disclaim, recant, or explain the
controversial doctrines, he did not even mention the definition
of faith. What was to Bernard a distinction of the most fundamental categories, was to Abelard a mere quibble of words.
But Abelard also confused understanding with opinion. He
referred to his rational explanation of the faith as expounding
the sense of his own opinion [20] and as defining by plausible and
most honest reasons [21]— using the word *verisimilis* which was
for Bernard definitive of opinion.[22] Bernard compared him
with the sceptics of the Academy, who pretended to know
nothing,[23] but at the same time accused him of pretending to
know everything except the words "I don't know." [24] These
inconsistent criticisms were both valid from Bernard's point
of view. Abelard pretended both to know everything and to
know nothing. Bernard, on the contrary, definitely knew
what he knew and definitely did not know what he did not
know. How could Bernard argue with a man who would not
concede the tenets either of faith or of understanding as

[17] E.g., hate, fear, or love. *Steps of Humility* 4, 14.
[18] Est quippe fides existimatio rerum non apparentium, hoc est sensibus
corporis non subjacentium. 981. c.
[19] *Abelard's Errors* 4, 9: Non est enim fides aestimatio, sed certitudo
(*Opera* 1450).
[20] Non tam nos veritatem dicere promittentes, quam opinionis nostrae
sensum quem efflagitant, exponentes. 980 a.
[21] Verisimilibus et honestissimis rationibus diffinire. 1085 c.
[22] *Consideration* 5, 3, 5 (*Opera* 1075).
[23] *Abelard's Errors* 4, 9: Academicorum sint istae aestimationes, quorum
est dubitare de omnibus, scire nihil (*Opera* 1450).
[24] *Ibid.* 1, 1: Nihil, praeter solum Nescio, nescire dignatur (*Opera* 1442).

infallible premises? How could Abelard argue with a man who would reject every proposition he considered arguable as not belonging to either faith or understanding? It was impossible for two men to understand each other who approached theology from such different points of view.

Two great attempts were made, in the early Middle Ages, to fulfill the impossible task set by Augustine — the task of faith seeking understanding.[25] These attempts were made by Anselm and Abelard. Anselm succeeded by sacrificing reason; Abelard, by sacrificing authority. Anselm's orthodoxy was irreproachable, but anybody who has read his works knows the far-fetched arguments, ingenious rather than convincing, by which he makes faith intelligible. Abelard's logic, if not above criticism, at least tried to be cogent, but he reserved the dangerous privilege of making such interpretations of the faith as might be necessary to make it logical. The difference between them is best shown by their attitudes toward apparent discrepancies between faith and reason. Anselm maintained that the traditional faith, as interpreted by the Fathers and especially by Augustine, is incontrovertible, and that if any person cannot understand it, he must accept it as faith, and attribute its apparent irrationality to the imperfection of his own reason. (Anselm was never forced to this extremity himself, but he counseled it for others less intelligent.) [26] Abelard, on the other hand, maintained that, since faith is intelligible, reason should guide us in interpreting it, and irrational interpretations should be rejected as unorthodox, alleged authority notwithstanding.[27] In spite of this difference, however, Anselm and Abelard agreed in their fundamental

---

[25] Augustine never pretended to have found understanding of such a sort as to supersede faith; and it is not clear whether to do so was his ideal. Cf. the retractation of *De Utilitate Credendi*: Non quia in hac vita nihil veri omnino inveniri potest quod mente cernatur, non fide credatur; sed quia tantum est quidquid est, ut non faciat beatissimos. Neque enim quod ait Apostolus, *Videmus nunc per speculum in aenigmate*, et, *Nunc scio ex parte* (1 Cor. 13. 12); non cernitur mente: cernitur plane, sed beatissimos nondum facit. (*Retr.* 1, 14, 2, *Pat. Lat.* 32, 606.)

[26] *Pat. Lat.* 158, 263 b.

[27] 1051 b.

doctrine, that faith is essentially intelligible, and that the task of theology is to understand it.

Bernard, a clearer thinker than Abelard, saw the impossibility of this task and abandoned the patristic position. Assigning faith and understanding to separate domains, he demanded no harmony between them beyond the lack of definite inconsistency which is implied by the fact that both are true. He did not, any more than Abelard, consider faith to be an end in itself. But for Bernard faith is consummated in mysticism, which gives understanding indeed,[28] but an ineffable understanding based on direct vision; whereas for Abelard faith is consummated, so far as this life is concerned, in the understanding of discursive reasoning,[29] which is, as Anselm said,[30] a kind of knowledge intermediate between faith and vision. For Bernard, consequently, the monastic virtues of humility and charity, which lead to mystical contemplation, are all-important for the lover of wisdom, while the study of logic is an innocent but unimportant pastime; whereas for Abelard the study of logic is the most essential preparation for knowledge. Both sought to comprehend the tenets of faith, but Abelard sought to comprehend them by disputations of logic, while Bernard sought to comprehend them by sanctity of life.

We know these truths. Do we think that consequently we also comprehend them? Not disputation but sanctity comprehends them; if indeed that which is incomprehensible can in any way be comprehended. But unless it could, the Apostle would not have said: *That ye may be able to comprehend with all saints.* The saints, therefore, comprehend. Do you ask how? If you are a saint, you comprehend, and know; if not, be one, and you will know by your own experience.[31]

[28] Cf. *Consideration* 5, 3, 6 (*Opera* 1075).

[29] 1051 d.

[30] *Pat. Lat.* 158, 261 a.

[31] *Consideration* 5, 14, 30: Novimus haec. Num ideo et arbitramur nos comprehendisse? Non ea disputatio comprehendit, sed sanctitas: si quo modo tamen comprehendi potest quod incomprehensibile est. At nisi posset, non dixisset Apostolus: *Ut comprehendamus cum omnibus sanctis* (Eph. 3. 18). Sancti igitur comprehendunt. Quaeris quomodo? Si sanctus es, comprehendisti, et nosti: si non; esto, et tuo experimento scies. (*Opera* 1093.)

We see, therefore, that Abelard was loyal to the patristic tradition, while Bernard was a precursor of the later scholastic doctrine of faith and reason exemplified by Thomas Aquinas.[32] While the later scholastics may have defined the frontier between the domains of faith and understanding more precisely, none of them formulated the principle of their separation more clearly than Bernard. Abelard, on the other hand, surpassed all his predecessors in his perfect confidence in the ability of faith to find understanding. Bernard's victory over Abelard was the defeat of the old optimistic confidence in the intelligibility of Christian revelation and the triumph of the new logical discernment between what can be, and what cannot be, understood by human reason. If we can define the difference between the patristic and the scholastic theologies by their opposed answers to the basic problem of the relation between faith and reason, we can say that Abelard was the last of the Fathers and Bernard the first of the Scholastics.

[32] According to Thomas Aquinas, we can understand the tenets of faith only in the sense of deducing their consequences, not in the sense of proving them. (*Sum. Th.* I, 1, 8, resp.) Theology, strictly so called, is the understanding or rather elucidation of the faith in this sense; whatever can be proved by reason alone is not properly called a tenet of faith, and the understanding of such things is philosophy rather than theology. Faith, therefore, is the foundation, not the scaffolding, of theology. (For the whole question, see E. Gilson, *Reason and Revelation in the Middle Ages*, N. Y., 1938.)

BIBLIOGRAPHY

BIBLIOGRAPHY

1. BIBLIOGRAPHIES

Bibliographia Bernardina. In *Xenia Bernardina* (Vindobonae, A. Hölder, 1891), Pars Quarta. Contains a bibliography of 129 MSS and 2761 editions of works by or about Bernard.

É. Gilson, *La Théologie Mystique de Saint Bernard* (Paris, J. Vrin, 1934). Contains a bibliography of works on Bernard's mystical doctrine.

2. BIOGRAPHIES

Vitae Sancti Bernardi. The contemporary lives are included in the standard editions of his works.

E. Vacandard, *Vie de Saint Bernard* (1894; 8° mille, Paris, J. Gabalda, 1927), 2 vol. The standard biography, scholarly and interesting.

A. J. Luddy, *Life and Teachings of St. Bernard* (Dublin, M. H. Gill, 1927). Emphasizes Bernard's doctrine.

W. Williams, *Saint Bernard of Clairvaux* (Manchester, University Press, 1935). Emphasizes Bernard's political activities.

3. STANDARD EDITIONS

Opera Omnia, edited by John Mabillon, 2 volumes in 4 parts. 1st ed., 1667. 2nd ed., 1690. 3rd ed., 1719. 4th ed. (Paris, Gaume, 1839), cited as *"Opera"* (in all cases "Volume I" is to be understood); cited in the notes to the text as "Mab."

Migne, *Patrologia Latina*, vols. 182, 183, 184, 185, 185 bis. The letters and essays are in vol. 182; the sermons are in vol. 183.

4. CRITICAL EDITIONS

Sermones de Tempore, de Sanctis, de Diversis. In *Xenia Bernardina* (Vindobonae, A. Hölder, 1891), Pars Prima. Cited as "XB" (in all cases "Part I" is to be understood).

Select Treatises of S. Bernard of Clairvaux: De Diligendo Deo, edited by W. W. Williams; *De Gradibus Humilitatis et Superbiae*, edited by B. R. V. Mills (Cambridge University Press, 1926). Cited as "Ed. Cant."

Of Conversion. Text of the Anchin MS, edited by Watkin Williams (London, Burns Oates & Washbourne, 1938).

5. English Translations

S. J. Eales, *Life and Works of Saint Bernard* (London, J. Hodges, 1889–1896). The four volumes published include the letters, the essay on *Abelard's Errors*, the first 19 sermons *de Tempore*, and the sermons on Canticles.

Works, translated by a priest of Mount Melleray (Dublin, Browne & Nolan). The following have appeared: *Sermons on the Canticle of Canticles*, 2 vol. (1920). *Sermons for the Seasons & Principal Festivals of the Year* (*de Tempore* and *de Sanctis*, with a selection of the sermons *de Diversis*), 3 vol. (1921–1925). *Treatise on Consideration* (1921). (Of the two English translations of the sermons on Canticles, the Mount Melleray version is to be preferred; although it is very free and takes liberties with the text, it preserves the spirit of the original better than the more literal but prosaic translation of Eales.)

Saint Bernard on *Consideration*, translated by George Lewis (Oxford, Clarendon, 1908).

Of Conversion, translated by Watkin Williams (London, Burns Oates & Washbourne, 1938).

The Twelve Degrees of Humility and Pride, translated by B. R. V. Mills (London, S. P. C. K., 1929).

The Book of Saint Bernard on the *Love of God*, translated by E. G. Gardner (London, Dent, 1915). (Text, translation, introduction, and notes.)

The Book of Saint Bernard on the *Love of God*, translated by T. L. Connolly (N. Y., Spiritual Book Associates, 1937).

Concerning *Grace and Free Will*, translated by W. W. Williams (London, S. P. C. K., 1920). (Includes a synopsis.)

Life of St Malachy, translated by H. J. Lawlor (London, S. P. C. K., 1920).

6. Selected Works on Bernard's Doctrine

E. Géruzez, *Essai sur l'Éloquence et la Philosophie de Saint Bernard* (Paris, Hachette, 1839).

P. Rousselot, *Pour l'Histoire du Problème de l'Amour au Moyen Age* (*Beiträge zur Geschichte der Philosophie des Mittelalters*, VI, 6, Münster, Aschendorffschen Buchhandlung, 1908). (To be read critically.)

J. Schuck, *Das religiöse Erlebnis beim hl. Bernhard von Clairvaux* (*Abhandlungen zur Philosophie und Psychologie der Religion*, 1, Würzburg, C. J. Becker, 1922).

E. Vacandard, article "Bernard (Saint)," *Dictionnaire de Théologie Catholique* (Paris, 1923), II, 747.

C. Butler, *Western Mysticism*, 2nd ed. (London, Constable, 1927).

P. Guilloux, "L'Amour de Dieu Selon Saint Bernard," *Revue des Sciences Religieuses* (1926, pp. 499–512; 1927, pp. 52–68; 1928, pp. 69–90).

W. Tatarkiewicz, *Historja Filozofji* (Lwów, 1931), I, 281–284.

E. Piszter, *Chrestomathia Bernardina* ex operibus S. Bernardi collecta et ad systema quoddam theologiae redacta (Taurini, Marietti, 1932). (Not consulted.)

É. Gilson, *La Théologie Mystique de Saint Bernard* (*Études de Philosophie Médiévale*, 20, Paris, J. Vrin, 1934). (The best work on Bernard's doctrine.)

É. Gilson und P. Böhner, *Die Geschichte der christlichen Philosophie* (Paderborn, F. Schöningh, 1937), pp. 298–312.

7. Isaac of Stella

Isaac de Stella, *Opera*, Migne, *Patrologia Latina*, 194, 1683–1896.

F. P. Bliemetzrieder, "Isaak von Stella: Beiträge zur Lebensbeschreibung," *Jahrbuch für Philosophie und Spekulative Theologie*, XVIII (1904), 1–34.

F. P. Bliemetzrieder, "Isaac de Stella: Sa Spéculation Théologique," *Recherches de Théologie ancienne et médiévale*, IV (1932), 134–159.

W. Meuser, *Die Erkenntnislehre des Isaak von Stella* (Bottrop, W. Postberg, 1934).

INDEX

INDEX

(1)